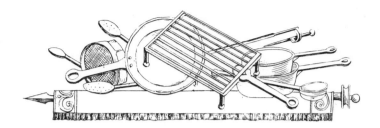

DAVENPORT'S DISHES

Philippa Davenport

JILL NORMAN

Jill Norman Ltd, 90 Great Russell Street, London WC1B 3PY

First published 1981
Copyright © Philippa Davenport, 1981

British Library Cataloguing in Publication Data

Davenport, Philippa
Davenport's dishes
1. Cookery
1. Title
641.5 TX717

ISBN 0-906908-04-3
ISBN 0-906908-29-9 Pbk

Typeset by Inforum Ltd, Portsmouth
Printed and bound in Great Britain at
Richard Clay
(The Chaucer Press) Ltd.,
Bungay, Suffolk

Contents

Preface

One of the most rewarding and enjoyable aspects of writing for newspapers is receiving letters from readers, letters telling me which of my recipes you have particularly enjoyed, and sometimes suggesting ingredients or techniques you would like me to write more about.

Amongst the mailbag of requests for copies of 'lost' recipes, there is quite a pile of letters asking when these newspaper recipes will be published as a book, enquiries typified by the lady who wrote 'I now have two drawers full of Davenport cuttings and it is almost impossible to find the recipe I want when I want it.'

This book has been compiled in response to those who have so kindly asked for such a book – a collection of some 250 of my recipes as published in the *London Evening Standard, Liverpool Daily Post* and other newspapers during the past three years or so.

The selection is based on your letters: these are the recipes most often asked for. They are a cross-section, suitable for all sorts of occasions and all sorts of weather. They include some baking, some store-cupboard items, and some decidedly special dishes, but the majority are recipes designed to meet the challenge every cook faces daily: how to feed our families delicious and varied meals without breaking the bank or our backs.

For some people cost is more important than speed, for others the reverse is true. For mothers and other cooks who are at home all or most of the day (and therefore place greater emphasis on economy than on speed of preparation) there are inexpensive and filling pies, stews and other composite dishes, including many which use eggs, cheese or vegetables, rather than meat, as the main ingredient. For the career woman or man, and anyone else for whom time is of the essence, there are quick and more original alternatives to the inevitable plain grilled chops, and a number of 'cold-start' casseroles which take five minutes to prepare in the morning and will cook in the cook's absence using an automatic oven timer. For the elderly, bachelors and students I have included some of my most popular, easy and nutritious dishes for one and two people.

Most of the ingredients used in these recipes are common-place and relatively cheap. My aim has been to make these ordinary foods into dishes that taste just that little bit special – not spectacular or fancy affairs, but practical and imaginative dishes that make such good eating that no-one will guess how relatively little time and/or money you have spent on their making.

I believe very firmly that good eating begins with good shopping. However ordinary the ingredients you buy it is always worth seeking out the freshest and best available. Limp, yellowing lettuce will never make a decent salad however much time and care you spend preparing it.

I am equally convinced that simple, careful cooking is best. It is not worth attempting elaborate chef's creations unless you have the resources of a chef. Far wiser to stick to fairly basic cooking techniques and to concentrate on executing them beautifully.

After all, the meals that linger in the memory as particularly delicious and distinguished are usually quite modest: not lobster à l'amoricaine, but a perfect cheese soufflé – perfect because it was made with newly-laid eggs and freshly-grated Parmesan cheese; perfect because it was cooked to just the right degree, trembling and towering with a beautifully creamy centre. In short, I believe it is not the budget but the care taken over shopping and cooking that determines how well you eat.

To judge by your letters, my three most popular recipes published to date are home-made yoghurt, sweet-pickled herrings and all-purpose tomato sauce (in that order). Such interest in these basic recipes reflects a heartening trend away from fancy foods towards the purer tastes of good, basic home-cooking. These three recipes are, of course, included in this book. I hope many others of your personal favourites are included as well. If some are missing, please bear with me — until my next book is published next year.

I should like to add my special thanks to Mary Ann Buckley for her invaluable help in assembling the recipes for this book.

1981   *Philippa Davenport*

Weights and Measures

For those cooks who have already 'gone metric' here are conversion charts for weights, measures and temperatures. All conversions are *approximate* so please use either metric or imperial for a recipe, never a mixture of the two. All spoon measurements used in this book are *level* unless otherwise indicated.

SPOON MEASUREMENTS		BAKING TIN, PAN SIZES,ETC.	
¼ teaspoon	1.5 ml	7 inch	18 cm
½ teaspoon	2.5 ml	8 inch	20 cm
1 teaspoon	5 ml	10 inch	25 cm
3 teaspoons } 1 tablespoon }	15 ml	12 inch	30 cm

LIQUIDS

Fluid ounces	Pints	Millilitres	Fluid ounces	Pints	Millilitres
1 fl. oz		25 ml	13 fl. oz		375 ml
2 fl. oz		50 ml	14 fl. oz		400 ml
3 fl. oz		75 ml	15 fl. oz	¾ pt	425 ml
4 fl. oz		125 ml	16 fl. oz		450 ml
5 fl. oz	¼ pt	150 ml	17 fl. oz		475 ml
6 fl. oz		175 ml	18 fl. oz		500 ml
7 fl. oz		200 ml	19 fl. oz		550 ml
8 fl. oz		225 ml	20 fl. oz	1 pt	575 ml
9 fl. oz		250 ml	25 fl. oz	1¼ pt	700 ml
10 fl. oz	½ pt	275 ml	30 fl. oz	1½ pt	850 ml
11 fl. oz		300 ml	35 fl. oz	1¾ pt	1 litre
12 fl. oz		350 ml	40 fl. oz	2 pt	1·1 litre

SOLIDS

Ounces	Pounds	Grammes	Ounces	Pounds	Grammes
½ oz		15 g	9 oz		250 g
1 oz		25 g	10 oz		275 g
1½ oz		40 g	11 oz		300 g
2 oz		50 g	12 oz	¾ lb	350 g
3 oz		75 g	13 oz		375 g
4 oz	¼ lb	120 g	14 oz		400 g
5 oz		150 g	15 oz		425 g
6 oz		175 g	16 oz	1 lb	450 g
7 oz		200 g		2 lb	900 g
8 oz	½ lb	225 g		3 lb	1·350 kg

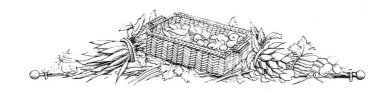

Soups

WILTSHIRE LEEK SOUP
(serves 4–5)

A delicately flavoured and attractive-looking soup which is quick and easy to prepare.

½ lb leeks (trimmed weight)
4 rashers streaky bacon
2 oz butter
2 slightly heaped teaspoons plain flour
1½ pt light chicken stock or water
a handful of chopped fresh parsley
¼ pt single or double cream
2 heaped tablespoons grated Parmesan cheese
salt and freshly-ground black pepper

Trim, thinly slice, thoroughly wash the leeks and pat them dry with kitchen paper towels. De-rind the bacon and cut it into snippets. Melt the butter in a saucepan, add the prepared leeks and bacon and turn for a minute or two to coat all over with the fat. Cover with a lid and cook over very gentle heat for 12–15 minutes until the leeks are tender. ·

Sprinkle on and stir in the flour. Pour on the stock or water and bring quickly to boiling point stirring all the while. Mix the Parmesan, cream, parsley and a good grinding of pepper together in a cup — add no salt at this stage because of the bacon and cheese. Reduce heat under the saucepan to very low and gradually whisk the contents of the cup into the soup. Let it heat through without boiling; check seasoning and serve immediately.

CAULIFLOWER CHEESE SOUP
(serves 4)

Cauliflower cheese is a very popular lunch or supper dish, and this soup is a variation on that theme. It makes a substantial main course soup for hungry people on a cold day.

1 lb cauliflower sprigs
1 large onion
3 oz butter
3 tablespoons plain flour
1 pt light chicken stock
1 pt milk
$\frac{1}{4}$ lb grated Cheddar cheese
4 slices of bread
1 teaspoon French mustard
salt and freshly-ground black pepper

Chop the onion finely and cut the cauliflower sprigs into tiny pieces. Melt the butter in a large pan over low heat. Add the vegetables and turn them to coat all over with fat. Cover and leave to sweat for 10 minutes. Then sprinkle on and stir in the flour. Pour on the liquids and stir continuously until simmering point is reached. Half-cover the pan and leave to simmer over the lowest possible heat for 8–10 minutes until the vegetables are completely tender.

Using a slotted spoon transfer most, but not all, of the vegetables to a blender goblet. Add some of the cooking liquor and reduce to a purée. (You could blend the entire contents of the pan to a purée but the texture of the finished soup is more interesting if it contains a few tiny pieces of vegetable.) Return the purée to the pan. Season with 6–8 tablespoons of the grated cheese, a little salt, pepper and set aside while you lightly toast the bread on both sides.

Spread the toast with the mustard mashed with a generous tablespoon of softened butter. Sprinkle the remaining cheese on top and return to the grill until golden and bubbling. Cut each slice of cheese toast into 20 or so tiny squares. Put half of them in a warmed soup tureen. Gently reheat the soup, check season-

ing and pour it into the soup tureen. Sprinkle the remaining
cheese toasts on top and serve immediately.

FRESH TOMATO SOUP

(serves 4–5)

This fresh-tasting, chilled tomato soup is a lovely way to make
use of end-of-season tomatoes which are often on sale quite
cheaply at the end of summer.

$2\frac{1}{4}$ lb tomatoes
1 small garlic clove
2 teaspoons caster sugar
2 teaspoons lemon juice
1 teaspoon concentrated tomato purée
salt and freshly-ground black pepper
$\frac{1}{4}$ pt soured cream
$\frac{1}{4}$ pt plain yoghurt
1 tablespoon each fresh chopped parsley, chives and
   mint

Drop the tomatoes into boiling water, a few at a time, for about
30 seconds to loosen the skins. Peel, chop roughly and put into a
liquidiser. Blend for several minutes until the flesh is reduced to
a fine purée and most of the pips have been completely broken
up.

Turn the fresh tomato purée out into a large bowl. Add the
garlic clove crushed with some salt, the concentrated tomato
purée and lemon juice beaten into the yoghurt, the soured
cream, a good grinding of pepper, and about half the fresh
chopped herbs. Then add the sugar.

Beat with a balloon whisk until all these ingredients are well
blended then cover and chill for several hours. Before serving,
check seasoning (depending on the type of tomatoes used you
may need to heighten the flavour with extra sugar, salt, lemon
or pepper, or all 4 of these things) and garnish with the
remaining herbs.

ITALIAN BEAN SOUP
(serves 4)

A homely, substantial meal-in-a-bowl. A particular favourite of mine because it is so easy. It takes no more than 5–10 minutes to prepare the ingredients; the casserole can then be left to cook gently in the oven for 4 hours – and it won't spoil if left for an extra hour or so.

> 8–10 oz haricot beans (soaked overnight in a large bowl of cold water)
> ¾–1 lb streaky belly of pork rashers
> 1 large onion
> 3 fat garlic cloves
> at least 6 heaped tablespoons fresh chopped parsley
> 1 large lemon
> 1 heaped teaspoon dried thyme
> scant teaspoon caster sugar
> salt and freshly-ground black pepper

Cut each rasher of streaky pork in half. Lay the pieces on the base of a large casserole. Crush the garlic with a little salt and spread it over the pork. Add the chopped parsley, thyme, lemon zest, sugar and a good grinding of pepper all mixed together.

Drain, rinse and drain the beans again. Mix them with the chopped onion and pile on top of the pork. Pour on the lemon juice plus 1½ pt hot – not boiling – water.

Cover with a lid and cook in the oven very gently, at 275–300F, 140–150C or gas mark 1–2 for about 4 hours, until the beans are soft and the pork is meltingly tender.

Stir in salt to taste plus extra pepper and/or lemon juice just before serving.

MANSION HOUSE SOUP
(serves 6)

I believe this is so called because it used to be served at the Lord Mayor of London's banquets, when it was made with turtle consommé. My version is a cheat recipe made with canned consommé (Sainsbury's is very good) or, better still, Lusty's consommé Madrilène which is prettily coloured and flavoured with tomatoes.

1½ pt canned consommé
3 large tomatoes
2 tablespoons dry sherry
½ pt soured cream
small jar mock caviar (red salmon or lumpfish)
2 lemons
salt and freshly-ground black pepper

Warm the consommé in a saucepan just long enough to melt the jelly. Stir in the sherry and a light seasoning of salt and pepper. Pour into a large bowl and leave in a cold place until set firm. Skin, peel and chop the tomato flesh and reserve separately.

When the consommé has set to a jelly, chop it with a damp knife and divide half of it between 6 soup cups. Sprinkle a few tomato pieces into each cup and cover with a dollop of soured cream. Add a spoonful of caviar, a squeeze of lemon juice and a grinding of pepper. Repeat the layers again, cover and chill until ready to serve. Serve garnished with wedges of lemon.

This makes a lovely dinner party dish, and can of course be made more economically by omitting the mock caviar.

POTAGE BONNE FEMME

Served with lots of piping hot, crisply fried bread croûtons, this economic and very good soup is enough for about 8 people. The croûtons, like the soup, can be cooked ahead, frozen and re-heated for serving.

1 lb thin leeks
1 lb potatoes
½ lb carrots
2 oz butter
2¼ pints water
2 teaspoons granulated sugar
1 heaped teaspoon dried tarragon leaves
salt and freshly-ground black pepper

Peel and dice the potatoes. Scrape and slice the carrots.

Thoroughly wash and slice the leeks, including most of the green parts as well as the white. Melt the butter in a very large saucepan. Add the vegetables and cook over low heat, stirring continuously for 3–4 minutes until all the ingredients are glistening with fat. Stir in the sugar, tarragon and a good seasoning of salt and pepper. Pour on the water, increase heat and bring to the boil fairly quickly, stirring occasionally.

Then cover the pan, reduce heat to low and simmer gently for 20 minutes until the vegetables are tender but in no way over-cooked.

Using a blender, reduce the soup to a smooth purée. Reheat it gently and adjust seasoning – adding extra sugar, salt and/or pepper to taste. Stir in a little fresh chopped parsley and a spoonful or so of cream if available. Serve immediately, handing round the dish of hot croûtons separately.

CHILLED MELON SOUP
(serves 6–8)

Fruit soups are highly regarded in Scandinavia but unusual in Britain. I must confess I dislike most sweet soups – they seem to me like puddings that have gone wrong – but I find this one deliciously refreshing, and it is extremely easy to make.

2 large ripe honeydew melons
4 juicy lemons
$\frac{1}{2}$ pt soured cream
a pinch of ground cinnamon
a few sprigs of mint
a few tablespoons of single cream or yoghurt

Halve the melons, scoop out and discard the seeds. Cut the melon flesh into rough chunks. Put a few of the melon chunks into a liquidiser, add the cinnamon and reduce to a purée. Gradually add the rest of the melon to the liquidiser, and reduce to a purée. You may have to add some of the lemon juice too to prevent the blender blades from sticking, and I find it is necessary to go on blending the mixture for quite a long while to reduce all the flesh to a really smooth purée. Beat in the remaining lemon juice, then turn the purée out of the blender into a bowl. Stir in a few lightly crushed mint sprigs, cover and chill for several hours. Chill the soured cream separately. Remove the mint sprigs from the soup. Beat the soured cream until perfectly smooth and creamy, then stir it into the chilled soup until thoroughly blended. Add a tablespoon or so of freshly-chopped mint and check seasoning. Serve garnished with a swirl of single cream or yoghurt.

TURKISH FISH SOUP
(*serves 4–6*)

This is really a cross between a soup and a stew. It will serve 4–6 people depending partly on appetite, and partly on whether you serve the soup as a meal in its own right, or follow it with cheese and fruit. A soup with a creamy smooth base and the piquancy of lemon – really excellent when you can lay your hands on salty fresh prawns.

For the stock:
2½ lb fishbones and trimmings (turbot head and sole bones are best) or 1½ lb whiting
1 large onion
a stick of celery complete with leaves
1 bouquet garni
6 peppercorns
6 coriander seeds
2 or 3 lemon slices
½ pt dry white wine or Bulmers no. 7 dry cider

For the soup:
1 lb haddock fillets
1½ pt fresh boiled prawns in the shell (or ½ lb shelled prawns)
2 lb fresh spinach (or 1 lb frozen spinach)
¾ lb potatoes
3 large egg yolks
4 tablespoons lemon juice
salt and pepper

Rinse the bones and trimmings or whiting thoroughly, place in a pan with the other stock ingredients plus 2½ pt water. Bring slowly to boiling point, cover and simmer for 25 minutes.

Strain the stock through butter-muslin into a clean pan, pressing lightly to extract full flavour. Reheat and boil until reduced to 2 pt.
Peel and finely dice the potatoes. Cook at a gentle simmer in half the fish stock together with the spinach until both vegetables are tender. Reduce to a purée in a liquidiser. Poach the haddock fillets in the remaining fish stock, adding the peeled prawns for the last 5 minutes to heat them through. When cooked, strain off the fish liquor and stir it into the vegetable purée. Skin and bone the haddock and divide the flesh into large chunks. Place in a warmed soup tureen together with the prawns.
Reheat the soup, seasoning it to taste with salt and pepper. Whisk the egg yolks and lemon juice together in a small bowl. Blend in a few spoonfuls of the hot soup, then blend the contents of the bowl into the soup pan, stirring all the time. Cook over gentle heat – on no account allow to boil – stirring until slightly thickened. Pour the soup into the tureen and serve with triangles of fried bread.

BEETROOT AND KOHLRABI SOUP
(serves 4–5)

Kohlrabi is a root vegetable with a rather delicate flavour which some people describe as a cross between turnip and cabbage. Be sure to buy a small one as large ones are inclined to be fibrous. Teamed with beetroot, kohlrabi makes a richly-coloured and slimline hot soup.

> raw beetroot weighing $\frac{3}{4}$ lb after trimming and peeling
> 6–8 oz kohlrabi
> 1 small onion
> 2 pt stock
> half a lemon
> a pinch of sugar
> $\frac{1}{4}$ pt soured cream
> chopped fresh parsley and chives (if available)
> salt and freshly-ground black pepper

Chop the beetroot and kohlrabi into small dice and chop the

onion finely. Put the beetroot and onion into a large pan. Add the stock, bring to the boil, cover and simmer gently for half an hour.

Add the kohlrabi to the pan and continue simmering until the vegetables are perfectly tender. This will probably take about half an hour — exact timing depends on the size of the vegetable dice.

Pass the contents of the pan through the medium blade of a vegetable mill. Season the soup with lemon juice, sugar and salt and pepper to taste, and reheat gently.

Serve the soured cream, mixed with fresh herbs if available, in a separate small bowl so everyone can help themselves.

LONDONER'S PEA SOUP
(serves 6)

This is what I call a meal-in-a-bowl. A soothing and nourishing dish that is really a cross between a soup and a stew. Perfect for Sunday supper with bread and cheese or a side salad. Good bacon stock can be made cheaply using knuckle of bacon, and chunks of meat cut from the knuckle can be used instead of bacon rashers for the substantial garnish.

    1 large onion
    1 leek
    2 celery stalks
    1 large carrot
    $\frac{1}{2}$ lb split green or yellow peas
    $\frac{1}{4}$ lb bacon fat or butter
    3 pt bacon stock
    1 fat garlic clove
    a large bouquet garni
    8–10 oz streaky bacon
    9 slices slightly stale bread
    4 tablespoons oil
    4 or more tablespoons each chopped fresh chives and parsley
    a little mace
    salt and freshly-ground black pepper.

Chop the fresh vegetables and sweat them in half the bacon fat or butter for 5–7 minutes. Add the crushed garlic clove, the rinds from the streaky bacon (tied in a bundle with a piece of string), the bacon stock and the bouquet garni. Bring to the boil, stir in the split peas (which do not need soaking in advance of cooking), cover the pan with a lid and simmer gently for about $1\frac{1}{2}$ hours or until the peas are completely softened.

When the peas are nearly tender, cut the bacon rashers into smallish pieces. Fry very gently over low heat until the fat runs, then over higher heat until crisp. Remove with a slotted spoon. Add the remaining 2 oz butter or bacon fat to the frying pan together with the oil, and fry the diced bread until golden and crisp. Drain well.

Remove the bouquet garni and bundle of rinds from the soup. Reduce the soup to a purée in a liquidiser. Reheat gently and season to taste with salt, pepper and mace. Stir in the bacon and chopped fresh chives. Sprinkle the parsley over the surface and serve accompanied by the bowl of fried croûtons.

AVGOLEMONO SOUP

(serves 2)

A Greek soup that can be made with fish, veal or chicken stock – home-made, of course. I find it very creamy and delicate, soothing and easily digested. The stock can be frozen but not the soup itself.

$\frac{3}{4}$ pt fish, veal or chicken stock
1 heaped tablespoon long grain rice
1 large egg
1 small lemon
salt and freshly-ground black pepper

Put the stock into a saucepan and bring it to the boil. Sprinkle on the rice, stir once, then cover the pan with a well-fitting lid, reduce heat as low as possible and simmer gently for 15 minutes until the rice is tender.

Beat the egg lightly in a small bowl. Add 1 tablespoon of freshly-squeezed lemon juice, a little salt and pepper and beat again. Add a few spoonfuls of the hot broth, stirring as you add them. Then slowly pour the contents of the bowl into the soup pan, stirring all the while. Continue stirring until the soup is very hot and slightly thickened (but do not allow it to come to the boil or the eggs will scramble and the soup will curdle) – about 5 minutes.

Then move the pan to the side of the stove and cover it with the lid and let it stand for another 5 minutes. Then taste it and add extra salt, pepper and/or lemon juice as you wish, and serve immediately.

VELVET FISH SOUP
(serves 4–5)

A creamy smooth fish soup, cheaply made with whiting and given a touch of delicacy and originality by the addition of wafer thin slices of raw mushroom. Raw scallops cut into papery slices make an exquisite alternative garnish. And for very special occasions you can replace half the whiting with prawns for rich shellfish flavour.

> 1 lb whiting fillet (or $\frac{1}{2}$ lb whiting fillet plus $\frac{1}{2}$ lb prawns in their shells)
> 1 lb fish bones and trimmings (if possible including sole bones and/or a turbot head)
> half a dozen or so cap mushrooms (or 2 fresh scallops)
> 1 leek
> 1 celery stalk
> 1 lemon
> a bouquet garni or 3 dried fennel stalks
> $\frac{1}{4}$ pt dry white wine or cider
> $1\frac{1}{2}$ oz butter
> 3 tablespoons plain flour
> $\frac{1}{4}$ pt single cream
> salt
> paprika and freshly-ground black pepper

Skin the whiting, sprinkle with the juice of half the lemon, some salt and pepper and set aside. Shell the prawns if using and set aside separately. Put the whiting skin, prawn shells and other bones and trimmings into a pan together with the chopped up leek and celery, sliced half lemon, herbs, wine or cider and water to cover. Put on the lid and simmer for 20 minutes. Strain and reduce the stock to $1\frac{3}{4}$ pt.

Poach the whiting gently in a little of the stock for 10 minutes, then reduce the contents of the pan to a perfectly smooth purée in a blender. If using prawns and scallops, also reduce the prawns and scallop corals to a purée.

Make a roux with the butter and flour; cooking it gently until straw coloured. Blend in the fish purée and the remaining fish stock. Bring to simmering point stirring all the while. Stir in the cream, simmer for 5 minutes or so without a lid and adjust seasoning to taste. Pour into soup bowls, garnish with the mushrooms cut into wafer thin slices or the white scallop discs cut papery thin, and top with a dash of paprika

LETTUCE CHIFFONADE SOUP
(serves 6)

A really healthy soup made with non-fattening salad ingredients. It can be served hot if the weather is beastly, or chilled if the weather is fine.

> A large bunch of spring onions
> a large well-hearted lettuce (or the outer leaves of several
>   lettuces if you wish to save the hearts for making salads)
> a bunch of watercress or a handful of spinach leaves
> 2 pt chicken stock
> $\frac{1}{4}$ pt plain yoghurt
> fresh or dried dillweed
> salt and freshly-ground black pepper

Trim the spring onions and chop them finely, green parts as well as white. Put them into a saucepan with the stock and bring quickly to the boil. Cover with a lid and simmer gently for 5 minutes.

Thoroughly wash, dry and finely shred the lettuce (and spinach if used). Chop the watercress, discarding any tough stalks. Add these ingredients to the pan and bring quickly back to boiling point. Reduce heat to very low, cover the pan again and simmer for a further 5 minutes or so until the vegetables are perfectly tender. Draw the pan to one side. Add the yoghurt, dill and a seasoning of salt and pepper. Beat with a balloon whisk to blend the yoghurt into the soup and, if serving hot, reheat gently without allowing the soup to reach boiling point. Serve garnished with wafer thin slices of cucumber or lemon.

SOUPE A L'OIGNON GRATINEE
(serves 6)

A very good and inexpensive, warming French soup. If you are feeling rich or particularly cold, bolster the soup by stirring in a couple of spoonfuls of brandy just before serving. Gruyère is the traditional cheese to use but I ring the changes sometimes: Danish Blue or Stilton or Dolcelatte mashed with a little butter make a delicious topping for the bread.

> $2\frac{1}{2}$ lb small onions
> 1 heaped teaspoon caster sugar
> 2–3 tablespoons oil
> 2–3 oz butter or good dripping
> 3 pt good beef stock
> 12 slices of French bread
> $3\frac{1}{2}$ oz Gruyère cheese
> salt and freshly-ground black pepper and a little nutmeg

Slice the onions thinly and put them into a large heavy-based flame-proof casserole in which you have melted the fats. Cook, stirring, over medium-low heat until the onions are glistening with fat, then fry for 15–20 minutes until golden brown. Stir occasionally to prevent sticking. Add the sugar, a pinch of freshly-grated nutmeg, some salt and pepper. Pour on the stock and bring quickly to the boil. Then reduce heat to a simmer, cover and cook for 30 minutes.

Meanwhile heat the oven to 400F, 200C, gas mark 6. Lay the slices of bread in a single layer on an oven shelf and bake for 5 minutes on each side.

Divide the soup between 6 ovenproof soup bowls or plates.

Heap the grated cheese onto the slices of bread and float them on the surface of the soup. Bake for 10 minutes so that the bread begins to soak up the delicious beef and onion flavoured liquid and the cheese melts.

LENTIL AND CABBAGE SOUP
(serves 6)

Pulses and fresh vegetables can be combined to make so many delicious and cheap soups — all the better for flavoursome home-made stock. This minestrone-style soup with Frankfurter sausages is almost a meal in itself.

6 oz brown lentils
half a small cabbage
3–4 carrots
3 leeks
3 tomatoes
4–6 celery stalks
2 garlic cloves
2 oz bacon fat or butter
3 pt bacon or beef stock
$\frac{1}{4}$ teaspoon oregano
2 tablespoons grated Parmesan cheese
$\frac{1}{2}$ lb Frankfurters

Do use whole brown lentils for this, not the split orangey ones. There is no need to soak them, but rinse them thoroughly and pick them over to remove any small bits of grit and debris.

Shred the cabbage. Skin and quarter the tomatoes, and slice the other vegetables. Stir them into the fat with the lentils and crushed garlic and cook gently until the fat is absorbed. Pour on the stock, bring to the boil, cover with a lid and simmer for 1 hour or until vegetables and lentils are tender.

Stir in the sliced sausages and any scraps of meat you can pick off the stock bones, and heat through. Add the Parmesan, oregano and some pepper.

CHILLED CUCUMBER SOUP
(serves 6–8)

A delicately flavoured and very pretty soup. Serve in plain white china bowls if possible.

2 large cucumbers
1 pt chicken stock
2 tablespoons tarragon vinegar
2 teaspoons caster sugar
fresh chives and parsley
salt and freshly-ground black pepper
$\frac{1}{2}$ pt double cream
$\frac{1}{2}$ pt thin cream

Reserve a few wafer thin slices of cucumber for garnish. Halve and de-seed, but do not peel the rest and roughly chop the flesh. Place in a pan with the chicken stock, bring to the boil, then simmer uncovered until quite tender. Add the sugar and vinegar and reduce to a purée in a liquidiser. Stir in 2 or more tablespoons each of chopped chives and parsley and, when cold, blend in all the double cream and $\frac{1}{4}$ pt single cream. Cover and chill in the fridge for several hours. Stir the soup well before serving, add more cream to thin if required and check for seasoning.

CURRY SOUP WITH APPLE
(serves 4)

A slightly odd sounding mixture perhaps, but one I find soothing and warming. The curry flavour is mild and the texture is creamy – diced apple gives a crisp finishing touch.

2 large onions
1 small Cox's apple
2 oz butter
1½ teaspoons curry powder
1 scant tablespoon plain flour
½ pt unsweetened apple juice (Just Juice or Waitrose own label)
¾ pt strong chicken stock
2 egg yolks
¼ pt double cream
a few spoonfuls coarsely chopped parsley
salt and freshly-ground black pepper

Quarter the onions and slice very thinly. Turn them in the melted butter, cover the pan and leave to sweat over low heat for 10–15 minutes. Meanwhile, beat the cream and egg yolks in a cup with some chopped parsley. Peel and dice the apple.

Add the curry powder and flour to the saucepan and cook stirring for a minute or so. Pour on the liquids and bring quickly to boiling point stirring continuously. Simmer for a couple of minutes.

Draw the pan to one side. Carefully whisk in the egg and cream liaison, adding it very gradually. Return the pan to low heat and cook the soup very gently until thickened to a delicate cream. Stir in the apple, adjust seasoning to taste (I sometimes add a squeeze of lemon juice) and serve immediately.

FISH CHOWDER
(serves 6)

Bacon goes well with smoked haddock, and the inclusion of lots of vegetables makes this colourful and well-flavoured soup a meal in itself. I simply serve bread and cheese afterwards.

1 lb smoked haddock fillet
6 oz green bacon in a piece
1 oz butter
1 onion
1 celery stalk

½ lb potatoes (peeled and diced weight)
1 green pepper
1 × 14 oz can of tomatoes
11–12 oz canned or frozen sweetcorn
1 pt milk
1 tablespoon cornflour
a bay leaf
salt and freshly-ground black pepper
chopped fresh parsley

Dice the bacon. Fry it in the butter with the chopped onion and sliced celery for 5 minutes. Add the green pepper cut into chunks and fry for a further 2–3 minutes. Add the potatoes, the roughly chopped tomatoes and their liquid, the bay leaf and a scant ½ pt boiling water. Cover and simmer gently for about 15 minutes until the potatoes are tender.

Meanwhile poach the haddock fillets gently in the milk for 5 minutes. Strain, reserving the milk, and when the fish is cool enough to handle, break it into large flakes. Blend the cornflour to a paste with a little of the milk, then blend in the rest of the milk.

Stir the milk into the soup pan together with the sweetcorn. Continue stirring until the liquid is slightly thickened and the sweetcorn heated through. Remove the bay leaf, and season to taste with salt and pepper. Add the flaked fish to the pan. Let it warm through again, then serve garnished with plenty of chopped fresh parsley.

JELLIED BORTSCH
(serves 6–8)

This excellent soup is best made with a good clear beef stock that is slightly jellied, but when none was available I once made it using 2 × 14 oz cans of Sainsbury's consommé plus water – and I boosted the setting qualities with a little gelatine powder.

¾–1 lb uncooked beetroot
2 large carrots
3 pt good, slightly jellied beef stock

2 dill-pickled cucumbers
1 large onion
2 inches cinnamon stick
2 cloves
a bay leaf, a few parsley stalks and a few sprigs of dill tied
   together with string (if fresh dill not available, use 3
   teaspoons dried dillweed)
about 3 teaspoons lemon juice
a little sugar, salt and freshly-ground black pepper
½ pt soured cream

Peel and grate the beetroot and carrots coarsely. Finely chop the cucumbers and onion. Put them into a very large pan together with the stock, cinnamon, cloves, bay leaf and herbs. Bring to the boil, cover and simmer gently for 45 minutes.

Remove from the heat and leave the pan, still covered, to stand for 30 minutes. Strain the liquid through a fine sieve lined with butter-muslin to extract vegetables and spicy sediment.

Season with a pinch of caster sugar, a good grinding of pepper, some salt and lemon juice to taste. When the soup is cold, cover and refrigerate until icy cold and set to a light jelly.

Serve the soup garnished with swirls of soured cream poured over the top of each bowl. Top with freshly-chopped dill leaves if available (or a few snipped chives) and/or – for a grand occasion – a spoonful of caviar or Danish lumpfish roe and wedges of lemon.

MOULES MARINIÈRE À LA CRÈME

I like to eat this popular Normandy dish in the fisherman's fashion – tucking a large napkin round my neck, tipping the mussels from shell to mouth with my fingers then spooning up the broth. Serves two (or four if served as a first course).

2 quarts fresh mussels
1 small onion
half a garlic clove
a small bunch of parsley
a few celery leaves
a small bay leaf

a small sprig of thyme
$\frac{1}{2}$ oz butter
$\frac{1}{4}$ pt dry white wine
scant $\frac{1}{4}$ pt double cream

Thoroughly wash the mussels, discarding broken ones and any that do not close when tapped. Chop the onion and garlic very finely. Cook the vegetables in the butter over low heat for 5–10 minutes until softened. Add the crushed parsley stalks, bay leaf, celery leaves and thyme tied together with string. Cover and set aside.

Bring the wine to the boil in a separate very large pan. Add the mussels, cover and cook over high heat for 4–5 minutes until the steam forces the mussels open. Strain the liquid through a muslin-lined sieve into the vegetable pan and let it simmer for a few minutes, uncovered, to concentrate flavour. Meanwhile, boil the cream until reduced by half. Also transfer the mussels to a hot soup tureen, throwing away any that have not opened.

Discard the bundle of herbs. Stir the hot cream into the broth. Check seasoning and add a handful of chopped parsley leaves. Pour the broth over the mussels and serve immediately.

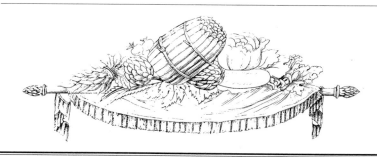

Starters

FRENCH BEAN APPETISER
(serves 2–3)

Delicious as a first course or side salad, and with a dressing that contains no oil. Double or treble quantities of all ingredients to serve more people.

> ½ lb pencil slim stringless French beans
> ¼ lb tomatoes
> 3 spring onions
> 1 tablespoon white wine vinegar
> 1 hard-boiled egg
> salt and freshly-ground black pepper

Top and tail the beans. Cook them in a little salted boiling water or — better still — steam them until just tender. Refresh them under a cold tap to arrest cooking and to help keep their fresh green colour. Drain very thoroughly and turn into a bowl. While they are still hot, pour the vinegar over them. Toss gently and leave for 10 minutes.

Meanwhile, plunge the tomatoes briefly in boiling water to loosen the skins. Drain and peel. Chop very finely or reduce to a purée in a liquidiser. Season generously with salt and pepper, and stir in the chopped spring onions (green parts as well as white). Lift the beans out of the vinegar, draining them well.

Arrange them in a shallow dish and pour the fresh tomato dressing over them. Chop the hard-boiled egg white finely and sprinkle them over the beans, then sieve the hard-boiled egg yolk over the top.

INDIVIDUAL BASIL AND TOMATO FLANS

Basil and tomatoes make perfect partners, and these little flans make a pretty and fresh-tasting first course or light lunch.

Shortcrust pastry made with 12 oz plain white flour and 6 oz butter.

For the filling:
$\frac{3}{4}$ lb tomatoes
1 teaspoon tomato purée
$\frac{1}{4}$ pt soured cream
2 × No 3 eggs
1 slightly heaped tablespoon fresh chopped basil
salt and freshly-ground black pepper

Heat the oven to 400F, 200C, gas mark 6, placing a baking sheet on the middle shelf. Use the pastry to line 6 small fluted flan tins with removable bases, measuring 4 inches across. Line with greaseproof paper and beans and blind bake for 12 minutes. Remove the paper and beans, brush the pastry bases with some of the white of 1 of the eggs, and bake for a further 12 minutes.

While the pastry is cooking, peel, seed and chop the tomato flesh. Season with salt, pepper, basil and tomato purée. Beat the whole egg, the remaining yolk and any left-over egg white together, stir in the soured cream and blend in the tomato mixture. Carefully pour the filling into the flans, reduce oven temperature to 375F, 190C, gas mark 5, and bake for a further 25 minutes. Let the flans cool for a minute or two before serving.

LENTIL AND ANCHOVY SALAD
(serves 6)

The combination of lentils and anchovies is smoky and interesting. This dish makes a lovely and rather unusual first course to serve in warm weather.

$\frac{1}{2}$ lb brown or slate grey whole French lentils
2 small onions

3–4 tablespoons olive oil
1 large garlic clove
the juice and zest of a lemon
about 3 tablespoons vinaigrette dressing
1 × 1¾ oz can of anchovy fillets
a bunch of parsley
1 large hard-boiled egg
salt and freshly-ground black pepper

Wash the lentils (there is no need to soak them) and slice the onions thinly. Warm the olive oil in a heavy-based pan, add the onions and lentils and stir over low heat until the oil is absorbed. Add the lemon juice and zest, the crushed garlic clove and about 1¼ pt cold water. Cover and simmer gently until the lentils are tender – about 1–1¼ hours. Drain off any liquid remaining in the pan, turn the cooked lentils into a shallow dish and toss lightly in the vinaigrette dressing. When the lentils are cold, gently stir in the drained and snipped anchovy fillets, a really generous quantity of coarsely chopped fresh parsley, and season to taste with salt and pepper.

Just before serving, sprinkle the top of the salad with the chopped hard-boiled egg white and the sieved yolk of the egg.

SWEET-PICKLED HERRINGS

I think these taste so much nicer than the harshly-flavoured roll-mops and pickled herrings you buy in shops, and they are amazingly easy to make. Packed into kilner jars and refrigerated, these herrings will keep well for up to 3 weeks – useful for standby meals.

8 fat fresh herrings
3 oz coarse salt
1½ pt cider vinegar
a small onion
4 tablespoons soft brown sugar
2 tablespoons pickling spices
1 teaspoon coriander seeds
1 teaspoon black peppercorns
1 bay leaf

Ask the fishmonger to prepare the herrings or do them yourself: remove heads and tails and gut the fish, cutting down the full length of the belly; lay the fish flesh side down and press the skin with the palm of your hand to flatten the fish and loosen the backbone. Turn the fish flesh side up, ease out the backbone with a knife, and divide the fish into two long fillets.

Put the fillets into a bowl, add the salt dissolved in $1\frac{1}{2}$ pt cold water. Leave the fish submerged in the brine for about 3 hours. Put all the remaining ingredients (except the onion) into a pan and bring to the boil. Immediately boiling point is reached, remove the pan from the heat, cover it and set aside until the liquid is cold.

Drain and dry the herrings. Lay them skin side down and put a few thin onion rings on each. Roll up each fillet, from wide to tail end, and secure with a cocktail stick.

Pack the fish into sterilised jars, and pour on enough of the strained pickling liquid to cover them completely. Cover with airtight vinegar-proof lids and refrigerate for a minimum of 3 days before serving.

SOUSED HERRINGS
(serves 4)

Delicious and fresh tasting. I serve these with lots of watercress, a little soured cream, and brown bread and butter.

    4 fat herrings filleted
    2 teaspoons coriander seeds
    2 teaspoons dillweed
    coarse salt and freshly-ground black pepper
    1 small onion
    white wine vinegar

Roll each fillet up neatly, from thick to tail end, with the skin on the outside. Lay the rolls, seam-side downwards, in a casserole, packing them tightly side by side in a single layer. Crush the coriander seeds with mortar and pestle. Mix them with the dillweed, some coarse salt and a generous grinding of black pepper. Sprinkle this mixture over the fish.

Slice the onion thinly and lay it on top. Pour on enough wine vinegar and water to immerse the fish completely using 2 parts of vinegar to 1 part of cold water. Cover with a lid, place in the oven and switch it on to 300F, 150C, gas mark 2. Cook very gently indeed for 2½–3 hours, reducing oven temperature to 275F, 140C, gas mark 1, or lower if the liquid begins to bubble vigorously.

This long, very slow cooking will completely soften the bones and impregnate the flesh with delicious flavourings. Thoroughly cool then refrigerate the soused herrings still immersed in their liquor, and drain well only just before serving. The herrings are excellent after 24 hours chilling; they will keep for 3 days or so during which time the vinegar flavour becomes gradually more pronounced.

CUCUMBER MOUSSE
(serves 4–6)

This looks very elegant served in a traditional white china soufflé dish but the delicate flavour and colour of the mousse will be ruined if it is not eaten on the day of making. Fromage blanc can be bought from good delicatessens and food stores. It is much nicer than cottage cheese, but cottage cheese could be used to replace half the fromage blanc if you wish. Remember to sieve cottage cheese before using.

> 10 oz thickened yoghurt (see page 246) or fromage blanc (Gervais green label is the best commercial variety I have tried)
> 1 large cucumber
> 2 teaspoons tarragon or white wine vinegar
> 1 teaspoon dried dillweed
> ¼ pt well-flavoured chicken stock
> 2½ teaspoons gelatine powder
> salt and freshly-ground black pepper

Measure the chicken stock into a small pan. Sprinkle on the gelatine powder and the dillweed. Leave to soak for 5 minutes then dissolve gelatine over low heat and set aside to cool. Wipe the cucumber skin. Cut off and slice 6 inches of the cucumber, reserve the rest. Put the cucumber slices into a liquidiser goblet together with the vinegar and half the fromage blanc or thick-ened yoghurt.

Beat the resulting purée into the remaining fromage blanc, then gradually beat in the cooling gelatine mixture. Adjust seasoning to taste, turn into a soufflé dish and chill until set. Garnish with the rest of the cucumber, cut into paper thin slices, just before serving.

FISHY AVOCADOS
(serves 4)

This piquant dish is like a fishy version of steak tartare. Prepare it well ahead to allow flavours to develop.

2 avocado pears
$\frac{1}{2}$ lb coley fillets
2 lemons
1 egg yolk
$2\frac{1}{2}$ fl. oz oil
$\frac{1}{2}$ teaspoon French mustard
1 teaspoon Worcester sauce
2 spring onions
3 midget gherkins
2 teaspoons capers
salt and freshly-ground black pepper
a small bunch of chives

Skin and flake the raw fish. Pour on the juice of 1 lemon and leave to macerate for $1\frac{1}{2}$ hours, gently turning the fish occasion-ally. About half an hour before the end of macerating time, make a piquant mayonnaise-type sauce – beat the egg yolk until sticky, season it well with salt, pepper and the mustard, gradu-ally beat in the oil, then thin it with the Worcester sauce. Chop the spring onions, gherkins and capers finely and stir them into the sauce. Halve and stone the avocados. Scoop out most of the flesh, leaving a thin wall of flesh in the shells. Dice the flesh and sprinkle both dice and shells with lemon juice.

Drain the fish and stir it gently into the sauce. Then carefully stir in the diced avocado. Pile the mixture into the shells, cover and chill for a minimum of 3 hours. Garnish with chopped chives just before serving.

PORK RILLETTES
(serves 4)

Suitable for serving at home or on a picnic, this pâté is tasty and very economic.

2½ lb lean belly of pork
½ lb pork back fat or flair
6 juniper berries, crushed with the back of a spoon then chopped into pieces
3 large garlic cloves crushed with plenty of salt
a large bouquet garni made up of a few sprigs of parsley and thyme tied together with a couple of bay leaves and a small sprig of rosemary
5 tablespoons white wine or very dry cider
freshly-grated nutmeg
freshly-ground black pepper

Remove bone and rind from the pork and cut both meat and fat into small cubes. Put them into a casserole together with all the herbs, spices, seasonings and wine or cider. Cover with foil and a lid and cook very gently indeed in a low oven (275F, 140C, gas mark 1) for 4–4½ hours.

Empty the contents of the casserole into a large sieve placed over a bowl. Remove the bouquet of herbs, then press the cubes of meat and fat lightly to help drain off excess fat.

Turn the meat and fat cubes into a large soup plate. Using 2 forks tear the cubes apart to make a soft shredded paste. Check seasoning and adjust to taste. Pack the paste, but not too firmly, into a dish or dishes. Spoon some of the melted fat over the top to seal. Decorate with fresh juniper and bay leaves when cold. Cover, refrigerate and eat within a week.

MUSHROOM FRITTERS WITH SKORDALIA

Deep-fried mushrooms in batter served with wedges of lemon or this Greek garlic-flavoured sauce make a tasty first course for 6 people.

$\frac{3}{4}$ lb flat mushrooms
a little vinaigrette

For the batter:
$\frac{1}{4}$ lb plain flour
a pinch of salt
2 tablespoons sunflower oil
10 tablespoons tepid water
2 small egg whites

For the skordalia:
$1\frac{1}{2}$ oz each fresh white breadcrumbs and ground almonds
4 or more fat garlic cloves
salt
lemon juice and olive oil

Sift the flour and salt into a bowl, and make a well in the centre. Add the sunflower oil and most of the water, and beat to make a very smooth batter. If it seems very thick (but bear in mind that the egg whites will lighten it later) beat in a little more water. Trim mushroom stalks level with caps. Brush each mushroom with a very little vinaigrette and set aside, gill side down, for half an hour.

Meanwhile make the sauce. Crush the garlic with mortar and pestle to make a paste. Soak the breakcrumbs in water and squeeze out excess. Gradually beat the breadcrumbs to a paste with the garlic. Season with salt then beat in the almonds. Gradually blend in as much olive oil as is needed to make a sauce the consistency of mayonnaise.

Add the oil drop by drop at first, making sure it is being properly absorbed, then thin it and flavour it with a little lemon juice.

Whisk the egg whites until stiff, fold them into the batter. Coat the mushrooms lightly with the batter and deep fry them in hot oil until golden and crisp on the outside but still juicy within. Serve piping hot with the chilled sauce.

COURGETTES À LA GRECQUE
(serves 4)

White wine is usually used when making this excellent appetiser, but I sometimes make it without — using 5 tablespoons water plus 1 tablespoon lemon juice in place of the wine

> 1 lb small courgettes
> 1 large onion
> 1 large garlic clove
> 4 tablespoons olive oil
> 6 tablespoons white wine
> 6 tablespoons cold water
> 2 tablespoons lemon juice
> 1 teaspoon coriander seeds
> a bay leaf
> parsley
> salt and freshly-ground black pepper

Warm the olive oil in a saucepan. Add the finely chopped onion and garlic, cover and sweat for 10 minutes over low heat. Mix the wine, water and lemon juice together in a cup, add the bay leaf, a few lightly crushed parsley stalks, and the coriander seeds lightly crushed with the back of a spoon. Tip the contents of the cup into the pan. Bring to the boil then leave to simmer, without a lid, for 3–4 minutes.

Meanwhile trim the courgettes, cut each one lengthways into 4 pieces, then cut across to make sticks about 2 inches long. Add the prepared courgettes to the pan, cover and cook gently for 5 minutes just stirring or shaking the pan occasionally to encourage even cooking. Add some salt and pepper and cook for a further 5 minutes — without the lid this time. Turn the mixture on to a serving dish and leave until cold. Remove bay leaf and parsley stalks and check seasoning just before serving.

PRAWNS WITH SHERRY
(serves 4–6)

Not a cheap dish but an easy and handsome starter – 1 lb crab meat can be used instead of prawns if you prefer.

> 3 pt freshly-boiled prawns in their shells
> 3–4 tablespoons sherry
> 4 tablespoons butter
> 2 tablespoons plain flour
> $\frac{1}{4}$ pt double cream
> $\frac{1}{4}$ pt single cream
> 2 tablespoons freshly-grated Parmesan cheese
> salt
> 2 tablespoons freshly-ground black pepper and a little nutmeg
> 2 oz toasted breadcrumbs

Peel the prawns, put them into a bowl, sprinkle with the sherry, toss lightly and set aside for half an hour. Use a little of the butter to grease 6 scallop shells or similar small shallow dishes that are heatproof. Use 2 tablespoons of the butter, the flour, the double and single creams to make a thick creamy sauce. Gently stir in the prawns and the juices that have collected in the bottom of their bowl. Cover and simmer very gently for 5–10 minutes until the prawns are heated through. Meanwhile heat the grill until very hot.

Remove the pan from the heat. Stir in the Parmesan cheese and season to taste with salt, pepper and a little nutmeg. Divide the mixture between the prepared dishes. Scatter the toasted crumbs over the shellfish mixture and top with the remaining butter cut into flakes. Flash under the grill until browned and piping hot, then serve immediately.

HUMMUS
(serves 3–4)

An unusual vegetable purée which is very popular in Arab countries. Tahini paste can be bought from most health food shops, as well as delicatessens, where you can also buy chick peas.

    2 oz chick peas
    2½ fl. oz tahini paste
    1 large juicy lemon
    1 large garlic clove
    a little fresh chopped parsley and a pinch of paprika or
        ground cumin for garnishing

Soak the chick peas overnight. Drain, rinse well under a tap, put into a saucepan and cover with plenty of fresh cold water. Do not add any salt – it will toughen the chick pea skins. Bring slowly to boiling point, then cover and simmer gently until the chick peas are quite tender. This takes 2 hours on average, but in my opinion it is almost impossible to overcook chick peas. Drain, reserving the cooking liquor separately from the peas.

Put the crushed garlic, lemon juice, chick peas and about 2 tablespoons of the chick pea cooking liquor into a blender. Reduce the mixture to a smooth purée.

Scrape the purée out into a mixing bowl and gradually beat in the tahini paste. Add some salt and thin the mixture to a very thick cream with extra cooking liquor or extra lemon juice (I find 3 tablespoons about right). Beat in a teaspoon of olive oil and add more garlic and/or salt to taste. Cover, chill and eat within 5 days. Garnish the purée with a little chopped parsley and a dusting of paprika or ground cumin just before serving.

CARROT AND CELERAIC REMOULADE

A lovely crunchy first course for 6 people. I also use it as a lunch dish for 3–4 in which case I add some sliced Frankfurter or bratwurst sausages just before serving and accompany the dish with plenty of good bread.

    ¾ lb carrots
    ¾ lb celeriac (trimmed weight)
    2 oz chopped walnut pieces

For the rémoulade sauce:
1 hard-boiled egg yolk
1 raw egg yolk
2 teaspoons French mustard
1½–2 tablespoons white wine vinegar
¼ pt oil
3 tablespoons yoghurt
salt and freshly-ground pepper

To make the sauce, pound the hard-boiled egg yolk to a fine powder. Carefully blend into it the raw egg yolk, then gradually beat in the mustard, vinegar, a little salt and pepper. Whisk in the oil, incorporating it very slowly at first then in a slow trickle. Finally beat in the yoghurt and adjust seasoning to taste.

Scrape the carrots clean and grate them coarsely. Grate the celeriac too. Mix it with the carrots and immediately (to prevent discolouration of the celeriac) stir the vegetables into the sauce, mixing in most of the nuts as well. Pile the mixture on to a serving dish and scatter the remaining nuts over the top. This can be made ahead but it is best to serve rémoulade fairly soon after the vegetables and nuts have been stirred into the sauce so that everything tastes really crunchy.

SMOKED MACKEREL MOUSSE
(serves 6–8)

Fish mousses are always popular, and the piquant flavourings and soured cream used here offset the richness of mackerel very well. It's a good recipe to remember when you've got some leftover egg whites.

2 medium-sized smoked mackerel
2 lemons
¼ pt soured cream

$\frac{1}{4}$ pt double cream
2 tablespoons grated horseradish
2 tablespoons French mustard
2 tablespoons chopped capers
2 tablespoons chopped spring onions
2 teaspoons gelatine powder
3 egg whites
salt
freshly-ground black pepper and cayenne

Finely grate the zest of $1\frac{1}{2}$ lemons and reserve. Squeeze the juice from $1\frac{1}{2}$ lemons into a small pan. Add 2 tablespoons water and sprinkle on the gelatine powder. Soak for 5 minutes, dissolve over low heat and set aside to cool. (Save the remaining half lemon to slice for garnishing the finished dish.)

Put the lemon zest into a blender goblet – or, better still, a food processor. Add the flaked fish and the soured cream and reduce to a smooth purée. If the blender blades stick, add some of the cooling gelatine.

Gradually beat in (the rest of) the cooling gelatine, the horseradish, mustard, capers, spring onions, and a good seasoning of salt and pepper. Whip the double cream softly and fold it in. Then whisk the egg whites and fold them in.

Check seasoning and turn into small ramekins or one large (about 3 pt) dish. Cover and chill until set. Garnish with lemon slices and cayenne pepper just before serving.

TOMATO ASPIC SALAD

This pretty salad will serve 8 as a first course or 4 as a lunch or supper dish.

2 lb tomatoes
1 small garlic clove
a sprig or two of fresh tarragon

¾ pt light home-made chicken stock
the juice of half a lemon
1 teaspoon caster sugar
2 teaspoons concentrated tomato purée
4 teaspoons gelatine powder

For the filling:
½ lb kipper fillets, poached, cooled and flaked
2 ripe avocado pears
vinaigrette dressing
a bunch of chives

Chop the tomatoes roughly. Put them into a saucepan with the herbs, the garlic crushed with salt, most of the chicken stock, lemon juice, sugar, tomato purée and a grinding of pepper. Cover and simmer gently until the tomatoes have disintegrated and are very tender. Sieve to extract tomato skins and seeds and the tarragon. Cool and adjust seasoning to taste.

Dissolve the gelatine powder in the remaining stock and blend it into the tomato liquid. When cold pour the mixture into a chilled 2 pt ring mould.

Cover and refrigerate until set firm. Turn out on to a serving dish and fill the centre with the cold fish which has been mixed with the diced avocados, snipped chives and a generous lubrication of vinaigrette dressing.

AVOCADO MOUSSE
(serves 6)

This is easily made and pretty looking. To turn it into a light lunch dish add extra goodies to the filling — chunks of tuna or chopped anchovies and quartered hard-boiled eggs.

2 large very ripe avocado pears
4 tablespoons chopped chives
4 tablespoons chopped parsley
2 tablespoons lemon juice
¾ pt soured cream
¼ pt light cold chicken stock
1 tablespoon gelatine powder

1 egg white
salt, freshly-ground black pepper and Hungarian paprika

For the filling:
Tomatoes peeled, quartered and dipped in vinaigrette dressing
a little chopped but not peeled cucumber
a small handful of black olives

Measure half the stock into a small pan. Sprinkle on the gelatine powder, soak for 5 minutes, dissolve over low heat and set aside to cool.

Meanwhile peel the avocados very carefully so that none of the dark green flesh close to the skin is lost. Stone and dice and put it into a blender with the lemon juice. Add the herbs and soured cream and the remaining cold chicken stock, and reduce to a perfectly smooth green purée. Gradually blend in the cooled gelatine, pouring it through the hole in the lid with the machine still running.

Season generously with salt and pepper – and extra lemon if you wish. Whisk the egg white softly and fold it into the mixture. Turn it into a ring mould that has been rinsed with cold water, cover and chill until set.

To serve (and this is a mousse which should be served on the day of making or the avocado will turn khaki coloured), unmould the mousse, dust it with paprika and fill the centre with the prepared tomatoes, cucumber and olives mixed together.

CHEESE AND ONION FLAN
(serves 4–8)

This makes a lovely first course for 8 people, or an inexpensive and excellent supper dish for 4. Prolonged baking of the pastry before adding the filling means that this flan is also very good cold – if there are any leftovers!

Shortcrust pastry made with 3 oz wholewheat flour, 3 oz plain flour and 3 oz butter

For the filling:
1 lb small onions
2 oz butter
1 tablespoon sunflower oil
2 eggs
$\frac{1}{4}$ pt soured cream
salt and freshly-ground black pepper
2 oz grated Cheddar cheese

Make the pastry and use it to line a 9 inch French fluted flan tin. Blind bake it at 400F, 200C, gas mark 6, on a preheated baking sheet – for 12 minutes with beans, then brush the pastry base with some of the egg white from the filling ingredients, and continue blind baking for a further 12 minutes.

To make the filling, halve then slice the onions. Sweat them in the butter and oil in a covered pan over gentle heat for 20 minutes – stirring occasionally to prevent sticking. Then uncover and cook for a further 5 minutes. Set aside and cool slightly while you beat the eggs and soured cream together with a very generous seasoning of salt and pepper. Stir in the onions and pour the mixture into the flan case. Sprinkle the grated cheese on top and bake – again using the preheated baking sheet and the same oven temperature – for 25–30 minutes until the filling is puffy and golden.

ASPARAGUS WITH MELTED LEMON BUTTER
(serves 6)

Thick white stems of asparagus are said to be the best. I am more than happy to settle for the thinner green sprue or 'sparrow grass' which is a good deal cheaper. It is usually sold loose rather than in bundles and, although most people rate it as suitable only for flans and soups, I think it is a waste of asparagus to cook it by any method other than steam-boiling.

3 lb asparagus
1 lemon
6 oz clarified butter
salt and freshly-ground black pepper

Choose asparagus stalks of the same thickness so they will all take the same time to cook. Wash carefully. Trim off woody bases making the stalks all the same length. Scrape the stems with a knife to remove scaly leaf points.

Set aside one stem, which will be used to test cooking time, divide the rest into 6 bunches and tie each bunch with soft string in 2 places.

Fill a tall saucepan with enough water to come two-thirds of the way up the asparagus stems. Salt it lightly, add a couple of lemon slices and bring to the boil.

Stand the bundles and single asparagus stem in the pan. Cover with a dome of foil taking care that it does not touch the asparagus tips. Bring back to simmering point and cook until tender — the tougher stems will cook in the water while the tender tips cook in the steam so the whole vegetable will complete cooking at the same time, 10–15 minutes depending on thickness.

To make the sauce simply heat the butter with the finely grated lemon zest. When very hot stir in $1\frac{1}{2}$ tablespoons lemon juice and season with salt and pepper to taste.

PRAWN AND APPLE COCKTAIL
(serves 4)

Prawn cocktails often seem to major on limp shredded lettuce and synthetic tasting pink sauce. Using crisp and crunchy salad ingredients and a home-made lemon-flavoured mayonnaise is a great improvement.

$1\frac{1}{4}$–$1\frac{1}{2}$ lb boiled prawns
1 large or 2 small Cox's or other crisp eating apple
2 tender celery stalks
1 oz cashew or walnuts
a few sprigs of watercress
about 8–10 tablespoons mayonnaise which is well flavoured
    with lemon juice and a little mustard

This may sound like a lot of prawns but don't forget that the shells account for over half the weight. The easiest way to shell a prawn is to hold it with its head in your left hand and its tail in your right hand. Uncurl the prawn and straighten it out as much as possible. Then press the head and tail towards each other in a straight line and then pull them apart again – the shell should come away in your right hand, leaving the head and body in your left hand. Then simply separate the head from the body.

Put the shelled prawns into a bowl and sprinkle them with a little salt.

Peel, core and cut the apple into smallish bite-sized pieces. Add them to the bowl together with the nuts and the chopped celery (choose tender small celery stalks taken from the heart). Add most of the mayonnaise and toss everything lightly together.

Add extra mayonnaise, freshly-ground black pepper and/or a little lemon zest to taste. Then pile the mixture into small glasses or individual soufflé dishes, each lined with a sprig or two of watercress.

PIGEON PÂTÉ

I make this using breast meat only (nearly all the meat on a pigeon is on the breast) and use the carcasses complete with leg and wing meat to make a delicious gamey soup. The pâté will keep for 10 days or so in a refrigerator and it is always best to leave 2 days between cooking and eating to allow the flavours to mature.

2 pigeons
$\frac{1}{4}$ lb pork back fat
$\frac{1}{2}$ lb lean pork
$\frac{1}{2}$ lb veal
$\frac{1}{4}$ lb pig's liver
6 oz streaky bacon
$\frac{1}{4}$ lb onions
2 large garlic cloves
12 juniper berries
4 tablespoons brandy

2 small eggs
salt and freshly-ground black pepper

Cut the breasts off the pigeons, peel away skin, dice the flesh and marinate in the brandy for 2–6 hours. Then cut the back fat into tiny cubes.

Mince the remaining meats, onion, garlic and juniper berries. Mix well with the lightly beaten eggs and a very generous seasoning of salt and pepper. Stir in the diced fat and pigeon meat together with the marinade liquid. Fry a marble-sized piece of the mixture if you want to check seasoning, then divide the mixture between 2 lightly oiled dishes each of $1\frac{1}{4}$–$1\frac{1}{2}$ pt capacity.

Cover with lightly oiled kitchen foil, place in a roasting tin with enough hot water to come half-way up the sides of the dishes and bake at 325F, 160C, gas mark 3 for 2–$2\frac{1}{2}$ hours: just how long depends on the shape and depth of the dish.

Remove the roasting tin and uncover the pâtés for the last 15 minutes of cooking time to allow the top to brown a little. Cover the pâtés again after cooking, top each with a plate and some weights and leave overnight in a cold place. Then, if wished, seal with melted fat and decorate with bay leaves, juniper berries and slices of orange.

DUCK PÂTÉ WITH BRANDY

This pâté is not the cheapest of mixtures but delicious and suitably festive for Christmas. I suggest that you make it in several small pots rather than in one large dish. This is because once cut open a pâté should be eaten within a day or so. If you don't have suitable pâté dishes, you can use small (1 lb size) Kilner jars instead.

1 × $4\frac{1}{2}$ lb duck (drawn weight)
6 tablespoons brandy
$\frac{1}{2}$ lb belly of pork (boned and de-rinded weight)
$\frac{1}{2}$ lb pig's liver
1 orange
8 juniper berries

1 oz pistachio nuts (shelled weight)
generous half teaspoon dried lemon thyme
3 oz fresh white breadcrumbs
salt and freshly-ground black pepper
½ lb pork back fat

Cut through the skin of the duck's breast. Peel it back and, using a small sharp knife, ease the meat away from the breast bone. Slice the breast meat into small slivers, put it into a small bowl, add the brandy, cover and leave in a cold place for several hours. Skin and bone the remaining duck meat and set it aside separately togehter with the duck liver. Make a good stock with the bones, skin and giblets.

Mince the belly of pork together with the pig's liver, the duck liver and all the duck meat excepting the breast meat. Mix these meats in a large mixing bowl with the juice and finely grated zest of the orange, the juniper berries (crushed with mortar and pestle), the lemon thyme, the pistachio nuts, fresh white breadcrumbs and a good seasoning of salt and pepper. Add the slivers of breast meat and the brandy in which it was marinated. Stir again to mix everything well. Then fry a tiny nugget of the mixture to check seasoning, and adjust to taste.

Cut the pork back fat into ¾ in slices, then into neat long strips. Lay the strips of fat in parallel lines, diagonally, across the base of your chosen dishes or pots (you will need a total capacity of about 2½ pt). Then lay more strips at right angles to the first strips to make a lattice pattern, and press strips of fat up the sides of the dish. Pack the duck pâté mixture into the prepared dishes. Top each with a lattice of pork back fat. Add a bay leaf then cover first with greaseproof paper and then with a foil 'lid'.

Stand the dishes in a roasting pan. Pour in enough boiling water to come half-way up the sides of the dishes. Then bake in an oven preheated to 350F, 180C, gas mark 4, for 2½–2¾ hours.

When the pâtés are cooked remove them from the roasting pan but do not uncover them. Cut a very thick piece of cardboard to fit neatly just inside the top of each dish. Put weights (or jars of jam) on top of the cardboard, and leave the dishes of pâté in a cold larder overnight.

Reduce the duck stock to a few syrupy spoonfuls and allow it to cool slightly. Meanwhile uncover the pâtés. If the meats have exuded a lot of fat, scrape off excess — taking care not to dislodge the lattice strips of pork back fat. Spoon a little of the syrupy glaze over the top of each pâté to seal it decoratively.

Cover and keep the pâtés under refrigeration until shortly before serving. Allow a minimum of 3 days between making and eating so that the pâtés have time to mature. Decorate the top of each pâté with a few bay leaves or a slice of orange just before serving or giving away as presents.

Eggs and Cheese

SIMPLE FLORENTINE
(serves 2)

When sweet-tasting summer spinach is in its prime this quick and easy recipe makes a good and inexpensive lunch or supper dish.

$1\frac{1}{2}$ lb fresh spinach
4 eggs
3 oz grated Cheddar cheese
$\frac{1}{4}$ pt soured cream
$1\frac{1}{2}$ oz slightly stale brown breadcrumbs
salt and freshly-ground black pepper
butter

Put the cheese, soured cream and a good grinding of pepper into a small bowl and stir together to make a creamy sauce. Wash the spinach very thoroughly in cold salted water, discarding any yellowing leaves and tough stalks. Drain, shake dry and pack into a large saucepan.

Boil the eggs for 5–6 minutes – until the whites are firmly set but the yolks are still liquid in the centre. Meanwhile, heat the grill and cook the spinach – taking great care not to overcook it or to reduce it to a slushy mess. The best method, I think, is to cook the spinach in a covered pan over medium heat for 2–3 minutes until the leaves have wilted (turn the leaves once or twice during this time to encourage even cooking). Then remove the lid and continue cooking, still stirring occasionally, for about 3 minutes more – until the spinach is just tender and most of the moisture has been driven off. Now, season the spinach with salt and pepper and stir in $1-1\frac{1}{2}$ oz butter cut up into small dice. Switch off the heat but leave the uncovered pan on the stove; residue heat will keep the spinach hot and evaporation will continue.

Butter a gratin dish and shell the eggs. Put the spinach into the dish, make hollows and lay the eggs in them. Pour the sauce over the eggs, sprinkle the breadcrumbs on top and cover with wafer thin flakes of butter. Cook under a medium-hot grill until the sauce is heated through and the crumbs are golden and crunchy.

GREEN HERB FLAN
(serves 4–6)

The fresh taste of green herbs, cream and buttery crisp pastry combine well in this dish, which could be cooked in 6 individual 4 inch flan tins if you prefer. If you make individual flans you will need pastry made with 12 oz flour and 6 oz butter.

> shortcrust pastry made with 3 oz plain flour, 3 oz wholemeal flour and 3 oz butter
>
> *For the filling:*
> enough fresh chopped herbs to come up to the $\frac{1}{4}$ pt level in a measuring jug (I use mostly parsley, a good quantity of chives and a little tarragon)
> 2 eggs
> 2 tablespoons freshly-grated Parmesan cheese
> $\frac{1}{4}$ pt single cream
> $\frac{1}{4}$ pt soured cream
> salt and freshly-ground black pepper

Line an 8 inch flan tin with the pastry, prick the base with a fork, line with greaseproof paper and weigh down with beans. Bake on a preheated baking tray at 400F, 200C, gas mark 6, for 10 minutes. Remove beans and paper, brush the pastry base with a little egg white and bake for a further 10–15 minutes.

Add the eggs, creams, cheese, salt and pepper to the herbs in the measuring jug. Blend together with a fork. Pour the mixture into the pastry case, reduce oven temperature to 375F, 190C, gas mark 5 and bake for about 25 minutes more until the herb custard is set. Serve warm or cold.

GNOCCHI ALLA ROMANA
(serves 4)

This excellent dish bears no resemblance whatsoever to semolina pudding! Italian friends of mine used to vary gnocchi – sometimes stirring in herbs as here, sometimes adding finely chopped ham, sometimes omitting the cheese topping and serving the gnocchi with a pesto sauce instead. I once made it replacing part (not all) the Parmesan with Cheddar cheese to keep costs down.

$\frac{1}{2}$ pt milk
$\frac{1}{2}$ pt water
4–5 oz semolina
4–5 oz Parmesan cheese
freshly-grated nutmeg
salt and pepper
6 tablespoons chopped fresh parsley (optional)
2 oz butter
2 small eggs

Bring the milk and water, seasoned with salt, pepper and nutmeg, to the boil. Tip in the semolina, stirring as you do so to prevent lumps forming (if very fine semolina is used 4–4$\frac{1}{2}$ oz will be enough, but 5 oz is usually best). Cook over gentle heat stirring continuously for about 8 minutes or until the mixture is so thick that the spoon will stand up in it.

Away from the heat, stir in the parsley and 3 oz of the grated cheese, then beat in the eggs one at a time. When well blended spread the mixture into a baking tray or other shallow tin measuring about 9 × 12 inches, which has been lined with oiled greaseproof paper.

Leave uncovered in a cold place overnight: the mixture will dry out sufficiently to cut up into pieces.

Next day, rub a gratin dish with some of the butter and let it heat up under a medium-hot grill. Cut the gnocchi mixture into 1–1½ inch squares. Arrange them in the dish, slightly overlapping like roof-tiles. Cover with flakes of the remaining butter and cook under the medium-hot grill until very hot and beginning to brown – about 6 minutes.

Baste the gnocchi with the buttery juices. Scatter 1–2 oz Parmesan over the top, increase heat and grill until the cheese is melted.

HERB OMELETTE WITH CROÛTONS
(serves 1)

An omelette made with newly-laid eggs, fresh herbs and good butter, is one of the quickest and best of all dishes.

> 3 large eggs
> 1 good tablespoon fresh chopped chervil (or tarragon, or a mixture of chives and parsley)
> salt and freshly-ground black pepper
> unsalted butter
> a small handful of tiny cubes of slightly stale bread, fried in butter until golden, well drained and kept hot

Set a 7 inch omelette pan over low heat to warm slowly. Meanwhile, chop the herbs with kitchen scissors in a small bowl. Crack the eggs into the bowl and add a little salt and a grinding of pepper. Use a fork to break up the yolks and stir them lightly into the other ingredients.

Add a good knob of butter to the pan and increase the heat. As soon as the butter has melted, swirl the pan to film the whole of the base and sides with fat.

Pour in the eggs and almost immediately tilt the pan away from you. Use the fork to draw the cooked egg towards you; the raw egg will trickle across the pan to take its place.

Set the pan down again — just for a moment or so until the whole base of the omelette is set but the surface is still deliciously soft and creamy.

Quickly scatter the croûtons over the top half of the omelette furthest away from you. Flick the part nearest you over the filling, and turn the omelette out on to a warm plate. Top it with an extra flake of butter and eat immediately.

WEST COUNTRY RAREBIT
(serves 1–2)

This variation of Welsh rarebit makes a very substantial snack. Or, if served with a watercress or chicory salad, it makes a good light lunch dish. Either way cider is the perfect drink to go with West Country Rarebit.

> 3 large slices granary bread
> 1 large crisp eating apple
> 3 thick slices Wiltshire ham
> generous $\frac{1}{4}$ lb farmhouse Cheddar cheese
> butter
> mustard (preferably Urchfont wholegrain mustard)

Lightly toast the bread on both sides. Spread the toast generously on one side, first with butter then with mustard. Then cut each slice of toast in half. Cut or fold the ham so that it will lie neatly on top of the bread. Peel, core and slice the apples fairly thinly. Arrange the apple slices on top of the ham. Finally, grate the cheese and sprinkle it over the apple.

Reduce the grill temperature to fairly low. Carefully place the slices of bread on the grid of the grill pan, and cook under fairly low heat for about 5 minutes or until the ingredients are well heated through.

Then increase the temperature a little and cook for a minute or so longer, until the cheese is bubbling and lightly browned. Serve straight away on hot plates.

BAKED EGGS NENETTE
(serves 6)

Baked eggs topped with a piquant cream make a good and very easy dinner party first course. I like to serve these with wholemeal toast.

>   6 large eggs
>   a little butter
> $\frac{1}{4}$ pt double cream
>   salt and freshly-ground black pepper
>   3 teaspoons French mustard
>   a scant teaspoon tomato purée
>   2–3 tablespoons each fresh chopped chives and parsley

Heat the oven to 375F, 190C, gas mark 5 and bring a kettle of water to the boil. Lightly butter 6 cocotte dishes, break an egg into each, and stand them in a roasting pan. Pour enough boiling water into the pan to come about halfway up the sides of the egg dishes. Cover the pan with a sheet of foil, or stand a baking tray on top of the egg dishes to cover them. Bake in the centre of the oven until the whites are set and the yolks still soft – 10–15 minutes depending on the idiosyncrasy of your oven, but take care not to overcook the eggs and remember that they will continue to cook slightly even after they are removed from the oven (due to the heat of the dishes).

Meanwhile measure the cream into a small saucepan and boil for a few minutes until slightly reduced. Away from the heat, stir in the mustard, tomato purée and a seasoning of salt and pepper. When smoothly blended, stir in the chopped fresh herbs. Pour the hot cream over the eggs and serve immediately.

BOMBAY EGGS
(serves 4–5)

Curried eggs make a cheap and satisfying supper dish. I serve them on a bed of rice, top them with snipped chives or parsley for colour and serve accompanied by lots of poppadoms. If you like really hot food increase the chilli powder.

10 hard-boiled eggs
$\frac{3}{4}$ lb onions
2 oz butter
2 teaspoons oil
1 teaspoon cumin seeds
1 teaspoon coriander seeds
$\frac{1}{2}$ teaspoon chilli powder
$\frac{1}{2}$ teaspoon turmeric
a pinch each of ground cinnamon and ground cloves
4 teaspoons plain flour
half a chicken stock cube dissolved in 1 pt boiling water
2 Cox's or other crisp dessert apples
4 tablespoons juice from a jar of mango chutney
2 tablespoons chives or parsley

Chop the onion and cook it gently in the butter and oil until slightly softened – about 5–7 minutes. Crush the cumin and coriander seeds with mortar and pestle. Stir them into the onion and, when the mixture smells warm and aromatic, sprinkle on the flour, chilli powder, turmeric, ground cinnamon and cloves all mixed together.

Stir briefly, pour on the hot stock and keep stirring until the mixture comes to the boil. Then reduce heat to very low and let it simmer uncovered for 15–20 minutes (just stirring occasionally) until the sauce is reduced to a good consistency and is well flavoured.

Meanwhile, peel, core and dice the apples. Halve the hard-boiled eggs and arrange them on a bed of hot, freshly-boiled rice (I allow 10 oz for 4 people with good appetites). When the sauce is ready, taste it and add a little salt – and extra chilli powder if you wish. Stir in the diced apple and 4 tablespoons juice from a jar of mango chutney. Pour the sauce over the eggs.

RAMSBURY SALAD
(serves 2)

This salad is full of goodies and makes an excellent main dish for a summery lunch or supper.

$\frac{1}{4}-\frac{1}{2}$ lb fresh young spinach leaves

2 thick slices of slightly stale bread rubbed with a cut garlic clove, cut into large dice, then fried in a mixture of oil and butter, and allowed to become cold

2 eggs

$\frac{1}{4}$ lb streaky bacon

a good grinding of black pepper

1–2 tablespoons vinaigrette dressing

First fry the croûtons, drain them well on kitchen paper and allow to become cold. Then hard-boil the eggs and also allow to cool. Wash the spinach very thoroughly in at least two changes of salted, cold water. Discard any yellowing leaves and tough stalks.

Drain the spinach very thoroughly, dry and turn it into a salad bowl. De-rind the bacon, cut into matchstick strips and put into a frying pan. Cook over gentle heat until the fat begins to run, then increase heat and fry until the bacon is deliciously crispy.

Pour the vinaigrette over the spinach (just enough to barely moisten the leaves) and toss lightly. Add the roughly chopped hard-boiled eggs, the crispy bacon and the hot liquid bacon fat. Toss the salad once more. Sprinkle the cold croûtons over the top of the salad bowl, and serve immediately.

PAN HAGGERTY

(serves 4)

A homely and substantial supper dish which is easy to cook and inexpensive to make. The potatoes need to be sliced fairly thinly: an electric slicer or mandoline does this job far quicker and more evenly than an ordinary kitchen knife.

2 lb potatoes

$\frac{3}{4}$ lb onions

5 oz mature Cheddar cheese

3 tablespoons melted bacon fat or good beef dripping

salt and freshly-ground black pepper

6–8 oz streaky bacon rashers (optional)

Peel and slice the potatoes quite thinly. Chop the onions finely, and grate the cheese. Melt 2 tablespoons fat in a large, heavy-based frying pan about 11 or 12 inches in diameter. Draw the pan aside from the heat and layer the ingredients in it — potatoes first (and also last) then onions, then cheese, sprinkling a good seasoning of pepper and a little salt between layers.

Cover the pan with a double-thickness of foil to make a well-fitting lid. Return the pan to the heat and steam fry gently for 30 minutes, by the end of which the vegetables should be tender. Remove the lid and increase the heat a bit, and cook for a further 3 minutes or so to drive off most of the moisture and to brown the underside of the potato cake. Meanwhile heat the grill until medium-hot.

Brush remaining fat over the surface of the potatoes, and cook under the grill for about 7 minutes to brown the top nicely. If using bacon, then lay the rashers across the top of the pan and grill for a further 2–3 minutes, turning the bacon as necessary, until crispy. Serve straight from the pan.

SCOTCH WOODCOCK

This piquant variation on scrambled eggs serves 4 as a first course or savoury, or 2 people as a quick snack.

> 6 fresh eggs
> 2 oz butter
> 1 can anchovy fillets
> 2 tablespoons double cream
> a little fresh chopped parsley
> a pinch of salt
> freshly-ground black pepper and cayenne pepper
> 4 rounds of thin brown or white bread

Drain the anchovies and mash half of them with half the butter to make a savoury paste. Toast the rounds of bread, spread them with the savoury butter, and keep hot.

Melt the remaining butter in a saucepan. Beat the eggs lightly with just a pinch of salt (because the anchovies provide quite a bit of salt), and a good grinding of black pepper. Add the eggs to the pan and cook, stirring continuously, over medium-low heat until gently scrambled.

Away from the heat, stir in the cream to stop the eggs from continuing to cook, and stir in a little chopped parsley. Pile the scrambled eggs on to the rounds of hot buttery toast, top each with strips of the remaining anchovy fillets and a sprinkling of cayenne pepper. Serve immediately.

CHEESE PUFF
(serves 4)

Grilled tomatoes and/or a green salad go well with this easy savoury pudding.

$\frac{3}{4}$ pt milk
butter
$\frac{1}{4}$ lb fresh brown breadcrumbs
6 oz grated Cheddar cheese
salt
pepper
cayenne
2 teaspoons mild mustard
2 tablespoons each fresh chopped parsley and chives
3 medium-sized eggs

Heat the oven to 425F, 220C, gas mark 7 and place a baking sheet on the shelf just above the centre. Measure the milk and 1 oz butter into a pan and bring to scalding point.

Away from the heat stir the crumbs into the hot milk. Add some salt, freshly-ground black pepper and a little cayenne and set aside for a few minutes. Meanwhile lightly butter a baking dish of 2 pt capacity (I use a Pyrex oval pie dish), grate the cheese, chop the herbs and lightly beat the eggs.

Beat all but about half an ounce of the cheese into the breadcrumbs.

When the oven has reached the correct temperature, stir the mustard and herbs into the breadcrumbs. Then add the eggs and beat thoroughly until everything is well blended.

Check seasoning adding more salt, mustard and pepper or herbs if you wish. Turn the mixture into the greased dish, scatter the remaining cheese over the top, and pop it on to the hot baking sheet in the oven. Bake for about 30 minutes until golden, slightly risen and smelling delicious.

LIKKY FLAN
(serves 4)

Early season tender young leeks have a lovely delicate flavour. Cooked in a creamy egg custard, and topped with a little bacon and cheese, they make a very good flan for lunch or supper.

> Shortcrust pastry made with 3 oz wholewheat flour, 3 oz plain flour and 3 oz butter
>
> *For the filling:*
> $\frac{1}{2}$ lb young leeks (trimmed weight)
> 1 oz butter
> 2 eggs
> $\frac{1}{4}$ pt single cream
> 1 oz grated cheese
> 2 or 3 rashers of streaky bacon
> salt
> freshly-ground black pepper and nutmeg

Put a baking sheet into the oven and heat to 400F, 200C, gas mark 6. Use the pastry to line an 8 inch fluted French flan tin. Line the pastry with a circle of greaseproof paper and weigh down with beans. Blind bake on the hot baking sheet for 10 minutes. Remove paper and beans, brush the base of the pastry with a little white of one of the eggs, and bake for a further 10 minutes.

Meanwhile thinly slice the leeks. Turn them in melted butter over low heat, cover the pan and sweat for 10 minutes to soften. Beat the eggs and cream with a seasoning of salt, pepper and freshly-grated nutmeg. Cut up the bacon into matchstick strips.

Stir the leeks and their buttery juices into the egg and cream mixture. Pour it into the partially baked pastry case. Sprinkle the cheese and bacon matchsticks over the top and bake for 25–30 minutes until the custard has just set, is puffed up and lightly golden.

ŒUFS SOUBISE

These eggs, bathed in a creamy onion sauce and garnished with lots of triangles of fried bread, make a good light lunch dish for 2 people. Or, if you hard-boil an extra egg, you can divide the mixture between 6 individual soufflé dishes and serve it as a first course for 6 people.

> 5 hard-boiled eggs
> $\frac{3}{4}$ lb onions
> 2 oz butter
> 2 teaspoons flour
> salt and freshly-ground black pepper
> a little freshly-grated nutmeg
> $\frac{1}{4}$ pt good stock
> $2\frac{1}{2}$ fl. oz soured cream or thickened yoghurt (see page 246)
> $\frac{1}{2}$ oz grated Gruyère or Cheddar cheese
> triangles of fried bread

Chop the onions fairly finely. Melt the butter in a saucepan. Add the onions, stir to coat well with fat, then cover and sweat for 10 minutes. Sprinkle on the flour. Stir it in. Pour on the stock and cook, stirring continuously, until the mixture comes to boiling point. Then reduce heat, add a seasoning of salt, pepper and nutmeg, half cover the pan and leave it to simmer gently for about 10 minutes. Stir the mixture occasionally during this time.

Turn the contents of the pan into a blender and reduce to a smooth purée.

Reheat gently, check seasoning and adjust to taste. If the consistency of the sauce is very thick, thin it with a spoonful of the soured cream. Arrange the halved eggs in a gratin dish, pour the sauce over the eggs, drizzle the soured cream over the top, then sprinkle on the grated cheese. Pop the dish under a hot grill for 2–3 minutes to heat the soured cream and to make the cheese melt and bubble. Garnish with triangles of fried bread and serve.

TOMATO, TARRAGON AND EGG MOUSSE
(serves 6 as a main course)

Basil is the classic herb for tomatoes, but this combination is equally good, and the mousse has an interesting texture as well as a deliciously fresh flavour.

    1¼ lb ripe tomatoes, skinned and finely chopped
    1 × 8 oz can of tomatoes
    2 tablespoons fresh chopped French tarragon
    8 hard-boiled eggs
    2 tablespoons lemon juice
    1 tablespoon each tomato purée and Worcester sauce
    4 teaspoons gelatine powder
    ¼ pt double cream and ¼ pt sour cream
    1½ tablespoons caster sugar
    salt and freshly-ground black pepper

Turn the canned tomatoes into a sieve placed over a small saucepan so that the juices drip through. Mix the canned and fresh tomato flesh together and pass them through a vegetable mill. Season with tarragon, lemon, sugar, tomato purée, Worcester sauce and plenty of salt and pepper.

Dissolve the gelatine in the tomato juice and blend it into the mixture. Stir in the sieved egg yolks and the finely chopped egg whites.

Stir the creams together then whip them softly and fold them into the egg and tomato mixture. Check seasoning and adjust to taste. Turn the contents of the mixing bowl into a soufflé dish or bowl of about 3½ pt capacity, cover and chill for a minimum of 4 hours. Decorate with a sliced tomato and a little fresh chopped tarragon just before serving.

QUICHE LORRAINE
(serves 4)

A classic quiche Lorraine is a delicate dish. It does not include cheese, and is never made with milk.

To make it correctly you will need:

> shortcrust pastry made with 4 oz flour and 2 oz butter
>
> *For the filling:*
> 5 oz smoked streaky bacon
> 2 medium-sized eggs
> 8 fl. oz cream (double cream for preference, but you can use single or a mixture of double and single cream)
> freshly-grated nutmeg, salt and freshly-ground black pepper

Make the pastry, use it to line an 8 inch fluted flan tin with removable base, and partially blind bake it at 400F, 200C, gas mark 6, using a little egg white from the filling ingredients to brush the pastry base and sides.

Remove the rinds from the bacon (it is worth buying freshly cut rashers of really good bacon for this dish rather than using vacuum-packed supermarket bacon) and cut the bacon into matchstick strips. Cook in a frying pan over gentle heat until the fat begins to run and the bacon is just coloured.

Beat the eggs with a fork. Add the cream, a grating of nutmeg, a generous grinding of black pepper, some salt and beat again.

Reduce oven temperature to 375F, 190C, gas mark 5. Scatter the bacon over the partially blind baked pastry base, and pour on the creamy custard mixture. Bake, standing the flan tin on a preheated baking sheet, for 25–30 minutes until the custard is puffed up, pale gold and just firm.

TORTILLA

Accompanied by hot crusty bread, this tasty and quickly cooked dish is ample for 4 people. Tortilla is also good cold, when I serve it with a salad.

> 8 medium-sized eggs
> 1 lb peeled potatoes cut into small dice

2 Spanish onions chopped
1 green pepper cut into dice
2–3 oz chorizio or other spiced sausage
olive oil
salt and freshly-ground black pepper

Choose a heavy-based frying pan about 11–12 inches in diameter. Heat 5 tablespoons olive oil in it. Add the diced potato and cook over medium-low heat for about 5 minutes, turning the potato as necessary. Add the chopped Spanish onions and continue cooking quite gently for a further 5 minutes until the vegetables are softened. Add a drop more oil if the potatoes begin to stick. Then turn up the heat, add the diced pepper and fry for 3 minutes to brown the vegetables nicely. Reduce heat again slightly and add a few drops more oil. Slice the sausage thinly and add it to the pan. Beat the eggs with a good seasoning of salt and pepper and pour them over the sausage and vegetable mixture. Leave to cook over medium-low heat for 4 minutes until the base of tortilla is golden brown and the centre top is beginning to set. Then transfer the pan to a preheated grill to colour and set the top of the omelette. Cut into wedges, like a cake, and serve.

SUPPLI AL TELEFONO

Use Italian rice (usually called arborio and available from Italian grocers and good delicatessens) to make this unusual and inexpensive dish. Serve it as a first course for 8 or as a main dish for 4 people, in which case a fresh tomato sauce makes a good accompaniment.

$\frac{3}{4}$ lb arborio rice
3 eggs
6 oz Mozzarella or Bel Paese cheese
6 oz ham cut in thick slices
a little flour
about 5 oz fresh breadcrumbs
salt and freshly-ground black pepper
oil for deep frying

Boil the rice in salted boiling water. Rinse and drain it well.

Turn it into a shallow dish, season it generously with pepper and a little salt, fork it lightly, and leave until completely cold. Whisk the eggs with a fork, then stir them gently but thoroughly into the cold rice. Chill the mixture for at least 2 hours, without covering it.

Cut the cheese into about 30 dice, each $\frac{3}{4}$ inch square, and dice the ham in the same way. Dust your hands lightly with flow. Put a tablespoon of rice in one palm and flatten it slightly. Lay a cube each of ham and cheese on top and cover with another tablespoon of rice. Gently press the mixture into a ball so that the cheese and ham are completely sealed in the centre of the rice. Roll each rice ball as it is made in fresh breadcrumbs until well coated all over, then leave the rice balls uncovered over-night in a cold larder or fridge to set firm.

To cook, heat oil in a deep-fat fryer until a cube of bread will brown in 30 seconds. Fry the rice balls − a few at a time to prevent sticking − for a couple of minutes until golden and crisp all over. Drain well and serve very hot. To eat, you pull the rice balls apart with your hands: the melted cheese will stretch like telephone wires − which is why the dish is called suppli al telefono!

CLASSIC CHEESE SOUFFLÉ

This makes an appetising first course for 4–6 people. Or, if served with triangles of fried bread and some grilled tomatoes and bacon, a good family supper dish for 3 people − in which case you may like to keep costs down by replacing the Parmesan and Gruyère cheeses with cheaper Cheddar cheese.

    3 large eggs
    7 fl. oz milk
    2 tablespoons butter
    2 tablespoons plain flour
    1½ oz Parmesan cheese
    2 oz Gruyère cheese
    1 tablespoon toasted breadcrumbs
    salt, cayenne and freshly-ground black pepper

Take the eggs out of the fridge at least half an hour before starting. Place a baking sheet on a shelf just above the centre of the oven and heat the oven up to 400F, 200C, gas mark 6.

Choose a soufflé dish — a thin fluted white china one is traditional and best for quick and even heat distribution, but earthenware can also be used. I use a 2 pt size: the dish will be over three-quarters full when you put the soufflé mixture into it, and when cooked, the soufflé will have risen nicely above the rim. Some cooks use a smaller dish so the soufflé towers high above the dish: this involves tying a stiff buttered paper collar round the dish to contain the soufflé during cooking, and then peeling the collar away before serving — not worth the extra effort in my opinion.

Butter the base and sides of your chosen dish, coat it with the toasted crumbs, tap gently and tip out excess. This generous greasing and light crumbing will encourage the soufflé mixture to glide up and cling to the sides of the dish.

Measure the milk into a saucepan, heat it over low heat and pour it into a jug (hot milk blends easily and minimises the chances of making a lumpy sauce). Put the butter into the pan and melt it over low heat. Away from the heat stir in the flour. When smooth return the pan to low heat and cook, stirring continuously, for 1 minute.

Away from the heat trickle the hot milk into the pan, stirring all the while to blend it well. Return the pan to the heat and cook, still stirring continuously, until the sauce is perfectly smooth, thickened and bubbling hot.

Remove the pan from the heat. Weigh the cheeses and grate them directly into the pan. The heat of the sauce is enough to melt the cheeses partially if not completely, yet their addition will sufficiently cool the sauce to enable you to add the egg yolks immediately afterwards.

Separate the eggs, reserving the whites in a large mixing bowl. Beat the yolks into the sauce, one at a time and until thoroughly incorporated. Turn the (by now beautifully glossy) sauce into your largest mixing bowl and season with salt, black pepper and cayenne — bearing in mind that the addition of egg whites will somewhat mute the flavour.

Check that the oven has reached the right temperature, then

whisk the egg whites using a manual rotary whisk – this gives better volume and therefore lighter results than an electric whisk. Move the whisk all round the bowl so the egg whites are all beaten to the same degree. Stop when the egg whites look shiny and fairly stiff. Overwhisking makes them grainy looking, too dry and stiff to fold in easily.

Tip the whisked whites on to the yolk mixture and fold in quickly, gently and thoroughly. Use figure of eight movements, cutting down through the mixture and lifting it over and up in a rather exaggerated way to keep everything really airy and light – the bubbles in the egg white must not be deflated.

Turn the mixture into the prepared dish. Dust the top with a little cayenne. Place the dish on the hot baking sheet, and close the oven door gently. Immediately reduce oven temperature to 375F, 190C, gas mark 5, and start timing. Depending on the type of soufflé dish you use, and on the idiosyncrasies of the oven, the soufflé will take about 25–30 minutes to reach perfection. Check after 25 minutes by shaking the dish gently. If the mixture wobbles violently, give it a few minutes more. If it trembles gently and feels just firm, serve it without delay.

SPINACH SOUFFLÉ

(serves 4)

Sometimes I serve this as a first course, sometimes as an unusual vegetable dish to accompany grilled meat or fish.

1 × 8 oz packet of Findus whole-leaf spinach
2 tablespoons plain flour
2 tablespoons butter
7 fl. oz milk
4 tablespoons grated Parmesan cheese
3 eggs
salt, freshly-ground black pepper and freshly-grated nutmeg

Put the frozen spinach into a sieve placed over a bowl and leave it at cool room temperature until completely defrosted – this takes several hours. Heat the oven to 400F, 200C, gas mark 6, placing a baking sheet on an upper shelf. Butter a 2 pt soufflé dish and dust it with a little of the Parmesan cheese. Make a thick white sauce with the butter, flour and hot milk. Away from the heat stir in most of the remaining grated Parmesan plus a good seasoning of salt, pepper and nutmeg. Press the spinach with a wooden spoon to extract as much moisture as possible, then chop it with a sharp knife and stir it into the sauce. Beat in the egg yolks one at a time and turn the mixture into a large bowl. Whisk the egg whites until stiff but not dry, fold them in, and turn the soufflé mixture into the prepared dish. Dust the top with the remaining Parmesan, and bake on the hot baking sheet for 25–30 minutes.

CHEESE AND HAM FRIES
(serves 4–6)

To make a more sophisticated version, called Croque Monsieur, simply replace the grated Cheddar and chutney with slices of Gruyère cheese and some French mustard.

12 slices of white bread
2 teaspoons chutney
6 thin slices of lean ham
6 oz grated Cheddar cheese
butter and oil

Spread the bread with butter, then spread a little chutney on 6 of the slices. Arrange the slices of ham over the chutney, sprinkle grated cheese on top, then cover with buttered bread. Press the sandwiches slightly to firm the filling, then cut each sandwich into 2 triangles. Shallow fry in a little butter and oil over medium heat for about 5 minutes on each side until the bread is golden and crisp. Drain well on kitchen paper and serve with a salad of tomatoes, mustard and cress.

CHEESE FONDUE
(a substantial snack for 4 or more)

You do not need a proper (and expensive) fondue set to make this. A heavy-based saucepan can be used as the fondue pot, and metal meat skewers can be used instead of fondue forks. Two or three nightlights in one of those inexpensive warmers intended for keeping coffee hot will keep the fondue bubbling gently while you dip into it.

6 oz each Gruyère cheese and Gouda cheese
¼ pt very dry cider
a cut clove of garlic
1 scant tablespoon cornflour blended with a few spoonfuls of cold water
half a glass of kirsch or brandy
nutmeg and freshly-ground black pepper

To dip into the fondue:
Chunks of hot crusty bread are traditional. I like to include also chunks of celery and apple, whole small mushrooms and perhaps a few thick slices of frankfurter sausage

Rub the inside of the pan with a cut garlic clove. Cut the cheeses into tiny dice and put them into the pan. Pour on the cider and add a grating of nutmeg and freshly-ground black pepper. Set the pan over medium heat and cook, stirring in figure of eight movements with a wooden spoon until the cheese is almost completely melted.

Draw the pan to one side and vigorously stir in the cornflour. Return to heat and continue stirring until the cheese mixture is very hot and very smooth. Add the kirsch or brandy and continue cooking and stirring for a further 2–3 minutes. The fondue is now ready to eat. Transfer from the stove to a table warmer to keep hot while you dip into it. Make sure it is steady, and extinguish the flames of the warmer when the pan is almost empty: a cheesy crust will form on the bottom of the pan, a treat to lift out and share at the end.

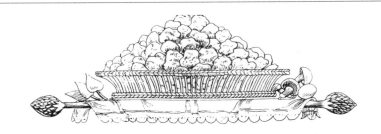

Fish

SUMMER HADDOCK
(serves 6)

This easy, quick and attractive looking main course salad makes a good lunch or supper dish.

> 2 lb smoked haddock fillets
> 6–8 hard-boiled eggs
> 1 × 6 oz can of sweet pimientos
> 2 dozen black olives
> 3 or 4 lettuce hearts
>
> *For the mayonnaise:*
> 2 egg yolks
> 2 teaspoons curry powder
> 4 teaspoons lemon juice
> $\frac{1}{4}$ pt olive oil
> $\frac{1}{4}$ pt vegetable oil
> a few drops of milk

Put the fish into a pan and pour on enough boiling water to cover completely. Quickly bring back to boiling point, then immediately remove the pan from the heat. Cover the pan and leave for 10 minutes before draining and skinning the fish. Spread out on a plate to cool quickly.

Beat the egg yolks with a little salt and the curry powder. Gradually beat in the oils (mixed together in a jug), drop by drop at first, then in a thin trickle. Season with lemon juice and salt to taste (but bearing in mind the saltiness of the fish), then thin the mayonnaise slightly by beating in a tablespoon or so of milk.

Drain the pimientos and cut the flesh into small chunks. When the haddock is cold, break it into bite-sized flakes. Add the fish to the mayonnaise together with most of the pimientos, most of the olives and the hard-boiled eggs cut into halves. Stir gently to mix the ingredients and to coat them with the sauce.

Arrange the lettuce leaves on a serving dish. Pile the fish mixture on top and sprinkle the remaining olives and pimientos over the fish.

BAKED MACKEREL WITH APPLES
(serves 4)

Slightly tart apples fried in butter go well with mackerel, and a mustardy soured cream sauce complements both apples and fish.

> 4 large mackerel
> a few slices of lemon
> a few stalks of parsley
> 2 cooking apples
> butter
> salt and freshly-ground black pepper
>
> *For the sauce:*
> $\frac{1}{4}$ pt soured cream
> 1 teaspoon French mustard, or add salt and freshly-ground
>   black pepper
> $1\frac{1}{2}$ teaspoons grated horseradish

Ask the fishmonger to bone the fish and cut each into 4 fillets. Lay the fillets, skin side down, in a single layer in a large shallow dish that has been well buttered. Dot a few slivers of butter on top of the fish (a generous half ounce), add a grinding of pepper, the slices of lemon and the parsley. Cover the dish with foil and set aside while the oven heats up to 425F, 220C, gas mark 7. Then bake for 20–25 minutes until the fish is tender – exact timing will depend on the size of the fish – basting the fillets with the buttery juices halfway through cooking.

While the oven is heating up, prepare the sauce: simply mix the ingredients together, season well with pepper and a little salt, turn into a sauceboat and chill.

While the fish is cooking, peel, core and slice the apples into rings. Sauté them in butter (unsalted is best as it is less likely to splutter and burn). Remove the parsley and lemon from the fish when cooked. Top with the fried apples and serve accompanied by the chilled sauce.

MUSSEL PANCAKES
(serves 6)

Mussels, bacon and spinach make a luscious pancake filling and mussel liquor makes a superb sauce.

> 18 × 6–7 inch pancakes
> 2 quarts (4 lb) fresh mussels
> $\frac{1}{2}$ lb green streaky bacon in a piece
> $\frac{1}{2}$ lb frozen whole leaf spinach
> 2 tablespoons butter
> 3 tablespoons plain flour
> 2 tablespoons white wine vinegar
> 6 tablespoons double cream
> salt and freshly-ground black pepper

Thoroughly clean the mussels, discarding any that are damaged or refuse to close when sharply tapped. Measure the vinegar into a large saucepan, add 8 fl. oz water and bring to the boil. Add the prepared mussels, cover and cook over high heat for 4–5 minutes – just shaking the pan occasionally to encourage even circulation of steam. Shell the mussels completely, discarding any that have not opened in cooking. Put them into a bowl and cover to prevent drying out. Strain the mussel liquor through a muslin-lined sieve to extract grit, and reserve.

Dice the bacon and cook over gentle heat until the fat runs. Slightly increase the heat to crisp the bacon a little. Add the butter, stir in the flour and cook for a minute or so before blending in 1 pt of the mussel liquor. Bring to the boil stirring and leave to simmer for 5 minutes.

Meanwhile cook the spinach. Squeeze it hard to dry it as

much as possible, chop and mix with the mussels. Add the bacon, removed from the sauce with a slotted spoon, and just over *half* of the sauce to bind the mixture. Taste and add extra seasoning if wished.

Stuff the pancakes with the mixture, roll them up neatly and lay them in a buttered gratin or baking dish. Cover with a buttered foil lid and cook in the oven at 400F, 200C, gas mark 6, for 15 minutes.

Stir the cream into the remaining sauce. Pour it over the pancakes and bake – without a lid this time – for a further 8 minutes or so until bubbling hot.

HERRING SUPPER SALAD
(serves 4)

A good, quick and inexpensive family supper or lunch dish. Make it using shop bought roll-mops, or better still home-pickled herrings (see recipe, page 31).

>8 fillets of sweet pickled herring
>$1\frac{1}{4}$ lb new potatoes
>1 cucumber
>$\frac{1}{2}$ lb (shelled weight) peas
>a large bunch of chives or some spring onions, finely chopped
>home-made mayonnaise made with 2 egg yolks and $\frac{1}{2}$ pt oil
>salt
>pepper
>2 generous tablespoons French mustard

Boil the potatoes and cook the peas. (I find fresh peas from the greengrocer are ungraded and often as hard as bullets so, if there are no fresh young peas in the garden, I use frozen peas). Drain and cool them slightly, then turn them into a salad bowl.

Season the mayonnaise with the mustard, thin it with 2–3 tablespoons milk and stir in the chopped chives. Pour it over the cooling vegetables and stir lightly to mix well.

Wipe the cucumber skin clean but to not peel it. Dice the cucumber and add it to the salad bowl. Unroll the herrings, discarding the onion slices, and chop the fish into large bite-sized pieces. Add these to the salad bowl. Toss gently to coat with the dressing, then serve the salad immediately.

FRIED TROUT WITH ALMONDS

An ideal dish for 2 since most frying pans will only take 2 whole fish at a time, and trout should be eaten as soon as cooked. Serve it with lots of good bread to mop up the buttery juices and follow it with a large fresh salad and cheese.

> 2 trout, each weighing 6–8 oz (frozen trout will do very well
>   if fresh trout are unavailable)
> 2½ oz clarified butter
> 1 oz flaked almonds
> a little plain flour
> a lemon
> salt and freshly-ground black pepper

Rub the skins of the cleaned and dried trout very gently with a good grinding of pepper: this gives delicious piquancy to the rich skin which, when crisply fried, is perhaps the best part of the fish. Then dust lightly with a little flour and some salt.

Choose a heavy-based frying pan large enough to take the 2 whole fish side by side. Warm it over medium heat. Add 2 oz of the butter cut into dice. When the foaming begins to subside add the fish to the pan, taking care to see that the underside of each fish is lying very flat. After 4–5 minutes steady cooking in the bubbling butter the skin on the underside of the fish should be crisp and golden brown.

Turn the fish carefully with a palette knife to avoid piercing the skin, and cook on the second side in the same way. Lift the fish out of the pan on to warmed plates. Wipe out the pan with kitchen paper towels. Add the remaining half ounce of butter and the almonds.

Cook, stirring occasionally, until the almonds are fried to a pale gold on both sides. Let the butter bubble a moment longer so it becomes a richer shade of gold.

Quickly add a generous teaspoon of lemon juice and a light seasoning of salt and pepper. Swirl to mix well, pour it over the trout and serve immediately with quartered wedges of lemon.

PEDRO'S KEBABS
(serves 2)

Chunks of filleted fish grilled on skewers with colourful and tasty vegetables, this dish is a good means of winning favour with those who dislike the skin and bones usually found in fish dishes.

6 oz fillet of coley or monkfish
6 oz fillet of smoked haddock
4 rashers of streaky bacon
½ red pepper
a medium-small onion
a few small cap mushrooms
2 tablespoons lemon juice
3 tablespoons oil
½ teaspoon each dried thyme and marjoram
salt and freshly-ground black pepper

Skin the fish and cut it into 1 inch cubes. Put it in a shallow dish with the onion cut into wedges, the pepper cut into chunks and the mushrooms with stalks trimmed level with caps. Pour on the lemon juice and oil, add the dried herbs and a good grinding of black pepper. Toss lightly, cover and leave to marinate in a cool place for about 1 hour.

Trim the bacon, cut each rasher in half and stretch with the back of a knife. Wrap a piece of bacon round each chunk of smoked haddock, thread the ingredients on to lightly oiled skewers, alternating white and smoked fish with vegetables. Grill under medium high heat for 10–12 minutes, turning the skewers and basting the ingredients with the marinade liquid as necessary. Serve with rice and a lettuce or watercress salad, preferably including a few slivers of raw fennel.

SMOKED MACKEREL WITH FLUFFY CUCUMBER SAUCE
(serves 6)

I like to serve this as a light lunch dish in summer. Plenty of good brown bread is the only accompaniment needed, although sunshine and a bottle of cool white wine make the meal even more agreeable!

6 large fillets of smoked mackerel
3 boxes of mustard and cress or bunches of watercress
1 firm large cucumber
$\frac{1}{4}$ pt double cream
3 teaspoons tarragon vinegar
1 tablespoon fresh chopped tarragon
$\frac{1}{2}$ teaspoon caster sugar
a pinch of icing sugar
salt and freshly-ground black pepper

Peel the cucumber, halve it and remove the seeds with a teaspoon. Chop up the flesh to make tiny dice and place in a shallow dish. Sprinkle on 1 teaspoon vinegar and $\frac{1}{2}$ teaspoon each salt and caster sugar. Toss gently and leave in a cool place for half an hour to draw out excess cucumber juices. Then drain the cucumber very thoroughly and pat it dry with kitchen paper towels.

Skin the fish and arrange them on a dish with clumps of mustard and cress or watercress.

Measure 2 teaspoons vinegar into a bowl. Add a good grinding of pepper and a pinch of icing sugar, and gently stir in the cream. Whip the mixture until it will hold a soft shape. Fold in the drained cucumber and adjust seasoning to taste.

SCALLOPS ON SKEWERS
(serves 2)

Because scallops are so expensive, it is common practice to 'stretch' them by combining them with other less costly ingredients and/or by coating them with a sauce. This recipe uses mushrooms and bacon which complement scallops beautifully.

6 large scallops
about $\frac{1}{2}$ lb large, very thinly-cut slices of streaky bacon
1 red pepper
$\frac{1}{4}$ lb button mushrooms
olive oil
lemon
dried basil
salt and freshly-ground black pepper

To prepare scallops, gently pull the coral away from the white. Remove the black intestinal thread, rinse well to remove any grit, and pat dry gently. Cut away the tough muscle from the edge of the white (it is a slightly different colour, so easy enough to find), then slice the white across into 2 or 3 flat discs depending on size.

Wipe the mushrooms clean, remove the seeds from the pepper and cut it into large chunks. Make a lemony vinaigrette and flavour it with a little basil. Spoon the mixture over the scallops, mushrooms and pepper, and leave to marinate for half an hour.

De-rind the bacon, halve each rasher by cutting across the stretch flat with the back of a knife. Wrap half a rasher round each well-drained piece of scallop and thread on to skewers, adding drained mushrooms and chunks of red pepper here and there. Grill, turning and basting with the marinade liquid as necessary, for 8 minutes or so until the bacon is crisp. Serve immediately with a dish of boiled rice, wedges of lemon and, ideally, a bowl of hollandaise sauce.

HOLLANDAISE SAUCE

The method given here is very easy. If you do not own a double-boiler improvise one: partially fill a saucepan with barely simmering water then fit a pudding basin over it so that the rim of the basin rests on the rim of the pan while the bottom of the basin is suspended *above* the water level.

¼ lb chilled unsalted butter
2 egg yolks
2 teaspoons lemon juice
2 teaspoons dry white wine or water
salt and freshly-ground black pepper
extra lemon juice to taste

Away from the heat, put the egg yolks into the top part of a double-boiler (or into the pudding basin) and beat with a balloon whisk for 2–3 minutes. Add a good pinch of salt, the lemon juice and wine or cold water, and beat for a further half minute.

Cut 2 pieces from the block of butter, each weighing half an ounce, and put them to one side. Cut the rest of the butter into small dice and melt in a small pan over low heat. Cover, to keep warm, and set aside.

Add one of the reserved lumps of chilled butter to the egg yolks and place the pan (or pudding basin) over the barely simmering water over a low flame. Stir the mixture with the whisk until the butter melts and amalgamates with the eggs. The mixture will soon become creamy and begin to thicken, then it will start to cling to the wires of the whisk so you will see the base of the pan (or basin) between strokes.

Remove the pan (or basin) from the heat, immediately add the remaining lump of cold butter and whisk until it is melted and absorbed by the eggs. Now, start whisking in the hot melted butter, just as if adding oil to make mayonnaise – drop by drop at first, then more rapidly. Adjust seasoning to taste when all the butter has been absorbed and the sauce is thick and smooth. Serve straight away or keep warm (covered and placed over a pan of hot water) for 30 minutes or so.

FISH PIE WITH CROÛTONS
(serves 4)

The combination of creamy fish filling and crunchy fried bread makes this a particularly pleasing variation on the fish pie theme.

1 lb cod or coley fillets
6 oz mushrooms
6 celery stalks
3 hard-boiled eggs (quartered)
3 oz butter
2 oz plain flour
$\frac{3}{4}$–1 pt milk
2 oz grated Cheddar cheese
a teaspoon of coriander seeds
4 tablespoons each chopped chives and parsley
salt and freshly-ground black pepper
$\frac{1}{2}$ lb crustless white bread cut into cubes
oil and butter for frying

Slice the celery thickly and sweat in half an ounce of butter for 10 minutes. Meanwhile, fry the croûtons, drain well and keep hot.

Add the fish to the celery pan. Pour on enough milk just to cover the fish and bring to boiling point. Remove the pan from the heat, cover with a lid and set aside for about 10 minutes or until the fish flesh has become opaque. Then strain the contents of the pan, reserving liquor and solid ingredients separately.

While the fish is cooking, slice and sauté the mushrooms in half an ounce of butter.

Make a sauce with the remaining 2 oz of butter, the flour and fish liquor. Stir in the cheese. Season with a good grinding of pepper, the coriander (I use a peppermill to grind the seeds), most of the herbs and salt to taste. Leave the sauce to simmer gently while you skin, bone and break the fish into large flakes.

Gently fold the mushrooms, celery, fish and eggs into the sauce and heat through. Turn on to a hot serving dish, surround with a ring of croûtons, sprinkle the remaining herbs on top and serve immediately.

SOLE COLBERT
(serves 4)

Fresh dover sole is a beautiful fish. The only thing some people have against it is the bones. In this recipe the sole is cooked on the bone in such a way that the bones can be removed in seconds just before serving.

> 4 sole, each weighing 10–12 oz
> salt and freshly-ground black pepper
> a little plain flour
> 2 lightly beaten eggs
> dried white breadcrumbs
> oil for frying
>
> *For the Colbert butter:*
> $\frac{1}{4}$ lb butter
> 2 tablespoons lemon juice
> 1 tablespoon meat jelly taken from underneath beef dripping
> 3 tablespoons fresh chopped parsley
> 1 tablespoon fresh chopped tarragon (or $1\frac{1}{2}$ teaspoons dried tarragon)

Choose fish that will fit your frying basket, and ask the fishmonger to skin them. Cut the flesh along the length of the backbone on the skinned side of each fish. Slide the knife under the flesh close to the bone and gently ease the flesh away from the bone until the fillets are attached only at the head, tail and fins. Then snip through the backbone with scissors near the head, in the middle and near the tail. Roll back the cut edges of the fillets a little to make an opening in the fish. (This will make it easy to remove the bone after cooking and will provide a pocket in which to place the savoury butter.)

Season the fish well with salt and pepper, dust lightly with flour, dip in beaten egg, coat generously all over with breadcrumbs and leave in a cold place for 1 hour to firm the coating. Meanwhile mash the butter and season it with salt, pepper, the herbs, lemon and meat jelly. Shape into a bolster, roll up in damp greaseproof paper and chill until solid.

Pour oil into a deep-fat fryer until one-third full. Heat very slowly to 275F/135C. Dip the basket into the pan to oil it. Lift it out, lay one fish in the basket, cut side up, lower gently into the pan and fry for 3–4 minutes until tender and golden. Drain well and keep hot while you fry the rest of the fish. Then use a knife to ease out the backbones, fill the pockets with pats of the chilled savoury butter and serve immediately.

PLAICE WITH MUSHROOMS AND PARSLEY
(serves 4)

Very fresh plaice are important if this simple and quick dish is to be really good. Serve with hot crusty bread to mop up the juices.

> 1½–2 lb fillets of plaice (or lemon sole)
> 1 small onion
> 4–6 oz mushrooms
> a handful of fresh chopped parsley
> half a lemon
> 1½ oz butter
> 4 tablespoons dry cider
> salt and freshly-ground black pepper

Season the fish generously with salt and pepper. Sprinkle with a good squeeze of lemon juice and set aside for 20 minutes.

Chop the onion finely. Melt 1 oz butter in a saucepan, add the onion and soften for 10 minutes. Turn the contents of the pan into a gratin dish. Stir in a handful of chopped parsley. Add another half ounce of butter to the saucepan (there is no need to wash it out). When hot, add the thickly sliced mushrooms and turn them over fairly high heat for 3 or 4 minutes.

Turn the fish fillets in the gratin dish to coat them with the parsley and onion butter, then fold each fillet in half. Pour on the cider and scatter the mushrooms on top. Add a seasoning of salt and pepper and lay a sheet of buttered greaseproof paper on top. Place the dish on the centre shelf of an oven heated to 375F, 190C, gas mark 5, and bake for 20 minutes until the fish is tender and hot. Baste with the buttery juices and serve immediately.

GRAVADLAX
(serves 6)

Now popular throughout Scandinavia, this ancient method of pickling fish originated in Sweden. It is very simple and delicious — a sort of home-prepared smoked salmon. Trout and even large mackerel can also be pickled this way.

2 lb tail end piece of salmon
a bunch of fresh dill or several spoonfuls of dried dillweed
4 teaspoons coarse salt
4 teaspoons granulated sugar
1 teaspoon black peppercorns

Choose a dish just large enough to hold the fish, then cut the salmon into 2 long fillets and lift out the backbone carefully.

If using fresh dill, chop it coarsely. Crush the peppercorns with mortar and pestle, and mix in the salt, sugar and dill.

Sprinkle a quarter of the dill and spice mixture into the dish. Lay one piece of salmon, skin side down, on top. Strew it with half the dill and spice. Cover with the second piece of salmon, this time skin side up and placing the thick end over the thin end of the first piece. Sprinkle on the remaining dill and spice mixture. Cover with a board and put heavy weights on top. Leave to pickle in a cold place – not the refrigerator – for about 24 hours or up to 4 days maximum.

When ready to serve, lift the salmon out of the pickle and gently scrape off the spices and dill. Carve the gravadlax into wafer thin slices exactly as though it were smoked salmon. Serve with wedges of juicy lemon or a sauce made by flavouring soured cream with fresh chopped dill and some French mustard.

Tiny new potatoes steamed in their skins and served piping hot are traditionally served with gravadlax in Scandinavia – dunk them as well as the fish into the dill and mustard sauce.

JUGGED KIPPERS
(serves 2)

Jugging is the easiest and cleanest way to cook kippers. It is well worth buying real kippers (easily recognised by their pale smoky colour). Herrings that have been dyed to a shade of mahogany are cheaper but not half as tasty.

2 plump kippers
2 oz unsalted butter
freshly-ground black pepper

Choose a large earthenware jug, tall and wide enough to hold the kippers so that only their tails appear above the rim. Fill it with boiling water and let it stand for a few minutes to warm through.

Empty the jug, stand the kippers in it and pour on fresh boiling water to immerse the fish. Cover the jug with a dome of foil and leave for 5–10 minutes, depending on the size of the kippers. Drain well and pat dry with kitchen paper towels. Lay the fish on very hot plates, grind pepper over, then top with slivers of butter and serve immediately.

COULIBIAC OF FISH

(serves 4)

This is often made using salmon or salmon trout, but turbot is much more reasonably priced and excellent. Coulibiac can be served cold, but it is at its most delicious when hot.

> 1 small turbot weighing about 2 lb
> 1 onion
> $\frac{1}{4}$ lb mushrooms
> 1 lemon
> 3 oz long grain rice
> 8 fl. oz chicken stock
> 1 small green pepper
> fresh chopped parsley and chives
> fresh chopped fennel or dillweed
> 2 hard-boiled eggs
> butter
> nutmeg
> salt and pepper
> 1 × 13 oz packet puff pastry
> $\frac{1}{2}$ pt soured cream
> 6–7 tablespoons natural yoghurt
> beaten egg

Ask the fishmonger to decapitate and clean the fish and cut it in half along the backbone. Wrap the 2 pieces in buttered foil, cook at 350F, 180C, gas mark 4, for 30–35 minutes, then skin, bone and flake the fish.

Meanwhile, sweat the chopped onion in 1–1½ oz butter for 5 minutes. Add the sliced mushrooms, 3 tablespoons lemon juice and a good seasoning of salt and pepper. Cover and cook gently, stirring occasionally, for 5 minutes. Uncover and cook for another 2–3 minutes.

Cook the rice in chicken stock until just tender. Then mix with the seeded and diced pepper, 3 tablespoons fresh chopped parsley, 2 tablespoons fresh chopped fennel fronds or dillweed (or 2 teaspoons dried dillweed), a good grating of nutmeg and plenty of salt and pepper.

Roll the pastry out to about 16 inches square, then cut it into 2 rectangles, one 7½ and the other 8½ inches wide. Place the larger piece on a baking sheet and spread half the rice mixture down the centre, leaving a 1 inch border all round. Cover the rice with the sliced hard-boiled eggs, and cover the eggs with the flaked turbot. Spoon the mushroom mixture on top and finally add the remaining rice mixture. Place the second piece of pastry over the top. Brush generously with beaten egg and seal the edges very firmly. Make a few slits for steam to escape and bake at 400F, 200C, gas mark 6, for half an hour.

Meanwhile, mix the sauce: beat the yoghurt into the soured cream and stir in a couple of tablespoons each of fresh chopped parsley and chives. Serve the sauce well chilled in a bowl.

OATMEAL HERRINGS WITH GOOSEBERRY SAUCE
(serves 2)

Coated with oatmeal, fried and served with a slightly tart gooseberry sauce, this is one of my favourite ways to serve herring.

2 herrings
3 tablespoons medium-ground oatmeal
½ teaspoon salt
a good grinding of pepper
about 1 tablespoon each butter and oil

For the sauce:
½ lb gooseberries
a little caster sugar
½ oz butter

Ask the fishmonger to prepare the herrings or do them yourself. Scale the fish and cut off their heads. Gut them, rinse them and open them out flat. Lay them flesh side down and press along the back to loosen the backbone. Turn the fish over, gently ease out the backbone, and cut off the fins. Coat the fish all over with the oatmeal and salt mixed together.

Rinse the gooseberries (there is no need to top and tail them). Put them into a small pan with just enough water to cover. Simmer gently until tender, drain well and rub the pulp through a sieve. Reheat gently with the butter and sweeten to taste. Keep hot.

Melt the butter and oil in a large frying pan. Lay the fish side by side in the pan and fry for 5–8 minutes, turning them over halfway through cooking time. Drain well on kitchen paper and serve immediately with the hot gooseberry sauce.

SOLE MEUNIÈRE
(serves 2)

It is hard to better really good fresh sole cooked in this simple, classic way.

1 fine sole weighing about 18 oz, skinned and filleted
¼ lb clarified butter
half a lemon
a small handful of parsley
a little plain flour
salt and freshly-ground black pepper

Season the fish generously with salt and pepper, then dust it with a fine, even coat of flour — you'll only need about a tablespoon of flour — and shake off any excess. Heat a large frying pan over medium heat. Add half the butter. When it has melted and the foaming begins to subside, add the prepared sole. Fry it gently until golden, turn it carefully and cook on the second side in the same way. Then lift the fillets out of the pan, put them on to a serving dish and keep warm.

Tip out the fat remaining in the pan. Wipe the pan clean with kitchen paper towels. Cut the remaining 2 oz clarified butter into dice. Add it to the pan and cook quickly to a golden brown colour. Away from the heat, quickly swirl a generous teaspoon of lemon juice and a small handful of chopped parsley into the pan. Pour the butter over the fish and serve immediately garnished with wedges of lemon.

PINWHEEL WHITING
(serves 2)

Fillets of white fish with a mushroom and herb stuffing make an attractive slimline dish — and most of the preparations can be done ahead if you wish.

> 2 whiting each weighing about 10 oz
> $\frac{1}{4}$ lb mushrooms
> 4 tablespoons chopped fresh parsley
> 1 tablespoon chopped fresh chives
> 1 garlic clove
> 4 tablespoons dry Vermouth
> a little butter
> salt and freshly-ground black pepper

Ask the fishmonger to skin and fillet the fish, then cut each fillet lengthways in 2 so you have a total of 8 long thin strips of fish.

Chop the mushrooms very finely indeed, crush the garlic and snip the fresh herbs.

Melt 1½ oz butter in a small saucepan. When hot add the mushrooms, garlic and herbs and cook over medium heat for 2–3 minutes stirring and turning the ingredients every now and then.

Scrape the contents of the pan into a sieve placed over a small bowl, season it well, and leave for 15–20 minutes so that the buttery juices drip away and the herb mixture cools. When cold spread the herb mixture on the fillets and roll each one up, from thin to thicker end.

Secure with cocktail sticks and lay in a single layer in a lightly buttered gratin dish. (Everything up to this stage can be done in advance).

Place a baking sheet on an upper shelf of the oven and heat the oven to 400F, 200C, gas mark 6. Add the Vermouth to the buttery juices, bring quickly to the boil and pour over the fish.

Add a little extra salt and pepper and dot with ¼ oz butter. Cover with foil and bake for 15 minutes.

Carefully turn the fish over and continue baking — this time without the foil — for a further 8 minutes.

SQUID SALAD

(serves 4–6)

Costing as little as 70p per lb squid is an inexpensive treat — and for me it always evokes happy memories of long lazy lunches in Mediterranean tavernas.

Some enterprising fishmongers now sell fresh squid caught in English waters. Alternatively frozen squid can be bought, usually by ordering in advance.

> 2 lb fairly small squid
> 4–5 tablespoons olive oil
> 2 fat garlic cloves crushed with salt
> 2–3 teaspoons lemon juice
> plenty of freshly-ground black pepper
> plenty of fresh chopped parsley

Don't be daunted by the thought of preparing squid: in practice it is much quicker and easier than it appears on paper. Put the squid into a bowl of cold water and swirl them around. Take them out one at a time and peel away the beautiful purplish veil of membrane that covers the body sac.

Hold the sac with one hand, use the other to pull the head and tentacles gently but firmly away from the body — the soft entrails from inside the sac will probably come away with the tentacles. Cut off the tentacles just in front of the eye and reserve them.

Throw away the head and entrails. Remove the transparent 'quill' from the body sac, and wash the inside of the body sac very thoroughly, removing and discarding anything it may still contain.

Dry the squid, cut the body into thin rings and, if the tentacles are very long, cut them into short lengths.

Put 4 tablespoons olive oil into a large frying pan over medium heat. When it is warm — don't wait until it is very hot unless the squid are really small, young and tender — add the squid and increase heat slightly.

Fry, stirring as necessary, for about 5 minutes. Then reduce heat to low and continue cooking very gently for a further 5 minutes or so until the squid are cooked through and quite tender.

Draw the pan to one side and stir in the crushed garlic. Add some pepper and 2 teaspoons lemon juice. Mix well and turn into a shallow dish to cool. Stir in plenty of parsley and extra oil, lemon, salt and pepper to taste just before serving.

TONNO E FAGIOLI
(serves 4)

Dried red kidney beans can be soaked for 4 hours, then cooked and used to make this salad (8 oz would be enough), but this version uses canned beans for the sake of speed.

1 × 15 oz can red kidney beans
½ lb fresh French beans or half a large cucumber
1 × 7 oz can tunny fish
4 hard-boiled eggs
12 spring onions
vinaigrette dressing
fresh parsley
salt and freshly-ground black pepper
2 tablespoons capers

Drain the canned beans from the liquid in the tin. Rinse under a cold tap and drain again. If using French beans, top and tail, steam until just tender, break in half if very long, and allow to cool slightly. If using cucumber, dice but do not peel. Trim the spring onions and chop them finely, green parts as well as white.

Put the vegetables into a salad bowl. Season them with salt and pepper and add at least 6 tablespoons coarsely chopped parsley. Pour on some vinaigrette dressing (made using a good proportion of vinegar on this occasion). Toss to mix and coat everything well.

Drain the tunny fish from the oil in the can. Break the fish into large flakes and stir gently into the salad. (If you are feeling lavish, add the contents of a can of anchovy fillets, snipping the fillets into pieces as you add them to the salad bowl.) Quarter the hard-boiled eggs, moisten them with a little vinaigrette. Arrange them round the edge of the bowl and scatter on the capers. Serve with hot crusty bread.

SCALLOPS WITH GARLIC
(serves 4–5)

A beautiful first course dish, but expensive so save it for special occasions. Fresh scallops are essential to the success of the dish – don't attempt to use frozen.

10 large fresh scallops
half a lemon
¼ lb mushrooms (large shaggy ones if possible)
1 large garlic clove

about 6 tablespoons chopped fresh parsley
1 tablespoon snipped fresh chives
1 heaped teaspoon chopped fresh basil (if available)
¼ lb fresh white breadcrumbs
clarified or unsalted butter
salt and freshly-ground black pepper

Prepare the scallops as described on page 78 then cut each disc of white scallop into 4 pieces. Leave the corals whole. Grate the lemon zest over the scallops, pour on the lemon juice, add a seasoning of salt and pepper, toss lightly and set aside in a cold place for about half an hour.

Chop the mushrooms very finely – a mezzaluna is the best tool for this – mix with the crushed garlic and chopped fresh herbs.

Fry the breadcrumbs in clarified or unsalted butter until golden and crisp. Drain well and keep very hot.

About 10 minutes before you plan to eat, turn the scallops into a sieve. Leave to drain off the lemon juice, then pat dry. Warm a frying pan over medium-low heat and melt about 2–2½ oz clarified or unsalted butter in it. Add the white scallop meat only and fry fairly gently (high heat will toughen scallops) for about 2 minutes to stiffen and colour the flesh on all sides. Add the corals and cook for 2 minutes more. Remove with a slotted spoon and keep warm.

Increase heat to medium-high. Add the mushroom mixture to the pan and cook, stirring almost continuously, for 2–3 minutes. Draw the pan away from the heat, stir in the scallops and season with salt, pepper and lemon juice to taste. Quickly divide between 4 small hot dishes, scatter with the fried bread-crumbs and serve immediately.

Poultry and Game

POLLO AL PARMIGIANO
(serves 6)

One of the joys of this chicken dish is that it can be prepared in
the morning before you go out to work and then left to marinate
all day. Preliminary cooking takes only 10 minutes in the
evening; the chicken is then left to complete cooking in a low
oven without any need of attention from the cook.

> 6 large pieces of boned and skinned chicken breast
> 3 tablespoons each olive oil and lemon juice
> 1 heaped teaspoon fresh chopped tarragon or $\frac{1}{2}$ teaspoon dried
>   tarragon
> plenty of freshly-ground black pepper
> 6 slices of ham (ideally prosciutto crudo from an Italian
>   grocer or good delicatessen)
> just over 2 oz freshly-grated Parmesan cheese

Choose a gratin or other flame-proof dish large enough to hold
the chicken pieces flat in a single layer. Measure the oil and
lemon juice into it, and mix in the tarragon and a good seasoning of pepper. Turn the chicken pieces in the marinade, cover
the dish and leave in a cold larder for several hours.

One hour before serving heat the oven to 300F, 150C, gas
mark 2 and heat the grill.

Uncover the gratin dish and place it under the grill, about 5
inches away from the source of the heat. Grill the chicken for 5
minutes on each side to colour it lightly.

Lay the slices of ham over the chicken, sprinkle the Parmesan cheese over the top and add another seasoning of pepper. Cover the dish with foil and bake for 45 minutes – it won't spoil if left for a little longer. Uncover and put under a hot grill for a minute or so just before serving.

COX'S CHICKEN DISH
(serves 4–6)

A purée of sweet apples, which have been cooked with the chicken, are used to make the sauce in this simple but comforting dish. Triangles of fried bread and peppery watercress complete the dish.

> 3–4 lb roasting chicken cut into 4–6 joints
> $\frac{1}{2}$ lb Cox's apples
> 1 onion
> $\frac{1}{4}$ pt unsweetened apple juice
> 1 teaspoon coriander seeds
> generous $\frac{1}{2}$ teaspoon dried rosemary
> scant $\frac{1}{2}$ oz butter
> 1 teaspoon oil
> 2 teaspoons each plain flour and softened butter mashed together
> plenty of salt and freshly-ground black pepper
> 2 bunches watercress and triangles of fried bread to garnish

Heat the oil and half the butter in a large frying pan. When foaming ceases add the chicken joints and fry fast until sealed and golden brown on all sides. Meanwhile chop the onion very finely and spread it over the base of a flame-proof casserole. Drain the chicken and lay it on top. Sprinkle with salt and pepper and the coriander and rosemary pounded together with mortar and pestle. Pour on the apple juice, bring to the boil, cover with a lid and put the casserole into an oven heated to 350F, 180C, gas mark 4.

Add the remaining butter to the frying pan. Peel, core and thinly slice the apples. Fry them over medium-high heat for 3 minutes, stirring and turning as necessary. Tip the contents of the frying pan over the chicken – don't stir it in – cover again and continue cooking in the oven for a further 15 minutes before reducing temperature to 325F, 160C, gas mark 3. Then cook for another hour.

Lift out the chicken pieces on to a warmed dish. Put the casserole on top of the stove and whisk so the apples disintegrate to a purée. Thicken the sauce by stirring in the mashed flour and butter and boil, stirring continuously, for a few minutes to get a good consistency. Check seasoning, pour the sauce over the chicken, garnish and serve.

AROMATIC GRILLED CHICKEN
(serves 2)

I prepare this dish a day ahead so the flavourings have plenty of time to seep deep into the chicken flesh. To make this dish for 4 people simply double all ingredients — but it is cheaper to buy a 3½ lb bird and to cut it into 4 portions yourself rather than to buy 4 ready-cut chicken pieces.

2 large chicken pieces (preferably breast)
½ teaspoon chilli powder
1 tablespoon lemon juice
½ teaspoon cumin seed
1 teaspoon coriander seed
1 very fat garlic clove
2 tablespoons yoghurt
2 teaspoons tomato purée
½ oz clarified butter
salt

Thoroughly defrost the chicken. Wipe it dry, loosen the skin, pull it gently away from the flesh and also remove any fat. Prick the chicken flesh deeply all over with the point of a knife, and make 2 or 3 deep slashes across the thickest part of the meat. Sprinkle on the chilli powder, pour on the lemon juice then brush the mixture all over the chicken and deep into the cuts.

Warm the cumin and coriander seeds in a small pan over low heat for a few minutes to bring out their aromas. Pound the seeds and crush the garlic with a mortar and pestle. Blend in the yoghurt and tomato purée. Spread the paste all over the chicken, pushing it deep into the slashes. Cover and leave in a cold place for 12–24 hours to flavour and tenderise the chicken. Heat the grill. Lay the chicken, bony side up, in a gratin dish. Season with salt and pepper, pour on the marinade juices and dot with the butter. Grill, several inches away from the heat, for about 12 minutes basting occasionally.

Turn the chicken over and grill for a further 8–10 minutes, again basting occasionally, until the chicken flesh is cooked and juicily tender, and the paste has formed a surface crust. Serve immediately with rice and a salad.

CORN AND CHICKEN PANCAKES
(serves 4)

Sweetcorn kernels scraped from fresh cobs and briefly boiled are best for this dish but canned sweetcorn kernels can also be used. A good recipe for using up leftover chicken.

For the batter:
2 oz each plain white flour and wholemeal flour
4 fl. oz milk
$\frac{1}{4}$ pt water
2 eggs
salt and 2 tablespoons melted butter

For the filling:
8 oz sweetcorn kernels
6–8 oz cooked chicken cut into slivers
8 spring onions, finely chopped

For the sauce:
2 tablespoons butter
1 tablespoon plain flour
1 × 8 oz can of tomatoes
1 generous teaspoon concentrated tomato purée
$\frac{1}{4}$ teaspoon caster sugar
$\frac{1}{4}$ pt soured cream
salt and freshly-ground black pepper

Use the batter to make 16 very thin and tender pancakes 6 inches across. These can be made a day ahead if you wish: interleave with circles of greaseproof paper, wrap in a foil parcel and refrigerate. To reheat, place the wrapped parcel in an oven heated to 375F, 190C, gas mark 5, for about 20 minutes. To make the sauce, make a roux with the butter and flour. Add the chopped tomatoes and their juices and bring to the boil stirring continuously. Add all the remaining sauce ingredients and leave to simmer very gently for a minute or two while you mix the drained sweetcorn, finely chopped spring onions (green parts as well as white) and chicken slivers in a bowl. Add a scant $\frac{1}{4}$ pt of the sauce to the filling to bind it, and use to stuff the pancakes. Roll up, tucking ends under, and lay in a buttered baking dish. Cover with foil and bake for 15 minutes at 400F, 200C, gas mark 6. Pour on the rest of the sauce and cook for a further 7–8 minutes, this time without a lid.

CHICKEN BREASTS WITH TARRAGON CREAM
(serves 4)

A very simple and special dish. Serve it with new potatoes and steamed broccoli. Don't butter the vegetables: the sauce will moisten them nicely.

> breasts of 2 chickens (i.e., 4 pieces, each about 6–8 oz)
> 2½ tablespoons fresh chopped French tarragon
> 4 fl. oz double cream
> 4 fl. oz soured cream
> salt and pepper
> freshly-ground coriander
> a squeeze of lemon juice
> 3½ oz unsalted butter
> 1 tablespoon olive oil

Rub the chicken meat with pepper and coriander and about 1 tablespoon lemon juice; leave at room temperature for an hour. Measure the creams into a jug, add the tarragon and season well. Cover and set aside so that the flavours infuse the creams.

Melt the oil and 1½ oz butter in a sauté pan. Add the chicken, skin side down, and cook for 6–8 minutes until lightly browned. Turn and fry the fleshy side for 2–3 minutes until sealed and coloured. Reduce heat as low as possible, cover the pan to stop any steam escaping and cook for 30–40 minutes.

When the chicken is tender, transfer to a hot serving dish.

Add the remaining butter, diced, to the sauté pan. When melted, increase heat to moderate and pour in the tarragon cream. Cook, stirring continuously, for 3–4 minutes until the cream and butter bubble up and blend together to make a smooth rich sauce. Pour over the chicken and serve immediately.

FARMHOUSE CHICKEN PIE
(serves 6)

A comforting dish and a good way to use up the chicken thighs and drumsticks left over from making Chicken Kiev (see page 105).

8–10 small chicken joints such as thighs or drumsticks
$\frac{1}{2}$ lb minced belly of pork (or best quality sausagemeat)
1 large onion
$\frac{1}{4}$ lb mushrooms
3 hard-boiled eggs
1 dozen pimiento-stuffed green olives
1 teaspoon dried thyme
6 tablespoons fresh chopped parsley
$\frac{1}{4}$ pt dry cider
chicken stock
3 tablespoons clarified or unsalted butter
a little plain flour
salt and freshly-ground black pepper
1 × 13 oz packet of puff or flaky pastry
beaten egg to glaze

Skin the chicken joints and dust with well-seasoned flour. Mix the pork or sausagemeat with the thyme and parsley, and a generous seasoning of salt and pepper. Divide into tiny pieces and roll into marble shapes using floured hands.

Heat a large flame-proof casserole until very hot. Add a little butter and, when the foaming ceases, fry the chicken joints, a few at a time, until well coloured. Remove, sauté the thickly sliced mushrooms then set them aside separately. Add the remaining butter to the pan and colour the onion and meatballs. Return the chicken joints to the pan (but not the mushrooms) and pour in the cider. Cover and simmer gently for 20 minutes. Turn the contents of the casserole into a 3 pt pie dish. Add the quartered eggs, sliced olives and mushrooms, tucking them in here and there. Check the liquid for seasoning and add extra as necessary. The liquid should come one-third of the way up the sides of the pie dish: add cold chicken stock if it is needed. Set the dish aside so the contents cool down. When the pie filling is cold, heat the oven to 425F, 220C, gas mark 7. Roll out the pastry to 1½ times the size of the top of the pie dish. Trim 1 inch wide strips from the edge of the pastry. Dampen the rim of the pie dish and press the pastry strips on to it. Dampen the pastry rim and lay the pastry 'lid' over the pie. Press lightly to seal the pastry edges, then trim away excess. Flute the edges and decorate the top of the pie with pastry trimmings. Glaze with beaten egg and cut a steam hole in the centre of the pastry. Bake in the centre of the oven for about 35 minutes.

CHICKEN PROVENÇALE
(serves 2)

This takes little more than 5 minutes to prepare and can be completely cooked in the cook's absence using the cold-start method and an automatic oventimer.

> 4 small chicken joints (thighs or drumsticks)
> 1 celery stalk cut into thin crescents
> 2 oz sliced leek or very finely sliced onion
> 2 garlic cloves crushed with salt
> 1 dozen small black olives
> a small handful of coarsely chopped parsley
> a good squeeze of lemon juice
> a pinch of caster sugar
> 1 × 8 oz can of tomatoes
> salt and freshly-ground black pepper

Season the chicken joints with plenty of pepper. Lay them in a single layer in a small casserole. Spread the crushed garlic on top and cover with the celery, leeks (or onion), olives and parsley mixed together. Roughly chop the canned tomatoes into their juices. Set half aside to use for another recipe or for making a Bloody Mary. Mix the rest of the tomatoes with sugar, lemon and plenty of salt and pepper. Pour this into the casserole, spreading it evenly over the vegetables. Lay a lightly oiled sheet of greaseproof paper on top and cover with a lid. Place the casserole on the centre shelf of a cold oven, and set time and temperature controls to give 3½ hours cooking at 300F, 150C, gas mark 2.

PERFECT ROAST CHICKEN
(serves 4–6)

If the skin is a crackle of gold and the flesh is juicily tender, roast chicken is truly delicious. The keys to success are to buy a fresh bird and to roast it breast down for the major part of cooking time – so that butter seeps into the lean breast meat and keeps it succulent.

> fresh roasting chicken, 4 lb drawn weight
> ¼ lb butter
> a frew sprigs of tarragon
> salt and freshly-ground black pepper
> chicken giblet stock
> a small glass of wine

Wipe the bird inside and out and remove the lumps of fat from inside the bird at the tail end. Strip the leaves from the tarragon, mash them into 1 oz butter together with a good seasoning of salt and pepper, and place inside the body cavity. Rub the chicken skin all over with a further 2 oz butter generously seasoned with salt and pepper – butter the thighs particularly generously.

Do not truss the bird. Lay it on its breast on a V-shaped rack in a roasting pan. Put the pan into an oven heated to 400F, 200C, gas mark 6, and immediately reduce the temperature to 375F, 190C, gas mark 5. Roast for 1 hour, basting the chicken with the buttery pan juices every 10 minutes or so.

Increase oven temperature to 400F, 200C, gas mark 6, again. Turn the bird breast up and roast for 20 minutes or so more until the breast skin is golden and crisp. Spluttering sounds and delicious smells will indicate when the chicken is ready, but double-check that the meat is thoroughly cooked by piercing the thickest part of the leg with the tip of a sharp knife: the juices should be clear. If they are pink, slightly reduce oven temperature and cook the chicken a little more.

Let the bird 'rest' while you make the gravy. Add the remaining 1 oz butter to the roasting pan, together with a small quantity of well-flavoured stock made from the chicken giblets and a small glass of wine. Boil until reduced to a syrupy, richly flavoured gravy, and stir in the mashed chicken liver just before serving. Potato purée and plenty of crisp green watercress are perfect accompaniments to roast chicken.

SIMPLE SPICED CHICKEN
(serves 4)

Barbecued food always seems to appeal to youngsters, and this chicken dish with its piquant barbecue sauce makes a popular school holiday lunch. Very easy to cook, I serve it with plain boiled rice to mop up the sauce, and a salad.

8 chicken drumsticks
1 large Spanish onion
2 tablespoons oil
4 tablespoons jelly marmalade
4 tablespoons soy sauce
2 tablespoons tarragon or wine vinegar
1 tablespoon French mustard
1 tablespoon tomato purée
1–2 garlic cloves
a few crushed coriander seeds
freshly-ground black pepper

Heat the oven to 400F, 200C, gas mark 6. Choose a gratin or baking dish which will take the chicken joints in a single layer. Pour the oil into it and swirl to coat the base and sides. Add the chicken, rolling them to coat all over with the oil then season with coriander and pepper. Push the fairly finely chopped onion into the gaps, turning it a little to coat with a thin film of oil. Bake just above the centre of the oven for 35 minutes. Meanwhile, crush the garlic clove and mash it into the jelly marmalade. Add the remaining ingredients and stir vigorously to mix well.

When the 35 minutes are up, spoon the sauce over the chicken. Bake for a further 30 minutes, basting the chicken with the sauce every 8–10 minutes. Serve piping hot.

CHICKEN AND HAM CROQUETTES
(serves 4–6)

If you buy a really large chicken for a Sunday roast, there should be enough leftovers to make these croquettes. A friend who has tried them says they freeze well after breadcrumbing: thaw at room temperature for 1–2 hours before frying.

$\frac{3}{4}$ lb cooked chicken meat (skinned and boned weight)
6 oz ham
3 tablespoons each butter, flour and grated Cheddar cheese
$\frac{3}{4}$ pt milk
1 heaped tablespoon fresh chopped tarragon (or 2 teaspoons dried tarragon)
1 whole egg and 1 yolk

For frying:
a little flour
beaten egg
about 6 oz toasted white breadcrumbs
oil

Make a white sauce with the butter, flour and milk. Away from the heat stir in the tarragon and cheese plus a little salt and a good grinding of pepper. Chop the chicken meat finely and mince the ham. Stir the meats into the sauce, then beat in one whole egg and one yolk to bind the mixture. Check seasoning, then spread the mixture thinly on a large shallow dish. Chill, preferably overnight, until cold and well dried out.

Divide the mixture into 16–18 portions. Roll each one into a small neat sausage shape. Dust the croquettes generously with flour, moisten them all over with beaten egg and coat with breadcrumbs. Deep fry in fat heated to 375F/190C for about 3 minutes. Drain well and serve immediately.

CHICKEN BENVENUTO
(serves 2)

This is one of those dishes that fills the kitchen with wonderfully inviting smells and is very easy to cook. It is a rich dish so I don't bother with a first course, and I follow the chicken with a large fresh-tasting salad and, say, a sorbet.

2 large chicken breast joints
2 oz unsalted butter
2 garlic cloves
$\frac{1}{4}$ lb mushrooms
5 oz tagliatelle
salt and freshly-ground black pepper

Melt half the butter in a large sauté or frying pan. Add 1 crushed garlic clove and the chicken pieces. Fry over gentle heat for a total of 30–40 minutes, turning the chicken from time to time to cook it evenly on all sides. The chicken is ready when the flesh is perfectly tender and juicy within and the skin is crisp and golden with a garlic flavoured crust. Transfer the chicken to a plate and keep hot.

Sauté the thickly sliced mushrooms in the fat remaining in the pan. Remove with a slotted spoon, adding them to the chicken.

Melt the remaining butter in the sauté pan. Add the remaining crushed garlic clove, some salt and a good grinding of black pepper. Remove the pan from the heat. Add the freshly boiled and drained pasta (which should preferably have been cooked in chicken stock) and toss lightly until coated with the garlic butter.

Turn the pasta onto a warm serving dish, arrange the chicken and mushrooms on top, and serve immediately.

CHILDREN'S CHICKEN SALAD
(serves 4)

Here is a very quick and easy salad that makes good use of leftovers from a roast chicken.

4 oz macaroni
7–8 oz skinned and boned chicken cooked meat
1 × 7 oz can of pineapple pieces in natural juice (not syrup)
1 × 7 oz can whole sweetcorn kernels
1 small green pepper or 2–3 oz young fresh or frozen peas
3 tablespoons olive or corn oil
3–4 tablespoons fresh chopped mint

Cook the macaroni in plenty of fast-boiling salted water until just tender. Drain well and allow to cool slightly while you make the dressing: 2 tablespoons of juice from the canned pineapple mixed with the oil and a good seasoning of salt and pepper.

Turn the macaroni into a large mixing bowl, pour on the dressing, toss lightly and leave until cold – 20 minutes or so.

Meanwhile, cut the chicken into bite-sized chunks, drain the pineapple and sweetcorn, chop the mint and either de-seed the pepper and cut the flesh into strips, or blanch the peas in fast boiling water for 2 minutes, drain, refresh under a cold running tap and drain again.

When the macaroni is cold, add the other ingredients to the bowl and mix lightly together. Turn into a serving dish lined with a bed of shredded lettuce, and serve.

INDONESIAN CHICKEN

Miniature kebabs suspended across a tiny bowl of sauce make an inviting first course. Or they can be served with boiled rice and fried bananas to make a main course – in which case these quantities are enough for 4 people.

2 lb chicken breasts
2 tablespoons each lemon juice, black treacle and peanut oil

For the sauce:
2½ oz onion (peeled and chopped weight)
2 garlic cloves
1½ tablespoons peanut oil
½ teaspoon chilli powder
1½ tablespoons each black treacle, lemon juice and soy sauce
5–6 tablespoons peanut butter
salt

Thoroughly defrost and dry the chicken breasts. Carefully skin and bone them, and separate the thin fillets of meat from the thick fillets. Lightly beat the thick fillets between sheets of clingfilm to flatten them. Cut all the chicken meat into narrow strips about 1 × ½ inch. Steep them in the well-mixed lemon juice, black treacle and peanut oil and leave in a cool place for about 4 hours. Then slide the chicken pieces, ribbon fashion, on to small skewers, spreading out the strips so they are almost flat. Reserve the marinade.

Liquidise the onions and garlic with the oil to make a thick purée. Put the mixture into a small pan and cook over very low heat for 10 minutes or until softened but not coloured. Add the remaining sauce ingredients and as much water as is needed to make a thick sauce. Cook stirring continuously until the sauce is perfectly smooth, glossy and very hot. Set aside and keep hot.

Pour the marinade over the skewered chicken and grill for 5 minutes or so, turning the skewers as necessary, until the meat is very tender and nicely browned. Divide the hot sauce between warmed small bowls, arrange the skewers across the bowls and serve immediately.

CHICKEN KIEV
(serves 6)

A great favourite in restaurants but usually much better cooked at home, where you will of course use fresh breadcrumbs instead of that revolting orange grit beloved of caterers, and you won't use any garlic – or just the merest hint.

the breasts of 3 × 3–3½ lb chickens (see method)
2 teaspoons fresh chopped chives (or a very small garlic clove)
1 tablespoon fresh chopped tarragon and parsley
6 oz unsalted butter
1 scant tablespoon lemon juice
salt and freshly-ground black pepper
3 small eggs
a little plain flour
about ½ lb fresh white breadcrumbs

It is best to cut the breast meat (complete with wing bones) off whole chickens for this dish rather than use shop-bought breast of chicken portions. Use the rest of the birds for casseroles or pies. Preparing the breast meat is easier to do than you might think, but it does take time – particularly if you have never done it before – so patience is the name of the game.

But first make the herb butter. Beat the softened butter with the lemon juice, herbs and plenty of salt and pepper. Using wet hands and wet greaseproof paper, shape the savoury butter into a block, wrap it and chill it until solid.

Lay one of the chickens on its back, pull the legs away from the body and cut them off. Cut down the length of the breast from the neck to the tail using a small, sharp knife. Completely peel away the breast skin and gently ease out the wishbone. Insert the blade between flesh and one side of the breast-bone and cut the meat free from the bone, gradually working the blade over the rib-cage down to the point where the wing joins the body. Cut through the wing joint so the wing is attached to the breast meat. Then cut off the wing pinion so that only the main wing bone remains attached to the breast meat, and scrape the meat back from the bone so it is clean.

When all 6 portions are prepared to this stage, separate the thin fillet from each portion. Beat both thin and main portions flat. I place them between sheets of clingfilm and beat them gently with a rolling pin.

Cut the savoury butter into 6 sticks. Lay one on each of the main portions and cover with a thin fillet. Fold the main breast meat over the fillet to encase the butter completely and make a neat, elongated parcel. Dust with well-seasoned flour, dip in egg beaten with a little water and coat generously with bread-crumbs. Leave for at least 2 hours (overnight if you prefer) in a cold larder or refrigerator to set the coating firmly.

Deep-fry 2 portions at a time in oil heated to 350–360F/177–182C. They will take 10–15 minutes to cook right through – reduce heat a little if the crumb coating is browning too fast. Drain well, decorate the meatless wing bones with paper cutlet frills and serve piping hot.

GRILLED CHICKEN WITH FIGS AND ORANGES
(serves 4)

Figs and oranges make aromatic partners for chicken and the smells that waft from the grill pan are marvellous.

        8 chicken thighs
        12 dried figs
        4 small thin-skinned oranges
        1 teaspoon dried rosemary
        2–3 tablespoons olive oil
        salt and freshly-ground black pepper

Remove the stalks from the figs and flatten each fruit as much as possible. Put them into a small bowl and pour on the juice of one orange and the olive oil; there should be enough liquid to cover the fruit. Set aside for at least 4 hours to soften the figs slightly.

Crush the rosemary to a powder with mortar and pestle. Put it into a shallow dish. Add a good grinding of pepper and the juice of 2 oranges. Prick the chicken all over with a fork, turn the pieces of meat in the dish and leave to marinate in a cold place for at least 4 hours.

To cook, thread the chicken pieces on to skewers, alternating meat with wedges of orange (the fourth orange, unpeeled and cut into 8 wedges). Brush the orange peel with olive oil, then grill the kebabs for about 20 minutes, turning and basting them with the marinade as necessary. About 6 minutes before the end of cooking time, add the figs to the ends of the skewers. The dish is ready when the figs are hot, the chicken skin deep gold with a few crackly dark blisters, and the orange peel is semi-charred. Sprinkle with salt and serve on a bed of watercress with the pan juices poured over. Whether you eat the orange segments or simply squeeze their juice over the chicken is up to you — I find them irresistible to chew.

RABBIT PUDDING
(serves 6)

Boneless rabbit meat can be bought from Sainsburys and from Bejam — ideal for this homely alternative to steak and kidney pudding.

$1\frac{1}{2}$ lb boneless rabbit meat
$\frac{3}{4}$ lb salt pork (boned and de-rinded weight)
2 onions
2 leeks
$\frac{1}{4}$ lb mushrooms
1 heaped teaspoon dried mixed herbs
the zest of a lemon plus 2 teaspoons juice
1 fat garlic clove
6 tablespoons chopped parsley
2 tablespoons tomato purée
3 tablespoons plain flour
$1\frac{1}{2}$ oz melted bacon fat (or a mixture of butter and oil)
1 × 14 oz can of tomatoes
plenty of salt and pepper

For the pastry
$\frac{3}{4}$ lb self-raising flour
1 teaspoon each salt, baking powder and dried thyme
6 oz shredded suet
about 7 fl. oz water to bind

Cube the pork and brown it, and remove from the pan. Add extra bacon fat or butter and oil to the pan as necessary, and brown the cubes of rabbit meat. Remove them from the pan. Sauté the sliced mushrooms, remove and reserve separately. Colour the chopped onion and leeks. Stir in the flour to absorb the fat remaining in the pan. Add the canned tomatoes and their juices (mashed together) and bring to the boil stirring. Return the meats to the pan (but not the mushrooms). Add the crushed garlic, fresh and dried herbs, lemon juice and zest, tomato purée and a good seasoning of salt and pepper. Cover and cook very gently indeed for 1½ hours – on top of the stove or in an oven heated to 300F, 150C, gas mark 2. Let the mixture become cold, adjust seasoning and stir in the reserved mushrooms.

To make the suetcrust pastry, measure the dry ingredients into a large mixing bowl and stir with a wooden spoon to mix well. Pour on and stir in enough cold water to make a soft dough. Roll out the dough to a large circle. Cut out and reserve a triangle of the pastry. Use the three-quarter circle to line a well-buttered pudding basin. Add the filling, and cover and seal with a 'lid' made by re-rolling the reserved pastry. Cover with a circle of buttered paper and pleated foil. Tie securely and steam or boil steadily for 1½–2 hours.

CASSEROLED RABBIT WITH OLIVES
(serves 4)

The sauce given here is small in quantity but deliciously rich in flavour and colour.

1½–2 lb rabbit, jointed
2 dozen black olives
½ lb streaky bacon rashers
½ lb onions, sliced
1 large garlic clove, crushed
rosemary
finely grated zest of 2 oranges
3 fl. oz Marsala
7 fl. oz good rabbit or chicken stock
a little butter and olive oil
¾ oz caster sugar
salt and freshly-ground black pepper

For the marinade:
1 teaspoon thyme
black pepper
2 onions
1 celery stalk
1 carrot
1 garlic clove
parsley stalks and bay leaf
$\frac{1}{2}$ pt wine or cider
2 tablespoons oil

Put the rabbit into a large bowl and sprinkle on 1 teaspoon of thyme and a generous grinding of black pepper. To prepare the marinade chop the vegetables and garlic clove finely and cook these gently in the oil in a covered pan for 5 minutes. Add a few parsley stalks and the bay leaf. Pour on $\frac{1}{2}$ pt of wine or cider and bring to the boil. Pour the marinade mixture over the rabbit, cover the bowl with a clean cloth and leave to marinate in a cool place for 24–48 hours, turning the meat occasionally.

Drain the rabbit from the marinade, pat it dry and dust it with the sugar. Heat a knob of butter and a spoonful of oil in a flame-proof casserole. Add the rabbit, a few pieces at a time, and brown and seal the meat well. Remove the rabbit joints with a slotted spoon, then lightly colour the onions, adding a little more fat to the casserole if necessary.

Return the rabbit joints to the casserole, burying them among the onions. De-rind the bacon rashers, roll each one up neatly, and tuck them here and there between the rabbit joints. Pour on the liquids, add the orange zest, garlic, a good pinch of rosemary and plenty of salt and pepper.

Bring the mixture to boiling point, then cover the casserole and transfer it to an oven heated to 300F, 150C, gas mark 2. Cook for 2 –2½ hours, or until the rabbit is tender, adding the olives to the casserole during the last half hour.

Just before serving, strain off the liquid and fast boil it until reduced and thickened to a syrupy rich coating sauce. Spoon the sauce over the rabbit and serve with a dish of steamed new potatoes.

BRAISED RABBIT
(serves 4–5)

It is always best to marinate rabbit for 24 hours before braising.
(For details on marinating rabbit see opposite page.)

> 1 × 2 lb rabbit, jointed
> 6 celery stalks
> $\frac{1}{2}$ lb carrots
> 8 small onions
> 1 fat garlic clove
> 2 teaspoons dried thyme
> 1 bay leaf
> $\frac{1}{4}$ lb large pitted prunes
> $\frac{1}{2}$ lb streaky bacon rashers
> a little olive oil
> about $\frac{1}{4}$ pt white wine or very dry cider
> fresh parsley
> 1 tablespoon each softened butter and plain flour kneaded
>   together to make a paste
> salt and freshly-ground black pepper

Marinate the rabbit joints for 24 hours. Drain off the liquid and
reserve it. Discard the marinade vegetables and dry the rabbit
joints carefully. Brown the meat, a few pieces at a time, in a
little hot olive oil in a flame-proof casserole, then colour the
halved onions, sliced carrots and celery and finely chopped
garlic.

Draw the casserole away from the heat. Bury the prunes
(which should not be pre-soaked) among the vegetables and
sprinkle on the thyme. Lay the rabbit pieces on top, tucking the
bay leaf among them, and season very generously with salt and
pepper. Pour on the reserved marinade liquid plus enough wine
or cider to make a total $\frac{1}{2}$ pt: the liquid should barely cover the
vegetables. Cover the rabbit with a 'blanket' of overlapping
bacon rashers, and lay a circle of lightly buttered greaseproof
paper on top. Cover with a well-fitting lid and braise in an oven
heated to 325F, 160C, gas mark 3, until the rabbit is very
tender – about 2–$2\frac{1}{2}$ hours.

Using a perforated spoon, transfer the rabbit joints, bacon and braising vegetables to a warm serving dish. Place the casserole over moderate heat, gradually stir in small pieces of the butter and flour paste, and simmer until the sauce is slightly thickened, smooth and hot. Add a handful of chopped fresh parsley, check the sauce for seasoning, pour it over the rabbit and serve garnished with triangles of fried bread.

BRAISED PIGEON WITH CABBAGE
(serves 4)

Long, gentle cooking is usually necessary to make pigeons tender. It is best to cook them breast downwards, as here, so that the lean meat doesn't dry out too much.

> 4 pigeons
> $\frac{1}{4}$ lb green streaky bacon in a piece
> 2 tablespoons dripping
> 1 tight green cabbage
> 2 carrots
> 1 Spanish onion
> $\frac{1}{2}$ pt chicken stock
> 2 teaspoons concentrated tomato purée
> 1 teaspoon Worcester sauce
> a bouquet garni
> a tablespoon or so of softened butter mashed with an equal
>   quantity of plain flour

Choose a large flame-proof casserole. Put the diced bacon into it and cook over low heat until the fat runs. Remove the bacon with a slotted spoon. Increase heat and add a little dripping. When it is very hot add 2 of the pigeons and brown all over. Remove and colour the remaining pigeons in the same way, then colour the diced onion and carrots. Remove them and add any remaining dripping. Add the cabbage cut into 4 wedges and turn to coat all over with fat. Return the other vegetables to the dish and bury the pigeons breast down, among them. Pour on the stock, add the bouquet garni, tomato purée and Worcester sauce. Bring to simmering point and cover the casserole with a lid.

Transfer the casserole to an oven heated to 325F, 160C, gas mark 3, and braise for about 2½ hours, or until the pigeons are tender.

Lift the cooked vegetables and pigeons out of the casserole on to a warmed serving dish. Remove and discard the bouquet garni. Place the casserole over direct heat. Stir in the mashed butter and flour, a nugget at a time, and boil for a few minutes stirring continuously until the sauce is slightly thickened and reduced to your liking. Season with salt and pepper as necessary and pour the sauce over the pigeons and cabbage.

DUCK WITH ORANGE SAUCE
(serves 4)

Chill-fresh ducks from Marks & Spencer are justly famed; both texture and flavour are excellent. Alternatively, this most savoury of sauces makes a delicious accompaniment for roast pork.

4½–5 lb duck
3 Seville oranges
¾ pt well-flavoured stock made from the duck giblets
2 fl. oz port (or 4 fl. oz red wine reduced to 2 fl. oz by fast boiling)
3 tablespoons sugar
1 heaped tablespoon each of butter and plain flour
salt and freshly-ground black pepper

Rinse and dry the duck thoroughly. Do not truss, but remove lumps of fat from just inside the tail end. Prick the skin all over with a sharp pointed knife and rub it with salt and pepper. Place on a rack in a roasting tin and roast at 400F, 200C, gas mark 6. I like the skin to be really crisp so I allow 25–30 minutes per lb, and drain the fat from the bottom of the tin every half hour.

Cook the port or reduced wine and sugar to a rich mahogany-coloured syrup. Pour on a little of the stock and stir until the caramel is dissolved, then blend in the rest of the stock. Make a brown roux with the butter and flour, blend in the prepared liquid and leave to simmer uncovered while you cut the orange skin into julienne strips, and blanch it for 5 minutes in fast boiling water. Drain well and reserve.

Squeeze the orange juice, strain it into the saucepan and continue simmering gently, stirring occasionally, until the sauce is reduced to a good consistency. Season generously with salt and pepper, add the blanched strips of zest and heat through, then turn into a warmed sauceboat and keep hot.

Check that the duck is thoroughly cooked. The juices should run clear when the thigh meat is pricked with a pointed knife. Cut the bird into 4 portions (simpler and better than trying to carve it), and serve garnished with bunches of watercress and boiled potatoes.

PERFECT ROAST TURKEY

Fresh turkey costs more than frozen, but tastes far, far better. I always buy mine from Marks & Spencer and – because I do not want to eat cold turkey for days after Christmas – I always buy a fairly small one, weighing no more than 10 lb.

> fresh turkey, up to 12 lb drawn weight
> about 7 oz softened butter
> a little dried tarragon
> salt and freshly-ground black pepper
> turkey giblet stock
> a small glass of wine

Let the turkey stand at room temperature for about 45 minutes before cooking it. Stuff the neck cavity and put a large lump of butter mashed with salt, pepper and some tarragon into the body cavity. (The body cavity can also be stuffed if you like, but only with a meatless mixture.) I think all poultry cooks more evenly if it is left untrussed.

Weigh the turkey *after* stuffing it and calculate roasting time accordingly. It will need 15 minutes per lb (turkeys weighing over 15 lb need a few minutes less per pound). Please note that this is *cooking* time. Add an extra half hour irrespective of weight to allow 10–15 minutes for basting the bird during cooking, and 15–20 minutes for 'resting' the bird between cooking and carving.

Smear the skin of the stuffed turkey with plenty of softened butter, well seasoned with salt and pepper – I allow at least $\frac{1}{2}$ oz butter per lb of turkey. Lay the bird breast down, not directly on the roasting pan base, but on a rack in the pan. (An inexpensive and useful rack, rather coyly called Roast-Rite, is available from John Lewis shops, Harrods and other stores. Consisting of 2 interlocking grids to make a V-shape which is ideal for roasting birds, it fits standard size roasting pans and folds away neatly for storage.) Cover the pan with a dome of foil, sealing the edges firmly round the lip of the tin, and roast at 375F, 190C, gas mark 5.

Half an hour before the end of cooking time, remove the foil. Turn the bird breast up, baste it with the buttery juices and sprinkle with salt and pepper. Complete roasting uncovered and baste frequently. Increase temperature slightly if necessary to get a really crispy golden finish to the skin. Check that the turkey is thoroughly cooked by piercing the thickest part of the leg with a skewer: the juices should be clear.

While the turkey 'rests' make an unthickened gravy by adding turkey giblet stock and a small glass of wine to the buttery pan juices; let them boil until reduced to a well-flavoured syrupy texture.

MUSHROOM STUFFING

A good stuffing improves turkey and helps minimise the chances of the meat drying out during cooking. Onion and sage are British favourites, but not my taste – and death to wine. This unusual combination of mushrooms, celery and rice makes an excellent alternative.

6 oz mushrooms coarsely chopped
1 large onion finely chopped
3 oz celery finely chopped
2 oz rice
2 oz coarsely chopped hazelnuts
¼ lb butter
stock
1 heaped teaspoon dried tarragon
salt, freshly-ground black pepper and a few crushed coriander seeds

Boil the rice in stock with the tarragon until tender and drain
well. Fry the onion in the butter quite gently for a few minutes
until slightly softened. Increase heat, add the celery and mushrooms and sauté. Away from the heat, stir in the cooked rice,
chopped nuts and a good seasoning of salt, pepper and coriander.

CREAMY BREAD SAUCE
(serves 6)

Bread sauce should be creamy, not a lumpy porridge reeking of
cloves — so don't stint on the liquids, and do try this alternative
flavouring of coriander, bay and mace.

½ pt milk
1 small bay leaf
a blade of mace
1 chopped onion
12 coriander seeds and 6 black peppercorns crushed with
mortar and pestle
3 oz fresh white breadcrumbs
3 oz butter
¼ pt single cream
salt and freshly-ground black pepper

Measure the cold milk into a small saucepan. Stir in the crumbled bay leaf, the mace, onion, coriander and peppercorns.
Cover and leave in a cold place overnight.

Next day bring the milk slowly to scalding point. Strain the
flavoured liquid on to the breadcrumbs and leave for 10
minutes. Then turn the swollen milky crumbs into the cleaned

out saucepan. Add the cream and 2 oz butter. Cook gently, stirring frequently, for about 3 minutes until the sauce is very smooth, slightly thickened and beautifully creamy. Season with salt and pepper, dot with the remaining butter, cover with a lid and set aside. Stir in the butter and reheat gently just before serving.

SUPERIOR CRANBERRY SAUCE
(serves 6)

All my friends seem to agree that superior is an apt description here.

$\frac{1}{2}$ lb fresh cranberries
finely-grated zest of half an orange
2 inches cinnamon stick
6 oz caster sugar
2 tablespoons dry white wine
4 fl. oz water

Grate the orange zest into a small pan. Add the cinnamon stick, sugar, wine and water. Stir over low heat until the sugar is dissolved. Add the rinsed and dried berries. Bring to the boil, then simmer very gently for 8 minutes until the fruit is tender and most of the berries have burst. Cover and set aside until ready to serve – the mixture will thicken as it cools, and the flavourings will develop nicely. Serve warm or cold, removing the cinnamon stick just before you transfer the sauce to a serving bowl or sauceboat.

Beef

SIMPLE PASTITSIO
(serves 6)

This is an inexpensive adaptation of a Greek dish, much simpler than lasagne and must more interesting than plain macaroni cheese. It can be completely prepared and assembled in advance.

For the meat sauce:
1 lb minced beef or lamb
4 rashers streaky bacon
1 onion
1 fat garlic clove
2 tablespoons oil
$\frac{1}{2}$ teaspoon each rosemary and thyme
$\frac{1}{4}$ teaspoon each marjoram and ground cinnamon
$\frac{1}{2}$ pt good stock
4 tablespoons tomato purée
a generous pinch of sugar

For the macaroni:
6 oz macaroni
2 oz butter
$1\frac{1}{2}$ oz plain flour
$\frac{3}{4}$ pt milk
$\frac{1}{4}$ pt plain yoghurt
$\frac{1}{4}$ lb mature Cheddar cheese
salt, pepper and nutmeg
3–4 tablespoons dry breadcrumbs

Fry the chopped onion in the hot oil until beginning to brown. Add the minced meat and matchsticks of bacon and colour. Stir in the crushed garlic, herbs, spices, seasonings, tomato purée and stock. Simmer uncovered, just stirring occasionally, for about 40 minutes. Season with salt and pepper to taste.

Meanwhile, boil the macaroni, and make a white sauce with the butter, flour and milk. Away from the heat, stir in half the grated cheese, a generous seasoning of salt, pepper and nutmeg, then the yoghurt and finally the drained macaroni. Put half the mixture in the base of a gratin or large soufflé dish, cover with the meat sauce, and top with the remaining macaroni mixture.

To reheat for serving, sprinkle the rest of the cheese and the breadcrumbs over the pastitsio and bake, uncovered, at 375F, 190C, gas mark 5, for about 45 minutes.

BEEF WITH MUSHROOM GRAVY
(serves 2–3)

If you have an automatic oven timer, you can prepare this comforting casserole in minutes in the morning. Put it into a cold oven and set the time and temperature controls so dinner will be cooked and ready to welcome you home in the evening.

1 lb trimmed and cubed chuck steak or skirt
2 oz finely chopped onions
$\frac{1}{4}$ lb mushrooms, thickly sliced
1 pig's trotter or piece of pork rind (optional)
3 fl. oz red wine
1 heaped tablespoon plain flour
$\frac{1}{2}$ teaspoon coriander seeds, crushed with the back of a spoon
$\frac{1}{2}$ teaspoon dried thyme
a pinch of ground cloves
a small bay leaf
salt and freshly-ground black pepper

Season the flour with coriander, thyme, cloves and plenty of salt and pepper. Dust the beef with it and put into a casserole. Add the bay leaf and trotter or rind. Mix the onions and mushrooms together with any leftover flour and press them down on top of the meat. Pour on the wine and cover.

Place in a cold oven and time to start cooking 3–3½ hours before you plan to eat, selecting oven temperature 300F, 150C, gas mark 2. Remove bay leaf and trotter or rind, and stir the casserole before serving.

HARVEST LOAF

(serves 6 or more)

A colourful meat loaf which includes carrots, onion and green peppers. It goes down a treat with baked potatoes and my favourite quick piquant sauce: chopped gherkins or sweet garlic cucumbers stirred into soured cream with a teaspoon or so of Worcester sauce.

½ lb stewing or braising steak
¼ lb ox liver
¾ lb salt pork or belly of pork (trimmed weights in each case)
1 large onion
1 green pepper
¼ lb grated carrot
¼ lb fresh brown breadcrumbs
a generous handful of chopped fresh parsley
1 fat garlic clove crushed with salt
1 tablespoon lemon juice
plenty of freshly-ground black pepper
2 or 3 bay leaves

Mince the meats fairly finely. Grate the carrot and onion, chop the pepper and parsley. Crush the garlic. Mix all the ingredients (except the bay leaves) very thoroughly together with your hands, including plenty of pepper – and salt unless the salt pork is very salty. Pack the mixture into a loaf tin lined with lightly oiled greaseproof paper (the paper is not vital but it makes turning out easier), doming the meat nicely. Press the bay leaves on top and cover with foil.

Stand the tin in a roasting pan, pour in enough boiling water to come halfway up the sides of the loaf tin and bake in the centre of the oven at 350F, 180C, gas mark 4, for 1 hour. Reduce oven temperature to 325F, 160C, gas mark 3, remove foil and bake for a further 30 minutes. Store the meat loaf in a cold larder or fridge overnight before serving to allow flavours to mature.

SCANDINAVIAN MEATBALLS
(serves 4)

This recipe is very quick and quite delicious – the meatballs can be fried or grilled. I like to serve them on a bed of garlic buttered noodles – with grilled tomatoes if the meatballs have been grilled, or with a tomato salad if the meatballs have been fried.

> $1\frac{1}{4}$–$1\frac{1}{2}$ lb best minced beef (I choose a nice piece of chuck steak and ask the butcher to mince it for me, or I mince it at home)
> 1 very small onion
> 2 tablespoons freshly-grated Parmesan cheese
> a few fresh basil leaves
> salt and freshly-ground black pepper
> a few bay leaves (optional)

Chop both the onion and the basil leaves very finely indeed. Put them into a mixing bowl. Add the minced beef and a good grinding of pepper (no salt at this stage). Sprinkle on the Parmesan cheese, then mix and knead the ingredients together – using your hands is the most efficient way.

Roll small pieces of the mixture between the palms of your hands to make small meatballs – somewhere between a hazelnut and a walnut in size.

Either thread the meatballs on to skewers, adding a bay leaf here and there. Brush them all over with oil and grill under fierce heat until crisp and brown on the outside but still tender and slightly pink within;

Or shallow fry the meatballs in hot oil, turning the balls as necessary so that they cook evenly.

Cut one of the meatballs in half to cool it quickly, then eat it to check whether the mixture is salty enough for your taste – I find the Parmesan usually provides enough salt. Turn the meatballs on to a serving dish, sprinkle with salt if you wish and serve immediately while piping hot and juicy.

A SIMPLE SPICED BEEF
(serves 2–3)

The sharp flavour of a good tomato pickle gives this stew interesting piquancy. Serve with lots of mashed potatoes to soak up the gravy.

    1 lb best stewing steak
    2 medium-sized onions
    a little beef dripping
    1 tablespoon tomato pickle (Marks & Spencer's is excellent if
        home-made is unavailable)
    $\frac{1}{4}$ pt beef stock
    salt and freshly-ground black pepper

Cube the beef, dust it with plenty of pepper and sear in the tiniest quantity of very hot dripping. Cook just a few pieces at a time to get them really crusty and brown all over. Remove with a slotted spoon. Add a little more dripping and brown the sliced onions in it. Return the meat to the casserole. Stir in the beef stock and tomato pickle and some salt. Cover tightly and simmer very gently on top of the stove or in an oven heated to 300F, 150C, gas mark 2, for 3 hours or until the beef is tender.

BEEFSTEAK AND KIDNEY PIE
(serves 6)

If your family are addicted to suet pastry, this beafsteak and kidney mixture can be cooked in a casserole for $1\frac{1}{2}$ hours only, then packed into a suet-lined basin (see recipe for rabbit pudding, page 108) and steamed for a further $1\frac{1}{2}$ hours.

    $1\frac{1}{2}$ lb chuck steak
    $\frac{3}{4}$ lb ox kidney
    $\frac{1}{2}$ lb small cap mushrooms
    2 medium-sized onions
    2 teaspoons lemon juice
    1 teaspoon Worcester sauce

14 fl. oz beef stock
2 oz beef dripping
3 tablespoons plain flour
a small bouquet garni
salt and freshly-ground black pepper
13 oz packet puff or flaky pastry
beaten egg to glaze

Trim mushroom stalks level with caps, and cut any largish mushrooms in half. Heat half the dripping in a large heavy-based flame-proof casserole. Fry the mushrooms in it stirring as necessary to colour them all over. Remove with a slotted spoon and reserve in a small bowl.

Add the rest of the dripping to the casserole. When it is very hot, brown and seal the steak and kidney — both meats should be cut into good size cubes, and they should be cooked in batches to make them really crusty and brown. Remove the meats from the casserole on to a plate.

Add the fairly finely chopped onions to the casserole together with a little extra fat if necessary, and cook until slightly coloured. Sprinkle on the flour, pour on the stock and cook stirring continuously until you have a smooth, slightly thickened, simmering sauce.

Season with salt and pepper, the lemon juice and Worcester sauce, and add the bouquet garni. Return the meats to the casserole (but not the mushrooms because they only need brief cooking). Push them well down into the gravy.

As soon as the contents of the casserole come back to simmering point, cover the casserole with a lid and cook in an oven heated to 300F, 150C, gas mark 2, for $2\frac{1}{2}$ hours. By the end of this time the meats should be beautifully tender and the sauce richly flavoured and of good texture. Remove the bouquet garni, check seasoning and adjust to taste. Then set the covered casserole aside until cold — this is important: the pastry topping will spoil if the pie filling it covers is already hot.

Stir the reserved mushrooms into the cold meat mixture and pack it into a large pie dish. Cover with a puff or flaky pastry lid in the usual way. Decorate, make a steam hole and glaze the pastry with beaten egg. Stand the pie dish on a preheated baking sheet and bake in the oven at 425F, 220C, gas mark 7, for about 35 minutes until the pastry is puffed up and a rich golden brown.

STIR-FRIED STEAK

(serves 2)

Stir-fried meat and vegetables are light and fresh-tasting and very quickly cooked – and must be served as soon as cooked. This sort of dish is ideal when you are cooking for one or two people only.

$\frac{3}{4}$ lb well-hung rump steak
$\frac{1}{2}$ lb beansprouts
$\frac{1}{2}$ lb Chinese leaves
3 tablespoons sesame, peanut or sunflower oil
1 heaped tablespoon very finely chopped fresh root ginger
1 fat garlic clove
$1\frac{1}{2}$ tablespoons soy sauce
1 teaspoon tarragon or white wine vinegar
salt and freshly-ground black pepper

Trim all fat from the steak. Cut the lean into tiny strips about 2 inches long and $\frac{1}{4}$ inch thick. Shred the Chinese leaves. Mix the soy sauce, vinegar, a very good grinding of black pepper and some salt in a cup. All these preparations should be done before you begin to cook because, once cooking starts, everything happens very quickly.

Put 2 tablespoons of oil into a 10–12 inch heavy-based frying pan. Add the crushed garlic clove and the ginger and place over medium-low heat until the oil is hot and aromatised with the flavourings. Tip in the Chinese leaves and the beansprouts and cook, stirring and turning the vegetables continuously with a pair of wooden spoons, for about 2 minutes. Lift out the vegetables, add the remaining tablespoon of oil and increase heat to very high. Add the strips of meat, then cook them, stirring and turning them continuously, until coloured on all sides – about 1 minute.

Reduce heat slightly, quickly return the vegetables to the

pan, pour on the contents of the cup, and cook, still stirring and turning, for a few seconds more — until all the ingredients are well mixed and very hot. Serve immediately.

CIDERED BEEF WITH CROÛTONS
(serves 8)

The sweetness of prunes, orange zest and coriander seeds are delicious with beef, but the cider must be very dry for this recipe.

3 lb chuck steak or thick flank
$\frac{3}{4}$ lb onions
16 large prunes
1 large garlic clove
3–4 tablespoons oil
1 pt dry cider
3 tablespoons flour
the zest of an orange
1 teaspoon crushed coriander seeds
salt and freshly-ground black pepper
12 thick slices of white bread cut into dice and fried until crisp and golden

Thoroughly brown and seal the cubed meat — a few pieces at a time — in very hot oil in a flame-proof casserole. Remove with a slotted spoon. Halve or quarter the onions if very large, then slice thickly and brown them in very hot oil. Add the garlic clove crushed with a little salt, sprinkle on the flour, pour on the cider and bring to the boil stirring continuously.

Return the meat to the casserole, bury the prunes here and there (there is no need to pre-soak them), add the finely-grated orange zest, crushed coriander, plenty of pepper and some salt. Cover and cook in a preheated oven at 300F, 150C, gas mark 2, for $2\frac{1}{2}$ hours.

Check seasoning before serving, and scatter the piping hot, crisply fried croûtons over the top.

THREE-DAY DAUBE PROVENÇALE
(serves 8–10)

Three days aren't really necessary; you can marinate the meat in
the morning, cook it in the evening and chill it overnight. Then
scrape off surface fat and complete cooking next day.

3 lb chuck steak or blade
1 pig's trotter
6 oz piece of smoked streaky bacon
1 large onion
4 tomatoes
1 orange
2 garlic cloves
a bouquet garni
2–3 tablespoons olive oil
2 teaspoons sugar
freshly-ground black pepper

For the marinade:
6 fl. oz red wine
1 small onion
4 cloves
1 garlic clove
the grated zest of ½ orange
a few black peppercorns
bay leaf, sprig of thyme and a few parsley stalks

For the provençale sauce:
6 anchovy fillets
1 tablespoon capers
1 large garlic clove
2 tablespoons chopped parsley
1 tablespoon olive oil
a handful of black olives

On the first day prepare the marinade. Peel and quarter the
onion, stud it with cloves and place on a piece of butter-muslin.
Add the sliced garlic and remaining marinade flavourings and
tie up loosely. Put it into a bowl, add the beef cut into 1½–2 inch
cubes, pour on the wine, cover and leave overnight in a cold
larder.

Next day drain the beef, reserving the wine, and discard the bag of flavourings. Thoroughly dry the beef, cut the bacon into large dice and chop the onion. Brown them all over in the olive oil. Add to the casserole the rinsed and dried trotter, the skinned, seeded and chopped tomatoes, the crushed garlic, the orange zest, bouquet garni, sugar and pepper – no salt at this stage.

Bring the wine to a fast boil and pour it into the casserole. Push the beef well down into the liquid, cover and cook at the gentlest possible simmer (250–275F, gas mark $\frac{1}{2}$–1) for $3\frac{1}{2}$–4 hours. Remove the trotter, discard bones, cut up the pork meat and return it to the casserole. Cover again and leave in a cold larder overnight.

On the third day, scrape off solid surface fat then reheat the daube slowly and gently. Meanwhile, pound the anchovies and capers until smooth, then blend in the crushed garlic, parsley and olive oil. Stir the sauce into the daube together with the olives about half an hour before serving. Check for seasoning after 15 minutes, adding salt, or straining off and reducing the sauce to concentrate flavour a little if necessary.

PORT AND LEMON STEAK
(serves 4)

This sounds unpromising but is very good, and it involves blissfully little work for the cook.

$1\frac{1}{2}$ lb chuck steak (trimmed weight – see recipe method)
2 tablespoons plain flour
1 large onion
1 large crushed garlic clove
$\frac{1}{4}$ lb button mushrooms
4 tablespoons each port and cold water
1 tablespoon lemon juice
2 teaspoons tomato purée
salt and freshly-ground black pepper

You want 4 slices of chuck steak for this, each weighing about 6–7 oz after trimming. Get the butcher to make them nice thick slices. Dust them with flour very well seasoned with salt and pepper, and lay them in a single layer in a large gratin dish or a roasting pan. Tuck the mushrooms into the gaps, and arrange the thinly sliced onion on top. Mix the crushed garlic, tomato purée and cold liquids together in a cup. Pour them over the meats. Lay a lightly buttered sheet of greaseproof paper immediately on top, then cover with a foil 'lid'. Place the dish in the oven, switch it on to 300F, 150C, gas mark 2, (the oven doesn't have to be preheated for this dish, so you could prepare the ingredients ahead and use the automatic oven switch so that the dish cooks in your absence). Cook for 3¼ hours. The onions will be tender by the end of this time but a little dry looking, so push them into the liquid before serving. Accompany with lots of creamy mashed potatoes to sop up the delicious gravy.

COTTAGE PIE WITH A DIFFERENCE
(serves 4)

The topping used here is rather less fattening than the puréed potato normally used.

1½ lb chuck steak
3 onions
2 teaspoons good dripping
½–1 teaspoon curry powder
1 teaspoon celery salt
2 teaspoons Worcester sauce
1 tablespoon each tomato ketchup and tomato purée
salt and freshly-ground black pepper

For the topping:
11 oz thickened yoghurt (see page 246)
2 eggs
1 oz plain flour
2 oz grated Cheddar cheese
plenty of freshly-ground black pepper

Trim any fat and gristle from the meat and mince it. Add half the dripping to a large sauté pan. When very hot, add the mince and brown all over. Tip the contents of the pan out into a dish. Add the remaining dripping to the pan and allow it to become very hot. Add the fairly finely chopped onions and fry over medium-high heat until slightly browned.

Stir in the curry powder — just enough to bring out the flavour of the meat, not to give the dish a distinctive curry flavour. Return the mince to the pan together with its juices, season well with salt and pepper and add the other flavourings.

Cover the sauté pan with a well-fitting lid to avoid evaporation, reduce heat to very low and cook the mince very gently for 30 minutes.

Meanwhile, heat the oven to 375F, 190C, gas mark 5, and prepare the topping. Sift the flour into a bowl and make a well in the centre. Lightly whisk the eggs; add the yoghurt and pepper and beat until smooth and creamy. Pour the mixture into the well, and gradually incorporate the flour to make a very thick cream. Stir in half the cheese. Turn the mince into a gratin or pie dish with a large surface area. Spread the topping over the mince and sprinkle the remaining cheese on top. Bake for about 35 minutes until puffy and golden.

MURPHYBURGERS
(serves 4)

The best mince is that which you mince yourself. Chuck steak is used here — 1 lb of it, stretched with carrots, to make 4 really meaty tasting large burgers.

> 1 lb chuck steak trimmed of fat and sinew
> 1 very small onion, very finely chopped
> $\frac{1}{2}$ lb grated carrot
> 6 tablespoons finely-grated, slightly stale mature Cheddar or
>   Parmesan cheese
> 3 oz fresh breadcrumbs soaked in $2\frac{1}{2}$–3 tablespoons milk
> salt and freshly-ground black pepper
> oil and butter for frying

Put the beef through the mincer twice. Mix well in a bowl with the onion, carrot, cheese, soaked breadcrumbs and a generous seasoning. Divide the mixture into 4 and shape each into a firm, neat patty about 1 inch thick and $3\frac{1}{2}$ inches in diameter. Dust all over with a little sifted flour, rolling them in the flour to dust the sides of the patties. Measure enough oil (or a mixture of oil and butter) into a large frying pan to cover the base by about $\frac{1}{4}$ inch and place over medium-high heat.

When the fat is very hot add the burgers one at a time, allowing a few seconds between each so that the fat regains frying temperature. Cook the burgers for about 3 minutes on each side so they are slightly charred on the outside and still slightly pink inside (or for 4–5 minutes on each side if you like well cooked beef). Turn the burgers and remove them from the pan in the same order in which you added them to the pan, and drain them on crumpled kitchen paper.

If you cooked the burgers in a mixture of oil and butter, you can add a crushed garlic clove to the fat remaining in the pan. Swirl it around, then pour it over a dish of boiled egg noodles and arrange the burgers on top.

BEEFEATERS HOTPOT
(serves 6)

This is very filling and economic — a good choice for a really hungry family on a cold day.

2 lb chuck steak (or skirt or thick flank)
$\frac{3}{4}$ lb onions
1 fat garlic clove
a little oil
1 slightly heaped tablespoon caster sugar
a good pinch of ground cloves
$1\frac{1}{2}$ oz plain flour
1 pt beef stock
3 tablespoons red wine vinegar
plenty of salt and freshly-ground black pepper
2 lb potatoes
1 oz melted butter
a handful of chopped fresh parsley

Cube the beef, brown and seal it in very hot oil in a flame-proof casserole. Remove the beef, add the thickly sliced onions to the casserole and brown them slightly. Stir in the garlic, sugar, ground cloves and a good seasoning of salt and pepper. Sprinkle on then stir in the flour, blend in the stock and vinegar, and bring to simmering point stirring all the while.

Push the meat well down into the gravy and cover the surface with layers of very thinly peeled and sliced potatoes (an electric slicer or mandoline makes quick neat work of slicing). Cover the casserole with a lid and cook in an oven heated to 300F, 150C, gas mark 2, for 2 hours, or until the potatoes feel quite tender when pierced with the point of a knife.

Remove the lid, brush the top layer of potatoes with the melted butter and cook for a further 50 minutes in the oven — this time without the lid. Scatter the potatoes with fresh chopped parsley just before serving to add extra colour and flavour.

THERMOS STEW
(serves 6–8)

Easter is a time when most families make an outing. The weather is usually too chilly for a traditional sandwich picnic. A warming stew is much more welcome; it travels well and is easily served from a wide-mouthed vacuum flask. This stew has a high proportion of vegetables to meat to keep costs down, and to give the family plenty of vitamin C.

> 2 lb stewing steak
> 3–4 lb mixed vegetables (such as onions, celery, carrots, parsnips and leeks) chopped
> 3 tablespoons olive oil
> 1½ oz flour
> 1 pt beef stock (or ¼ pt red wine plus ¾ pt beef stock)
> a large bouquet garni
> a large garlic clove crushed with salt
> 1 teaspoon each thyme and marjoram
> salt and pepper

Cube the meat, discarding gristle and excess fat, and toss in well-seasoned flour. Brown the meat in batches in hot oil in a flame-proof casserole. Remove the meat from the casserole, and stir any leftover flour into the fat remaining in the casserole.

Pour on the liquid and bring to the boil stirring. Return the meat to the casserole. Add the vegetables, herbs and seasonings, pushing them well down into the liquid. Bring back to simmering point and cover with a well-fitting lid. Cook gently on top of the stove or in an oven heated to 300F, 150C, gas mark 2, for 3–3½ hours, stirring the mixture occasionally.

BŒUF À LA MODE

A classic and spectacular party dish which will serve 8–10 people. A large green salad and hot herb bread make good accompaniments.

> 3½ lb topside larded with a few strips of pork back fat
> 4 garlic cloves
> ½ pt red wine
> 1 large carrot
> 1 large onion
> 3 tablespoons brandy
> 3 sprigs of thyme
> a large bunch of parsley
> 2 bay leaves
> 3 curls of thinly-pared orange rind
> 3 pig's trotters
> light beef stock
> 2½ lb baby carrots
> a handful of small black olives
> a little olive oil
> salt and pepper

Rub the joint all over with black pepper and 2 crushed garlic cloves, and leave to marinate overnight in the red wine.

Next day, drain the joint and dry it, reserving the marinade liquid. Brown all over in a deep flame-proof casserole or a heavy roasting pan in a little oil. Remove the joint. Add the chopped large carrot and onion and colour them together with 2 more chopped garlic cloves. Return the meat to the dish and flambé it with the brandy. Add the herbs, trotters, orange rind, the marinade liquid and enough light beef stock to cover the meat.

Bring to a bare simmer. Cover with foil and a lid and cook

very gently on top of stove or in an oven at 275–300F, 140–150C, gas 1 or 2, for 4 hours. Let the meat cool in the dish for 4 hours, then drain well, wrap in foil and chill. Strain the liquid into a bowl, season it well and chill until the fat solidifies on top. Scrape off the fat and just melt the jelly. Steam or boil the scraped baby carrots. Arrange them round the sliced beef, pour on the clear beef jelly and chill until set. Garnish with plenty of chopped fresh parsley and the olives just before serving.

MACARONI MARBLES
(serves 4)

Mince and cheese are firm favourites with most children, and not too expensive. This dish combines both ingredients making it a popular choice for school holiday lunches.

$\frac{3}{4}$ lb good quality, finely-minced beef
$\frac{1}{4}$ lb Cheddar cheese cut into dice about $^{1}/_{3}$ inch square
1 large slice brown bread
1 small egg
$1\frac{1}{2}$ teaspoons tomato purée
a generous dash of Worcester sauce
a good pinch each of dried marjoram and thyme
6 oz macaroni
$\frac{1}{2}$ lb onions
$1\frac{1}{2}$ tablespoons each oil and butter
salt and pepper

Reduce the bread to crumbs and put into a bowl. Add the beef, raw egg, tomato purée, Worcester sauce, herbs and some salt and pepper. Mix everything very thoroughly together. Take a small piece of the mixture in your hands, press a cube of cheese into the centre of it and roll into a neat ball so that the cheese is completely hidden inside (it's rather like making miniature Scotch eggs!), then roll on a lightly floured surface. You'll only need a scant tablespoon of flour to make the whole lot, about 24–28 marbles.

The marbles can be prepared an hour or two in advance, if you wish, in which case lay them in a single layer, cover and store in the fridge until ready to cook.

Warm the butter and oil in a large sauté pan. Add the chopped onions and cook gently for 5–10 minutes until softened. Meanwhile start to cook the macaroni in plenty of salted boiling water. Now push the onions to the edge of the sauté pan and add the marbles to the centre – in a single layer. Increase heat a little and cook, stirring and turning as necessary, for 8–10 minutes – by which time both meatballs and onion should be slightly brown and crisp on the outside, and the cheese will have melted to make a delicious semi-liquid pool in the centre of each marble.

Lift the marbles out with a slotted spoon. Switch off heat, add the cooked and well-drained macaroni to the sauté pan and swirl until coated all over with a glistening of fat and onion. Serve with the marbles piled on top.

PEPPERED BEEF

(serves 2)

The amount of liquid used in a cold-start recipe such as this one seems very little indeed, but it mingles with juices exuded by meat and vegetables during cooking to produce a good quantity of rich gravy.

2 thick slices of braising steak, each weighing about 6 oz
1 very small onion
1 small green pepper
1 teaspoon Worcester sauce
2 teaspoons anchovy essence
2 teaspoons tomato ketchup
2 tablespoons cold water
a little butter

Butter a small casserole or other ovenproof dish that will take the steaks in a single layer. Lay the steaks in the dish and tuck the very finely chopped onion into the gaps. Mix the liquids together in a cup and pour them over the meat. De-seed the pepper and cut it into chunks. Scatter the pepper over the steaks and lay a sheet of buttered greaseproof paper on top. Cover with a lid and place the dish on an upper shelf of a cold oven. Set timing and temperature controls so that the oven will switch itself on to 300F, 150C, gas mark 2, about 3 hours before you plan to eat – a little longer will do no harm. Serve with potatoes, rice, pasta or crusty bread to mop up the gravy.

COTTAGE BEEFCAKE
(serves 4–6)

I make two of these while I am at it. One to serve hot for supper and the other to slice when cold for packed lunches – the beefcake is even better cold, I think.

For a slimline sandwich, wrap each slice of cold beefcake in lettuce leaves. To cope with man-sized appetites, pack the slices into those envelopes of flat unleavened bread which we used to see only at take-away kebab houses but which are now to be found at some supermarkets.

Pack each envelope with some juicy salad ingredients too: slices of tomato, shredded lettuce and perhaps a dollop of home-made chutney.

> 1 lb braising beef such as chuck steak
> ¼ lb streaky bacon
> 1 fairly small onion
> 1 large garlic clove
> a good-sized bunch each of chives and parsley
> 1 teaspoon Worcester sauce
> 1 teaspoon curry powder
> 1 egg
> 2 slices of bread, reduced to crumbs and soaked in 2 table-spoons milk
> salt and freshly-ground black pepper

Trim away from the beef any fat, gristle and membrane. Put the meat through the fine blade of a mincer together with the bacon.

Chop the onion very finely and crush the garlic with half a teaspoon of salt. Put these ingredients into a mixing bowl. Add the meats, chopped herbs, curry powder, Worcester sauce, breadcrumbs, a grinding of pepper and the lightly-beaten egg.

Mix everything together very thoroughly – I find that using my hands is most efficient.

Pack the mixture into a loaf tin of $1\frac{1}{4}$–$1\frac{1}{2}$ pt capacity, pushing it well into the corners and levelling the top with a palette knife. Stand the loaf tin on a baking sheet and bake in an oven heated to 375F, 190C, gas mark 5 for 1 hour.

BEEFSTEAK AU MARCHAND DE VIN
(serves 2)

This is the sort of simple but showy dish men love to eat and love to cook. Potato sticks heated through in the oven and canned petits pois (Culina are good) warmed in their liquid with a knob of butter make excellent and trouble-free accompaniments.

> 2 fillet steaks (ask the butcher for well-hung meat and say you want steaks weighing 6–8 oz each, sliced about 1 inch thick)
> half a small onion
> 1 teaspoon olive oil
> $1\frac{1}{2}$ oz unsalted butter
> 3 fl. oz robust red wine
> salt and freshly-ground black pepper

Take the steaks out of the fridge 1 hour before cooking. Cut off any excess fat and wipe the meat with kitchen paper. Skin and chop the onion very finely indeed. When ready to cook, measure the oil and half an ounce of butter into a frying pan and place over medium heat.

When the butter ceases to foam, increase heat to fairly high and add the steaks. Use tongs or a fish slice and spoon to avoid splashing fat or piercing the meat, and leave a few seconds before adding the second steak so that fat regains frying temperature. Fry for 2–4 minutes depending on whether you want the steaks rare or medium. Then turn the steaks over, in the same order as you put them into the pan, and cook for a further 2–4 minutes. If you like well-done steaks, now reduce heat to medium and cook for an additional minute or two.

Remove the steaks in the order in which they went into the pan and drain on kitchen paper. Transfer to a hot serving dish and season with salt and pepper. Pour away the frying fat; add half an ounce of butter to the meaty sediment remaining in the pan and melt over low heat. Stir in the onion and cook gently for 2 minutes.

Pour on the wine and increase heat to high. Cook, stirring the base of the pan to scrape up meaty sediment, until the wine has reduced to a few spoonfuls. Switch off heat, stir in the remaining half ounce of butter cut into dice. As soon as it melts into the sauce, season to taste, spoon over the steaks and serve.

BEEF AND MUSHROOM STEW WITH DUMPLINGS
(serves 4)

I'm not very keen on huge stodgy dumplings, but these tiny ones are light, delicious and very quickly cooked.

$1\frac{1}{2}$ lb chuck or flank steak
$\frac{1}{2}$ lb onions
$\frac{1}{2}$ lb mushrooms
2 large garlic cloves (crushed)
2 tablespoons beef dripping
$\frac{3}{4}$ pt beef stock
1 tablespoon lemon juice
1 teaspoon dried thyme
1 heaped tablespoon softened butter mashed to a paste with
    1 slightly heaped tablespoon plain flour
6 tablespoons fresh chopped parsley

For the dumplings:
1 small egg
2 oz self-raising flour
2 oz fresh brown breadcrumbs
2 oz shredded suet
1 teaspoon lemon zest
3 tablespoons fresh chopped parsley
salt and pepper

Thoroughly brown and seal the cubes of beef and roughly chopped onions — a little at a time — in very hot dripping in a flame-proof casserole. Add the garlic, thyme, lemon juice, stock, a good seasoning of salt and pepper and bring to the boil.

Cover and cook in the oven at 300F, 150C, gas mark 2, for 1¾ hours. Then push the thickly sliced mushrooms well down into the gravy and cook for a further 45 minutes. Strain off the liquid and keep the solid ingredients hot in the oven while you cook the dumplings.

Make the dumplings. Lightly beat the egg. Mix the remaining dumpling ingredients in a bowl, then stir in and bind them with the egg. With floured hands shape the mixture into 24 tiny balls. Drop them into the boiling liquid, cover and cook at a fast simmer on top of the stove for 10–12 minutes. Using a perforated spoon, lift out the dumplings and add them to the meat and mushroom mixture. Add nuggets of the mashed butter and flour mixture to the liquid and let it simmer, stirring continuously, until slightly thickened. Pour the gravy over the stew, sprinkle with parsley and serve.

BEEF WELLINGTON
(serves 6)

Fillet of beef is wildly expensive, but if you can afford to indulge in the occasional very special meat, this is certainly a magnificent dish.

2 lb well-hung fillet of beef
2 teaspoons brandy
1 oz clarified butter
1 onion
¼ lb mushrooms
1 small garlic clove
2 oz creamy-texture pâté
salt and freshly-ground black pepper
1 × 8 oz packet puff pastry
beaten egg for glazing

Trim all fat and membrane from the beef. Rub it with the cut garlic clove, then with a good grinding of pepper, then brush it with the brandy. Tie it into a neat bolster shape.

Choose a heavy-based frying pan large enough to hold the joint. Make it very hot. Add the butter and, when the butter foam dies down, add the beef. Brown and seal the meat all over.

Then reduce heat and fry the beef more gently for another 10 minutes, turning the meat to cook it evenly. Remove from the pan and cool.

Sauté the chopped mushrooms, then soften the finely chopped onion and garlic in the fat remaining in the pan. Drain off all fat, mix the vegetables and season them well.

When the meat and vegetables are cold, roll out the pastry until it is rather wider than the beef and more than twice its length. Remove the string from the beef, lay the meat on the pastry and spread the pâté over the beef. Lay the vegetables on top. Brush the pastry borders with beaten egg, fold the pastry over the meat, seal the edges securely and decorate with pastry trimmings. Chill the parcel for half an hour.

Glaze the pastry with beaten egg, make a few steam slits and bake for 20 minutes at 425F, 220C, gas mark 7. Then reduce oven temperature to 350F, 180C, gas mark 4, and bake for a further 10–15 minutes, depending on how rare or well cooked you like beef.

CHILLI CON CARNE

A hot favourite with many people and pleasantly easy on the housekeeping budget. I find it will serve 4–6 depending on how much rice you serve with it.

> 1½ lb chuck steak, thick flank or skirt
> 2 large onions
> 6–8 oz dried red kidney beans
> a little olive oil
> 1 teaspoon plain flour
> 1 × 14 oz can of tomatoes
> 1 large green pepper
> the juice of half a lemon
> salt and freshly-ground black pepper

For the spiced paste:
1 red pepper
1½ teaspoons chilli powder
2 fat garlic cloves
1 teaspoon cumin seeds
1 teaspoon coriander seeds
2 tablespoons olive oil

Warm the cumin and coriander seeds in a small pan over low heat until they smell aromatic, then pound with mortar and pestle. Put into a blender with the chopped and de-seeded red pepper, chopped garlic, chilli powder and oil. Reduce to a paste – stopping the blades every now and then and pushing the ingredients well down into the goblet with a rubber bladed spatula. When the spiced paste is quite smooth put it into a shallow dish. Add the meat cut into large cubes, turn to coat evenly, cover and leave in a cold place overnight.

Turn the canned tomatoes and their juices into the blender and whizz – to reduce them to a purée and to collect any spicy paste still stuck in the blender. Turn into a bowl and reserve. Soak the beans overnight in plenty of cold water.

Next day scrape the paste off the meat and add it to the tomatoes. Heat a very little olive oil in a large flame-proof casserole and brown the beef in batches. Then brown the roughly chopped onions. Stir in a teaspoon of flour to sop up any oil remaining in the casserole, then return the meat. Add the tomato mixture and lemon juice and bring to the boil. Cover tightly and simmer (or transfer to an oven heated to 300F, 150C, gas mark 2) for 1 hour.

Stir in the drained and rinsed beans and cook gently for 1 hour more. Add the chopped green pepper (and a little boiling water if the dish looks a little dry) and cook for another hour. Season generously with salt and pepper before serving, plus extra chilli powder to taste.

This is a good-tempered dish and can be kept hot in a low oven without spoiling for an extra 45 minutes or so.

CURRIED MEATBALLS
(serves 6)

Served on a generous bed of boiled rice, with some poppadoms and a dish of thinly sliced bananas sprinkled with a little lemon juice (allow one banana per person) this makes an unusual, inexpensive and easy supper dish.

1 lb lean beef
½ lb onions
2 oz fresh white breadcrumbs
1½ teaspoons curry powder
1 teaspoon grated fresh root ginger
1 egg
a little flour
salt and pepper

For the sauce:
1 oz butter
1 tablespoon oil
1 garlic clove
1–2 teaspoons curry powder
2 tablespoons plain flour
the juice of 1 lemon
12 fl. oz beef stock
3 tablespoons juice from a jar of mango chutney
¼ pt yoghurt

Mince the beef and onions finely. Mix with the breadcrumbs, curry powder, ginger, some salt and a little pepper. Bind with the egg. Using floured hands, divide the mixture and roll into 40 small meatballs.

Heat a large sauté pan. Add the butter and oil. Fry the meatballs, in batches, over high heat, turning them until golden brown and well sealed all over. Remove them from the pan with a slotted spoon. Stir the flour, curry powder and crushed garlic into the fat remaining in the pan. Blend in the beef stock and cook, stirring continuously until the sauce is smooth thick and bubbling hot. Add the lemon juice and juice from the jar of mango chutney plus a good seasoning of salt and pepper.

Return all the meatballs to the pan. Reduce heat to the gentlest possible simmer, cover the pan with a well-fitting lid and cook for 25 minutes. Lift the meatballs out of the pan with a slotted spoon, and arrange them on a bed of boiled rice. Away from the heat, stir the yoghurt into the sauce. Warm through gently, pour over the meatballs and serve immediately.

Lamb and Veal

LAMB PASTIES
(makes 6)

Pasties are a good way of making a little meat go far. These are good hot and even better cold – try them for a picnic or office lunchbox.

$\frac{3}{4}$ lb raw, boneless shoulder or leg of lamb cut into $\frac{1}{2}$ inch cubes
$\frac{1}{2}$ lb courgettes (thickly sliced if slim or cut into small dice if large)
8 spring onions – green parts as well as white – finely chopped
$1\frac{1}{2}$ teaspoons lemon juice
1 generous tablespoon chopped fresh mint
a pinch of caster sugar
salt and pepper
shortcrust pastry made with 10 oz flour
a little beaten egg for glazing

Heat the oven to 425F, 220C, gas mark 7. Roll out the pastry and, using a tea plate or saucer as template, cut out six circles $6\frac{1}{2}$ inches in diameter. Mix the small cubes of lamb, courgettes, spring onions, lemon juice, sugar, mint, salt and pepper together in a bowl – using your hands is most efficient. Place a dollop on one half of each of the pastry circles. Brush pastry edges with beaten egg. Fold each circle in half and pinch the raw pastry edges together very firmly to seal the filling inside. Lay the pasties on a baking sheet, make a steam hole in the top of each. Glaze the pastry with beaten egg and bake for 40–45 minutes until the pastry is golden, the meat is tender and the smell coming from the oven is deliciously inviting.

SHOULDER OF LAMB WITH APRICOT AND WALNUT STUFFING

(serves 6 or more)

Shoulder of lamb is sweet meat, but a little fatty, and it is a difficult joint to carve. Boned and stuffed with a slightly tart apricot mixture, it is a treat to carve and makes excellent eating.

> shoulder of lamb weighing about $4\frac{1}{2}$ lb
> 3 oz dried apricots
> $1\frac{1}{2}$ oz walnut pieces
> $1\frac{1}{2}$ oz long-grain rice
> a little butter
> a few springs of tarragon
> light chicken stock
> salt and freshly-ground black pepper

Ask the butcher to bone the lamb or do this yourself, carefully cutting and easing the bones out from the fleshy side so that the skin remains intact. Trim away the fatty corner completely.

Melt a knob of butter in a small pan over low heat. Turn the rice in it until transparent. Add some salt, sprigs of tarragon and light chicken stock, cover and simmer gently until tender. Put the apricots into a separate small pan. Cover them with cold water or cold tea. Bring very slowly to the boil, cover and simmer for 2 minutes, then set the covered pan aside for half an hour. Drain the apricots reserving their juices. Chop them roughly, mix them with the walnuts and cold cooked rice. Season generously with salt and pepper and add a spoonful or two of the apricot juices to moisten and bind the mixture. Spread the cold stuffing over the fleshy side of the boned joint. Roll it up into a neat bolster shape and tie securely at intervals with string. Now weigh the joint and calculate roasting time, allowing 21–25 minutes per pound, depending on whether you like pinkish or well-cooked lamb.

Rub the fatty surface of the joint generously with salt and pepper. Stand the joint on a rack in a roasting pan and roast in a preheated oven for 20 minutes at 425F, 220C, gas mark 7, then reduce oven temperature to 375F, 190C, gas mark 5, and complete roasting. Let the joint 'rest' in a warm place for 10–15 minutes before carving.

FRENCH LAMB
(serves 2)

A marvellously easy dish, which takes less than 5 minutes to prepare in the morning, and then takes 15 minutes or so to cook when you get home in the evening. Serve with a large salad.

> 2 leg steaks or large chump chops
> a scant teaspoon of dried rosemary
> 1 teaspoon each dried basil and thyme
> 1 very small garlic clove
> 1 tablespoon olive oil
> a good squeeze of lemon juice
> salt and freshly-ground black pepper

Measure the dried herbs into a gratin dish which will take the chops or steaks in a single layer. Add a good grinding of black pepper (no salt at this stage – it would draw out the meat juices), mix together and crush lightly with a wooden spoon to break up any very spiky bits of rosemary. Add the oil, lemon juice and crushed garlic clove and mix again.

Add the lamb, turning it and pressing the herb mixture into the meat on both sides with the back of the wooden spoon. Check that all of the meat is coated with a thin film of olive oil. Cover the dish lightly and set it aside in a cold place for a minimum of 3 hours or up to 9 hours. If the meat is set aside for more than 5 hours, scrape off and discard the herbs just before grilling or the herb flavourings will be very strong.

To cook, lay the lamb on a rack suspended across the gratin dish. Grill under very fierce heat for 2 minutes on each side. Then reduce heat and grill for a further 5–7 minutes on each side depending on whether you like lamb medium-rare or well cooked. Sprinkle with salt just before serving.

SEVILLIAN LAMB
(serves 4)

Here is a delicious summery casserole of lamb. It contains no flour to offend the calorie conscious but is thickened with vegetables.

> 1 best end neck of lamb consisting of 6 cutlets, boned and rolled, tied into a bolster shape with string, then cut into 4 thick slices
> 1 × 8 oz can of tomatoes
> 1 × 6½ oz can of sweet pimientos
> 4 small to medium-sized onions, quartered
> 16 pimiento-stuffed olives
> 1 teaspoon olive oil
> ½ teaspoon rosemary
> 1 teaspoon lemon juice
> a pinch of sugar
> salt and freshly-ground black pepper

Heat the oil in a heavy-based stewpan or flameproof casserole. Add the lamb and brown it all over. Remove the meat with a slotted spoon, add the onions and colour them too. Then add the tomatoes, rosemary, lemon juice, a pinch of sugar and a good seasoning of salt and pepper. Bring the mixture to boiling point, then return the lamb to the pan, burying it among the vegetables. Cover with a lid and reduce heat to a very gentle simmer. Cook gently for 50 minutes.

Drain the pimientos and cut the flesh into strips. Slice the olives. Turn the slices of lamb over and sprinkle the pimientos and olives over them. Cover the pan again and continue cooking for a further 10–15 minutes until the olives and pimientos are heated through and the lamb is perfectly tender. Check seasoning and serve.

MOUSSAKA
(serves 6–8)

Always popular and all the preparations can be made ahead leaving only the baking to be done at the last moment.

$2\frac{1}{2}$–3 lb aubergines
2 lb lean boneless shoulder of lamb
2 onions
a little olive oil
1 teaspoon coriander seeds and $\frac{1}{2}$ teaspoon dried rosemary
  pounded together with mortar and pestle
1 large garlic clove
1 × 14 oz can of tomatoes (or 1 lb fresh tomatoes skinned
  and chopped)
salt and pepper

For the topping:
3 tablespoons each butter and plain flour
$\frac{3}{4}$ pt milk
2 oz Cheddar cheese
salt, pepper and nutmeg
3 eggs
a few spoonfuls of dry breadcrumbs

Slice the aubergines thickly, sprinkle with salt, lay in a colander, weigh down with a plate and set aside for at least 30 minutes to drain off the juices. Rinse, dry, and fry the aubergines in oil until golden. Drain well and set aside.

Mince the meat. Brown with the chopped onion in a little oil. Add pounded rosemary and coriander, crushed garlic and tomatoes. Simmer, half-covered for 30–40 minutes, stirring occasionally. Then cook without lid for a few minutes more. Season well and set aside to cool.

Make a sauce with the butter, flour, milk and grated cheese. Season with salt, pepper and nutmeg. Allow the sauce to cool slightly then beat in the eggs one at a time.

Layer the aubergine slices and minced lamb mixture in a large shallow dish, beginning and ending with the aubergine. Pour the sauce over the top, sprinkle on the breadcrumbs and bake at 350F, 180C, gas mark 4, for 50–60 minutes until the moussaka is piping hot and the crumbs are golden.

OVEN-BARBECUED BREAST OF LAMB
(serves 2–3)

I am particularly pleased with this recipe – in fact I think it is one of the best barbecue dishes I have ever eaten. The meat is tenderised by lengthy marinating, then baked at high temperature so that excess fat is rendered down, while the marinade liquid is re-used to make an accompanying sauce. To serve 4–6 people, double all the ingredients. You will need 2 roasting tins and 2 racks. Allow about 1 hour 10 minutes for cooking time; start with one tin just above the centre and the other just below the centre of the oven, then swap their positions after 35 minutes.

> 1 × 1¾–2 lb breast of lamb
> 1 tablespoon cornflour
> 1 tablespoon soy sauce
>
> *For the marinade:*
> the zest and juice of 2 large lemons
> 2 fat garlic cloves crushed
> 3 tablespoons Worcester sauce
> 2 tablespoons concentrated tomato purée
> 2 tablespoons soft dark brown sugar
> 8 pimiento-stuffed green olives finely chopped

Trim away the fat from the corner of the breastbone at the thick end of the joint. Using a sharp, heavy-bladed knife – and not inconsiderable personal strength – chop down between the riblets to divide the joint into narrow strips. If in doubt, ask the butcher to do this for you.

Stir all the marinade ingredients together in a large bowl. Add the lamb, turn it until well coated with the mixture, then cover and leave in a cool place (not the fridge) for 8 hours or a little longer. If possible turn the mixture once or twice during this time.

Heat the oven to 400F, 200C, gas mark 6. Pour a generous ¼ pt of cold water into the bowl of marinated lamb, then turn the contents of the bowl into a sieve placed over a saucepan, and leave for at least 10 minutes so that the liquid drains off.

Scrape most of the little bits of olive and lemon zest off the lamb into the saucepan and lay the strips of meat in a single layer on a rack in a roasting tin (the very thin boneless strips of meat can be folded in two to make them the same thickness as the pieces containing bone).

A rack is vital: if the lamb were placed directly on the pan base it would cook in its own fat instead of crisping and browning — use the rack from your grill pan or a cake cooling rack. Bake for 40–45 minutes or until the meat is crusted to a rich dark brown. Reduce heat towards the end of cooking time if necessary to prevent burning.

Put a tablespoon of the cold marinade liquid into a cup, heat the rest. Stir a scant tablespoon of cornflour and a tablespoon of soy sauce into the cup and stir until smooth. Then stir the contents of the cup into the saucepan and cook, stirring, for about 3 minutes until the sauce is slightly thickened and piping hot.

Accompany the crispy strips of lamb with boiled rice or Chinese egg noodles (I allow nearly 3 oz per person if the lamb is to serve 3 people) and serve the sauce separately in a jug or sauceboat.

LAMB FINGERS
(serves 6)

Always choose large breasts of lamb, weighing about $1\frac{3}{4}$–2 lb each, with a good meaty layer. Small lightweight pieces are inclined to be all bone — disappointing and less good value.

> 2 × $1\frac{3}{4}$–2 lb breasts of lamb
> stock
> 2 large carrots
> 1 onion
> 1–2 celery stalks
> 1 large bouquet garni
> salt, pepper and mustard powder
> a little flour
> 2 eggs
> a few slices of bread
> 2–3 tablespoons grated Parmesan cheese
> oil for frying

Trim away the corner fat from the breastbone at the thick end. Lay the meat in a roasting pan, tucking the chopped vegetables and bouquet garni into the gaps. Pour on hot stock to cover the meat, fit a baking tray on top and weigh it down to prevent the meat from rising out of the liquid during cooking. Cook at 325F, 160C, gas mark 3, for 3 hours or until the bones pull out easily.

Pull out riblet bones and trim away excess fat. Cut and ease out the corner of breastbone and pieces of cartilage – neatly, avoiding tearing the meat. Match the two pieces of meat, placing one on top of the other. Cover, weigh down and refrigerate overnight. Reduce the bread to crumbs and leave to dry out at room temperature overnight.

Cut the pressed lamb into narrow strips about the size of fish fingers. Dust with flour seasoned with mustard powder, salt and pepper. Dip in beaten egg and coat with the breadcrumbs and Parmesan mixed together. Chill for 1 hour before shallow frying in hot oil over moderate heat until golden brown. Drain well and serve with soy sauce, potatoes and a green vegetable.

LAMB WITH MUSHROOM BUTTER
(serves 6)

This is an excellent way to make grilled lamb chops taste slightly special. The butter is also good with pork chops and grilled fish. I have used it, too, as a delicious and unusual filling for baked potatoes.

> 6 lamb chops
> 3 oz butter at room temperature
> 1½ oz mushrooms
> 1 small garlic clove
> 1 dozen coriander seeds
> salt and freshly-ground black pepper

Mash the butter with a fork or beat it with a wooden spoon until soft and creamy. Crush the garlic with some salt. Chop the mushrooms very finely indeed – you don't have to use caps for this recipe, mushroom stalks left over from another recipe are full of flavour and would do perfectly well.

Crush the coriander seeds with the back of a spoon. Add them to the butter, together with the chopped mushrooms and garlic, and a good grinding of black pepper. Mash to mix everything together well.

Brush a small sheet of greaseproof paper with cold water to damp it thoroughly. Wet your hands under the tap. Put the butter on to the paper and use your hands to shape it into a small bolster. Wrap the butter in the paper and refrigerate it until firm (or pop it briefly into the freezer).

Season the lamb chops with a little pepper and coriander, but no salt. Brush with oil and grill under fierce heat until cooked to your liking. Slice the mushroom butter into rounds and place a pat on top of each chop as it comes sizzling from the grill. The butter will melt and mingle with the meat juices to make a delicious sauce.

ROMAN LAMB STEW
(serves 4)

Choose tender, delicately-flavoured young English lamb for this dish, which is traditionally made with milk-fed lamb.

$1\frac{1}{2}$–$1\frac{3}{4}$ lb lean boneless shoulder of lamb, cut into large cubes
4 teaspoons each butter and olive oil
1 small onion finely chopped
2 oz Parma ham, cut into strips (or diced unsmoked back bacon)
1–2 celery stalks finely chopped (if available)
$\frac{1}{4}$ pt dry white wine or a very dry cider such as Bulmer's No. 7 or Norfolk Dry
$\frac{1}{4}$ pt light chicken stock or water
a few parsley stalks and a sprig of oregano tied together with string
1 tablespoon lemon juice
2 large egg yolks
2 tablespoons chopped parsley
salt and freshly-ground black pepper

Using a large flame-proof casserole, heat 1 teaspoon butter and 1 teaspoon olive oil and fry one-third of the lamb until golden.

Remove with a slotted spoon. Add more fat and colour the remaining meat in the same way. Then colour the onion, celery and ham. Return the meat to the pan. Pour on the wine or cider. Let it simmer uncovered for 10 minutes.

Add the stock or water, the bunch of herbs and a good grinding of pepper and bring back to simmering point. Cover, reduce heat as low as possible and cook very gently for 45 minutes. Stir and turn the meat once or twice during this time.

Lightly beat the lemon, egg yolks and parsley together in a cup. Stir in a few spoonfuls of liquid from the casserole, then stir the contents of the cup into the casserole. Cook, stirring, for 5 minutes, while the sauce thickens slightly. Do not allow the mixture to boil. Season to taste with salt and pepper. Remove the bunch of herbs, squeezing them between two spoons so that the juices drip back into the casserole.

STUFFED PEPPERS
(serves 4)

A sauce of cold yoghurt flavoured with crushed garlic goes well with these peppers, which can be served hot or cold.

> 4 red or green peppers (each weighing about 4 oz)
> $\frac{1}{2}$ lb lean minced lamb
> $\frac{1}{4}$ lb finely chopped onions
> 2 garlic cloves crushed with salt
> $\frac{1}{4}$ lb long grain rice
> 6 tablespoons olive oil
> 3–4 tablespoons chopped fresh basil or mint
> a large pinch of cinnamon
> 1 oz raisins
> 1 lemon
> 1 pt canned tomato juice
> lots of salt and freshly-ground black pepper

Heat the oil in a saucepan. Add the onion and lamb; cook, stirring for 4–5 minutes, until browned. Add the garlic and rice and cook over lowest possible heat, stirring frequently, for 15 minutes. Add cinnamon, basil or mint, 1 teaspoon lemon juice and $7\frac{1}{2}$ fl. oz tomato juice. Stir once, cover and simmer very gently for 15–20 minutes. Drain off and reserve any liquid remaining in the pan (probably only a spoonful or so). Season the rice generously, stir in the raisins and spread out on a plate to cool a little.

Heat the oven to 350F, 180C, gas mark 4. Cut a small slice off the top of each pepper. Scrape out the seeds and the pith carefully.

Check the seasoning of the rice mixture again now it is cool, adding more lemon, herbs, cinnamon and/or salt and pepper to taste. Pack the peppers firmly with the filling (they will probably take only two-thirds of it), stand them in a casserole, arranging the leftover rice mixture round them to help support them. Heat any reserved pan juices together with the remaining lemon and tomato juices.

Season with salt and pepper and pour it round the peppers; it should come about half-way up the sides of the peppers; if necessary add some hot chicken stock. Cover the casserole with a lid and cook for 45 minutes.

CURRIED LAMB TRIANGLES
(makes 6)

This is a neat way to use up a little leftover rice, good and economic lunchbox food.

> Shortcrust pastry made with 5 oz each plain flour and
>   wholemeal flour
> $\frac{3}{4}$ lb lean boneless lamb
> $\frac{1}{4}$ lb dried apricots
> 2 onions
> 4–6 tablespoons cold boiled rice
> 1 tablespoon garam masala
> salt and freshly-ground black pepper
> beaten egg for glazing
> a spoonful of sesame seeds

Chop the apricots, cover them with water and bring slowly to boiling point. Cover the pan and set aside for 10 minutes. Drain the fruit reserving about 2 tablespoons of the liquid. Stir the garam masala into this liquid and use it to moisten and flavour the rice.

Chop the onion very finely, and cut the lamb into $\frac{1}{4}-\frac{1}{2}$ inch dice. Mix the 2 ingredients together, then stir them into the rice and apricots and season with salt and pepper.

Roll out the pastry and cut into 6 squares. Spoon some lamb mixture on to half of one of the squares, brush the pastry rim with water and fold the pastry over the filling to make a triangle. Seal firmly and decorate. Glaze with beaten egg, sprinkle with a scattering of sesame seeds and make a steam hole. Prepare the other triangles in the same way.

Chill for 10 minutes then bake at 425F, 220C, gas mark 7, for 40 minutes. Serve cold, alone or with salad.

WHITTONDITCH CHUMP

(serves 1)

Spread the chop with savoury butter 1 hour before grilling and the flavour will be very mildly spicy; let the butter soak into the chop for several hours and the flavourings will become more pronounced.

> 1 lamb chump chop
> $\frac{1}{2}$ oz butter
> a good $\frac{1}{4}$ teaspoon English mustard powder
> a good $\frac{1}{4}$ teaspoon curry powder
> nearly $\frac{1}{2}$ teaspoon Worcester sauce
> salt and freshly-ground black pepper

Beat the butter until creamy and softened. Sprinkle on the mustard powder, curry powder and Worcester sauce and beat again until you have a smooth and well-blended paste. Spread this on both sides of the chop and set it aside in a cool place for 1 hour or more.

Then heat the grill until very hot. Lay the chop on the grid of the grill pan or balance it across a small heatproof gratin-type dish. Grill for slightly longer and using slightly fiercer heat than normal (because the butter coating will slow down the rate at which the heat penetrates the meat).

Sprinkle with salt and pepper and serve piping hot on a

generous bed of mashed potato with the buttery pan juices
poured over.

LAMB IN A SAUCEPAN
(serves 1)

This is a good way to cook an entire main course in one saucepan
— quick, easy and not too expensive.

1 chump chop
1 small onion
$\frac{1}{2}$ oz butter
1 teaspoon oil
2–3 oz mushrooms
2 oz rice
1 × 8 oz can of tomatoes
a good pinch of dried tarragon
salt and freshly-ground black pepper

Heat the butter and oil in a saucepan until very hot. Add the
chop and sprinkle finely chopped onion round it. Fry the chop
for about $1\frac{1}{2}$ minutes on either side until well browned and
sealed, then lift it out of the pan. Add the thickly sliced
mushrooms to the pan and fry, stirring as necessary, for about 1
minute until coloured on all sides.

Chop the tomatoes roughly, add them and their juices to the
pan and bring to the boil stirring all the time. Add the rice,
tarragon and a generous seasoning of salt and pepper. Stir once
or twice then, without waiting for the mixture to come back to
the boil, lay the chop on top of the rice and vegetables and
reduce heat to very low.

Lay a circle of buttered paper directly on top of the chop and
cover the pan with a lid. Simmer as gently as possible for 25
minutes. By the end of this time the lamb should be cooked
right through and beautifully tender and the rice will have
absorbed the tomato juice. Lift out the chop, fluff the rice and
vegetables with a fork and serve immediately.

REDCURRANT LAMB
(serves 2)

This is a simple and good way to make the best of imported lamb. Shoulder chops (also called blade chops and shoulder slices) are large, economical and well suited to this recipe.

> 2 large lamb chops
> 2 celery stalks
> half a small onion
> 2 tablespoons redcurrant jelly
> 1 tablespoon freshly-squeezed orange juice
> a good pinch of finely grated orange zest
> scant $\frac{1}{2}$ teaspoon dried rosemary
> a little butter
> salt and freshly-ground black pepper

Butter very lightly the base and sides of a small casserole or ovenproof dish. Trim any excess fat from the chops, and lay them side by side in the dish. Pound the rosemary to a powder with mortar and pestle, mix with orange zest and plenty of pepper, and sprinkle over the meat. Cut the celery into thin crescents, chop the onion very finely, mix together and scatter into any gaps between the chops and over them. Break up the redcurrant jelly with a fork, blend in the orange juice and pour over the meat. Lay a sheet of lightly buttered greasproof paper directly on top of the ingredients, and cover the dish with a lid. Place the dish on an upper shelf of a cold oven. Turn the oven on to 300F, 150C, gas mark 2, and cook for $2\frac{1}{2}$ hours, or set automatic timing and temperature controls so that the oven will switch itself on to this temperature $2\frac{1}{2}$ hours before you plan to eat. Season the gravy with salt (and extra pepper if you wish) just before serving.

DEVONSHIRE LAMB PIE
(serves 8–10)

Many cooks seem to find shortcrust easier to make and to mould than hot-water-crust pastry (and many people seem to prefer its taste too) so I have used it for this cold meat pie.

$2\frac{1}{2}$ lb lean boneless lamb cut into tiny dice
$\frac{1}{2}$ lb apples
8 spring onions
2 fat garlic cloves
6 tablespoons chopped fresh mint
3 tablespoons redcurrant jelly
$\frac{1}{2}$ teaspoon allspice
$\frac{1}{4}$ lb unsmoked streaky bacon
salt and freshly-ground black pepper
shortcrust pastry made with 1 lb plain flour and $\frac{1}{4}$ lb each
  butter and lard
a beaten egg for glazing the pastry

Mix the diced lamb with the peeled and diced apples, the chopped bacon and chopped spring onions (green parts as well as white). Add the crushed garlic, mint, redcurrant jelly, allspice and a good seasoning of salt and pepper. Mix everything together very thoroughly with your hands.

Use two-thirds of the pastry to line the base and sides of a 9 inch cake tin with springclip sides and removable base, having lightly greased the tin first. Pile the filling into the tin, mounding the centre.

Roll out the remaining pastry to make a lid. Brush the edges with a little beaten egg seasoned with some salt. Place the lid on top of the pie, pinch the raw pastry edges together to seal them firmly, and trim. Then gently ease the sealed pastry edges slightly inwards and upwards so that the pastry rim stands clear of the sides of the tin. This is important: if the pastry is sealed against the sides of the tin it may stick during unmoulding. Glaze with beaten egg, decorate with trimmings and glaze again. Make a large steam hole in the centre of the pastry lid and hold it open with a piece of rolled card.

Stand the pie on a baking sheet and bake for 30 minutes at 400F, 200C, gas mark 6. Reduce oven temperature to 350F, 180C, gas mark 4, glaze the pastry again and bake for a further $1\frac{1}{2}$ hours. Cool the pie for at least 5 hours before unmoulding and serving.

FRECKLED LAMB

(serves 2–3)

Quick, easy and delicious but it is best to cube and marinate the lamb at least an hour before cooking.

1 lb lean boneless lamb
1 tablespoon lemon juice
$\frac{1}{2}$ teaspoon rosemary
$\frac{1}{2}$ oz butter
1 tablespoon oil
1 onion finely chopped
$\frac{1}{4}$ pt stock
2 tablespoons plain yoghurt or soured cream
salt and freshly-ground black pepper
a little finely grated lemon zest and a handful of parsley

Cube the lamb. Sprinkle it with a good grinding of black pepper, the crumbled rosemary and the lemon juice. Toss lightly and set aside in a cool place for at least an hour, then drain off and reserve the liquid.

Heat the butter and oil in a large frying or sauté pan. When it is very hot, thoroughly brown and seal the lamb, cooking it in batches and adding the chopped onion with the last batch. Return all the meat to the pan, pour on the stock and the reserved juices. Bring quickly to simmering point, push the meat well down into the liquids and reduce heat to fairly low. Let it cook quite gently for about 15 minutes, just stirring and turning the meat occasionally. Then lift out the meat and keep hot while you boil the juices remaining in the pan until reduced and concentrated in flavour. Season with salt and pepper, stir in the cream or yoghurt and let it warm through gently. Pour the sauce over the lamb, sprinkle with parsley and lemon zest and serve with new potatoes.

CROWN ROAST OF LAMB

(serves 6)

Some people like to stuff the centre of a crown roast with mixtures of such things as rice, sausagemeat and dried apricots.

Good though these ingredients may be I think it is best to serve such a choice cut of meat really simply — let the meat speak for itself. Besides, stuffing the central cavity covers the lamb fat and therefore prevents it from crisping really well. And, when there are two beautiful cutlets per person, are extras really necessary?

> 2 fine pieces of best end neck of lamb, each piece consisting of
>   6 cutlets
> 1 garlic clove
> a little olive oil
> a good bunch of fresh mint
> salt and freshly-ground black pepper

Choose the leanest, meatiest best ends of neck available. Ask the butcher to chine the joints (that is to make a saw cut along the length of the thick back or chine bone which runs at right angles to the tapering cutlet bones; doing this makes it easier to remove the chine bone later) and to make a parallel saw cut across the top (spiky and virtually meatless) ends of the cutlet bones — this is usually done in such a way as to leave the ends hinged to the main part of the joint rather than to detach them completely. He will probably do both these jobs without having to be asked, will also skin the joints and make no charge for any of this.

Allow 1 hour for roasting the joint, then work out your time schedule so that roasting is completed just before you carry the first course into the dining room. This will allow the joint to 'rest' while you eat the first course and it will be ready to serve just when you want it.

Bring the meat out of the refrigerator into room temperature 1 hour before starting to roast. About 30 minutes before roasting switch the oven to 425F, 220C, gas mark 7, and prepare the meat. Following the butcher's saw line, cut away the hinged bony flap, then remove the chine bone, scraping and easing it away from the meaty base of the cutlets with a sharp knife. Make cuts about 1 inch long between the tips of the cutlet bones, then scrape the thin layer of meat clean away from the tip of each bone (save these scraps and all other trimmings for stock-making) and wrap the bare bone tips in foil to protect against burning during roasting. If the backs of the joints are heavily fatted, trim away excess.

Rub the cut part of the halved garlic clove all over the meat, fat and bones to flavour the joints delicately. If you like a more pronounced garlic flavour, make tiny slits here and there in the lamb fat and insert slivers of garlic into them.

Stand the two joints back to back, so the two fatty sides face each other and all the cutlet bones point upwards. Gently curve the joints to make a circle or crown and sew them together to hold in shape, stitching the last bone of one joint to the first bone of the other. Use a fine string, but not one which contains nylon — it will melt in the heat of the oven.

It is sometimes necessary to make small nicks near the base of the cutlets in order to curve the joints nicely. If you have to, do so of course, but keep them to the minimum as gashes can distort the crown shape and cause it to topple slightly during cooking. Cuts also encourage meat juices and flavour to leak out.

Lightly brush the crown all over with olive oil. Then rub the fat, but not the lean parts, very generously with salt and pepper. Using fingers is a bit messy but most effective.

Stand the joint on a rack in a roasting tin (I use the rack from my grill pan; if yours is too large for the oven, use a small cake cooling rack instead). Oil the rack lightly first to prevent the meat from sticking to it during cooking. Roast in the preheated oven for 20 minutes. Then reduce temperature to 375F, 190C, gas mark 5, and roast for a further 35–40 minutes. No basting is necessary at any time.

Transfer the roasted meat to a warmed serving dish lined with a bed of fresh mint. Remove the foil from the bone tips and decorate with cutlet frills. Make a gravy with the meaty pan juices if you wish — I think the meat is juicy enough not to need gravy — and let the joint 'rest' in a warm place for 10–15 minutes before serving and carving.

WILTSHIRE HOTPOT
(serves 2)

With apologies to Lancastrians, this is my version of their
famous hotpot. I think the inclusion of tarragon, apple and a
few spoonfuls of wine make for excellent flavour, and it is a
recipe that involves blissfully little work for the cook.

> 4 small lean or 2 large lean lamb chops
> $\frac{1}{2}$ teaspoon dried tarragon
> 1 smallish onion
> half a Cox's apple
> 4 tablespoons dry white wine
> $\frac{3}{4}$ lb potatoes
> a little butter
> salt and freshly-ground black pepper

Choose a small casserole or ovenproof dish which will take the
chops in a single layer. Butter the base and sides. Lay the meat
in the dish and sprinkle it with plenty of pepper and the
tarragon. Peel and dice the apple (don't be tempted to use the
whole apple: it is the hint of sweetness which is so good) and
tuck it into any gaps between the chops. Chop the onion finely,
sprinkle it over the meat, and pour on the wine. Slice the
potatoes very thinly and lay them, overlapping like tiles, over
the meat. Season generously with salt and pepper between the
potato layers, and cover the top layer of potatoes completely
with thin flakes of butter. Do not cover the dish with a lid. Place
the dish on an upper shelf of a cold oven. Switch on to 300F,
150C, gas mark 2 and bake for 3 hours, or set automatic timing
and temperature controls so that the oven will turn itself on to
300F, 150C, gas mark 2, 3 hours before you plan to eat.

GENEVA VEAL CHOPS

Pork chops can also be cooked this way – a quick and luxurious way to cheer up chops, which appeals greatly to gin drinkers.

    4 veal chops
    6 juniper berries
    3 tablespoons gin
    2 oz unsalted butter
    $\frac{1}{4}$ pt double cream
    salt and freshly-ground black pepper

Crush the juniper berries with mortar and pestle. Mix them with some pepper, rub the mixture over the meat and leave in a cool place for 1 hour.

Choose a heavy-based frying or sauté pan large enough to take all the chops at once. Heat it, add half the butter and, when foaming ceases, add the chops and brown them all over. Add the rest of the butter, reduce heat to very low, cover the pan tightly and cook very gently for 25–30 minutes until the meat is cooked through and tender. Turn the chops once or twice during this time.

Remove the chops and keep them hot. Add the gin to the pan. When it is hot draw the pan away from the heat, ignite the gin and tip the pan so the flames spread. When the flames have died down, return the pan to the heat. Pour on the cream and boil until the sauce is smooth, hot and thickened. Season with salt and pepper, pour the sauce over the chops and serve straight away.

VEAL FRICASSÉE
(serves 6)

This summery casserole can be cooked in advance almost completely. Reheat it gently but thoroughly about 20 minutes before serving and add the egg and cream liaison at the last minute.

    2 lb lean shoulder, leg or pie veal (boneless weight)
    2 oz butter
    $\frac{1}{4}$ lb celery

$\frac{1}{4}$ lb carrots
18 bulbous fat spring onions
$\frac{1}{2}$ lb button mushrooms
$\frac{1}{2}$ lb broad beans (shelled weight)
4–5 teaspoons plain flour
2 tablespoons lemon juice
$\frac{1}{2}$ pt good veal or chicken stock
plenty of fresh chopped parsley
2 egg yolks
3 fl. oz double cream
salt and freshly-ground black pepper

Cut the veal into large cubes. Cut the celery into big chunks, slice the carrots, and peel the bulbous heads of the spring onions (save the green parts for snipping over a salad).

Melt the butter in a flame-proof casserole over low heat. Add the cubes of veal in batches and cook gently, turning them to coat them all over with fat, until just coloured – but don't really brown the meat.

Remove the meat with a slotted spoon. Add the celery, carrots and spring onions to the casserole and cook gently until slightly softened.

Sprinkle on and stir in the flour. When it has been smoothly absorbed by the fat, pour on the stock and lemon juice and bring to simmering point stirring continuously. Season generously with salt and pepper and return the meat to the casserole.

Cover with a well-fitting lid and cook at a very gentle simmer for about 50 minutes – either on top of the stove or in an oven preheated to 300F, 150C, gas mark 2.

Stir in the whole button mushrooms and the broad beans. Bring the casserole gently back to simmering point, cover it again and cook, very gently as before, for a further 30 minutes or so until the meat is perfectly tender and all the vegetables are cooked.

Beat the egg yolks with the cream in a cup. Carefully stir in a few spoonfuls of the simmering casserole liquid, then pour the contents of the cup into the casserole, adding it in a slow trickle and stirring the casserole all the while.

Cook very gently indeed for a few minutes longer, without

letting the liquid approach boiling point, until slightly thickened.

Check seasoning and serve immediately, lavishly garnished
with coarsely chopped parsley and piping hot croûtons of fried
bread.

WIENERSCHNITZEL
(serves 4)

Most of my favourite veal dishes are Italian, but this Viennese
classic always looks lovely and I particularly like the contrast of
chopped hard-boiled eggs with meat fried in breadcrumbs.

> 4 escalopes of veal, each weighing $\frac{1}{4}$ lb, trimmed of all fat and
> membrane and flattened to $\frac{1}{4}$ inch thickness
> seasoned flour
> 1 raw egg beaten with 1 tablespoon water
> 3 oz stale breadcrumbs
> oil and unsalted butter for frying
> 1 tablespoon lemon juice
>
> *To garnish:*
> 2 hard-boiled eggs
> slices of lemon
> 8 anchovies
> 2 tablespoons capers
> fresh chopped parsley

Lightly dust the veal in well-seasoned flour, moisten with
beaten egg and coat with a fine even layer of breadcrumbs.
Cover and leave in a cool place for 1 hour.

Meanwhile, prepare the garnish – sieve the hardboiled egg
yolks, chop the whites finely and reserve separately. Roll the
anchovies up neatly.

Fry the escalopes two at a time, in a large pan over medium
heat. You will need 1 oz butter and 1 tablespoon oil for each
batch and it will take about 3–4 minutes for the meat to cook
through. Reduce temperature a little if the crumb coating is
browning too fast. Drain the cooked veal on kitchen paper
towels, arrange them on a hot dish and garnish. Remove any fat

and crumbs remaining in the pan and wipe the pan clean with kitchen paper towels. Add 1½ oz fresh butter to the pan. Melt gently and continue cooking until it smells nutty and begins to brown. Draw the pan to one side. Add 1 tablespoon lemon juice and a little salt and pepper. Swirl the pan to mix everything, and warm it briefly. Pour it over the veal and serve immediately.

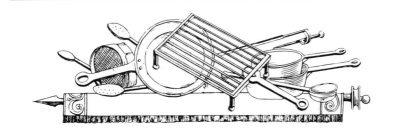

Pork, Bacon and Offal

ORIENTAL CHOPS
(serves 2)

This is one of those useful dishes that can be left to cook while you are out. Serve it with lots of rice, noodles or mashed potatoes to sop up the sauce.

> 2 large pork chops
> a small garlic clove
> 3 tablespoons each English mustard powder and soft brown sugar
> 1½ tablespoons tarragon or white wine vinegar
> 1 teaspoon soy sauce
> freshly-ground black pepper

Mix the mustard powder and sugar in a gratin dish. Add the crushed garlic clove, vinegar, soy sauce and a good grinding of black pepper and blend everything together well with a fork.

Remove the rinds from the chops and trim away excess fat. Make snips into the fat here and there to prevent curling during cooking. Lay the chops in the gratin dish and turn them until generously coated all over with the pungent mixture. Cover the dish with a foil lid and place it in a cold oven.

Set the automatic time-switch so that the oven will turn itself on to 300F, 150C, gas mark 2, 3 hours before you plan to eat. By the end of this time the meat will be tender and richly flavoured with the sauce.

LOIN OF PORK WITH PRUNES
(serves 6)

This is a fairly rich and quite expensive dish, suitable for a party.

$3\frac{1}{4}$–$3\frac{1}{2}$ lb loin of pork
1 pt extra dry cider – Bulmers No. 7 is good
$\frac{1}{2}$ lb pitted prunes
$\frac{1}{2}$ pt double cream
a few spoonfuls soured cream
salt, pepper and coriander
rounds of fried bread

Bone and rind the loin (or ask your butcher to do this), reserving the bones and rind, and rub it all over with salt, pepper and coriander. Roll it up, tie into a neat bolster shape and weigh again. Place the meat on a rack, put the bones, rind and 5–6 tablespoons of cider in the base of the pan, and roast at 350F, 180C, gas mark 4, allowing 35 minutes per lb and 30 minutes over.

Put the prunes into a small flame-proof casserole with $\frac{3}{4}$ pt cider. There is no need to presoak them if using a good quality such as Sunsweet. Bring to simmering point on top of the stove, cover and place on the floor of the oven for the last half hour of roasting time.

When roasting time is up, discard rind and bones and pour off all but a few spoonfuls of the fat (save the fat for delicious fried potatoes). Strain the prunes and add their liquor to the roasting pan. Allow it to bubble up and reduce to a thinnish syrup. Gradually blend in a scant $\frac{1}{2}$ pt double cream and a few spoonfuls of soured cream.

Cook for 5 minutes or so, stirring, until you have a hot, shiny and thickened sauce. Season it well. Arrange the pork in thin slices down the centre of a hot dish, pour the sauce over and arrange the prunes on rounds of fried bread round the edge of the dish.

PORK PASTIES
(makes 6)

Absolutely delicious whether served hot or cold, this variation on a Cornish pasty makes a good supper dish or food for a packed office lunch or picnic.

> Shortcrust pastry made with 5 oz each plain white flour and wholemeal flour and butter
> a small egg beaten with a little salt for glazing the pasty
> 13 oz boneless belly of pork taken from the lean end
> 1 medium-small onion
> 1 large cooking apple
> 2 oz Cheddar cheese
> salt and freshly-ground black pepper

Mince the pork coarsely or cut it into $\frac{1}{4}$ inch dice. Chop the onion very finely. Cut up the apple and cheese into dice the same size as the pork. Mix the ingredients well in a large bowl, seasoning them with salt and freshly-ground black pepper.

Divide the pastry into 6 pieces. Roll each piece into a circle $6\frac{1}{2}$ inches in diameter. Spoon the pork mixture on to one half of each circle, leaving a clear pastry rim round the edge. Brush the rim with beaten egg. Fold the pastry over the filling and seal the raw pastry edges firmly together. Make a steam hole in each pasty, glaze the pasties with beaten egg and bake on a baking sheet for 35–40 minutes in an oven preheated to 425F, 220C, gas mark 7.

MISSISSIPPI BEANS
(serves 4–6)

A substantial and warming dish that is cheap and very easy to cook. Beans cooked by this method (but usually with pork and tomato flavourings only) are the original baked beans!

1 lb haricot beans
1½ lb belly of pork (fresh or salt) in one piece
2 bay leaves and a bunch of parsley stalks tied together with
     string
1 large garlic clove
1 onion
1 large green pepper
3 tablespoons black treacle
1 × 8 oz can of tomatoes
salt and freshly-ground black pepper

Soak the dried beans (and the pork if salt) in plenty of cold water for several hours. Drain thoroughly. Lay the beans in a large casserole with the chopped onion and belly of pork buried among them. Add the bay and parsley and enough cold water to just cover the beans. Cover with foil and a lid and cook for 2½ hours at 325F, 160C, gas mark 3.

Remove and discard the herbs. Lift out the pork, remove the bones and cut the meat into 2 inch cubes. Stir the treacle into the casserole, then the tomatoes and their liquid, the de-seeded and chopped green pepper, the crushed garlic, some salt (go carefully if using salt pork) and plenty of pepper. Stir to mix everything well. Lay the pork cubes on top. Return the dish to the oven – without a lid this time. Reduce heat to 300F, 150C, gas mark 2, and bake for a further 1½–2 hours until the pork has sunk into the beans in a rich crusty glaze.

OVEN-BARBECUED SPARE RIBS

Delicious and very easy indeed to prepare. Serves 4 as a substantial first course.

3 lb spare ribs of pork
2 fat garlic cloves
2 tablespoons soft dark brown sugar
2 tablespoons Worcester sauce
2 tablespoons tomato purée
2 tablespoons soy sauce
1 lemon
1 orange

Heat the oven to 350F, 180C, gas mark 4. Cut the spare ribs to make 4 large pieces. Put them into a roasting pan, and cover the pan with a foil lid. Bake for 45 minutes.

Meanwhile prepare the barbecue sauce. Chop the garlic cloves, sprinkle them with sugar and crush. Grate the orange and lemon zest finely and squeeze the juice. Stir both zest and juice into the sugared garlic, and blend in the Worcester sauce, tomato purée and soy sauce.

When the 45 minutes are up, remove the foil lid from the roasting pan and increase oven temperature to 400F, 200C, gas mark 6. Tip the melted pork fat out of the pan. Pour on the barbecue sauce and turn the meat in it to coat on all sides. Cook, uncovered, for 40–50 minutes, basting and turning the spare ribs occasionally. Divide the ribs into individual bones just before serving.

SPARE RIB WITH CAPER SAUCE
(serves 1)

Lean spare rib chops (n.b. chops, not Chinese-style spare ribs) are cheaper than loin chops and good for this dish. Boiled and buttered noodles and spinach make good accompaniments.

> 1 meaty and lean spare rib chop
> about 1 teaspoon oil
> 1 small onion
> $\frac{1}{2}$ chicken stock cube dissolved in $\frac{1}{4}$ pt boiling water
> 1 heaped teaspoon capers
> scant teaspoon French mustard
> $\frac{1}{2}$ oz butter
> freshly-ground black pepper

Heat a 6 inch or 7 inch frying pan with just enough oil to film the base. When it is very hot add the chop and cook over fairly high heat for a minute or so on each side until nicely browned. Chop the onion finely and tuck the bits round the chop. Pour on the hot stock — standing back while it bubbles up. Then reduce heat to very low, cover the pan with a foil 'lid' and let the chop cook very gently for about 12 minutes — turning the chop halfway through.

Then remove the lid and let the meat continue cooking gently for a further 7 or 8 minutes (again turning the chop once). By the end of cooking time the meat should be beautifully tender and the stock reduced to a few spoonfuls. Lift the chop out of the pan. Stir in the mustard, chopped capers and the diced half ounce of butter. Increase the heat and cook, stirring continuously for a minute or so until the butter has melted to give a piping hot syrupy-textured sauce. Season with pepper, pour the sauce over the chop and serve immediately.

PORKBURGERS
(serves 4 or more)

Belly of pork, taken from the thicker, leaner end, makes delicious mince, and these very inexpensive burgers have become great favourites with my family.

> $1\frac{1}{4}$ lb lean belly of pork (boned and derinded weight)
> 3 oz fresh breadcrumbs
> $\frac{1}{2}$ tablespoon concentrated tomato purée dissolved in 1 tablespoon water
> $1\frac{1}{2}$–2 teaspoons salt
> a good pinch of allspice
> a bay leaf crumbled to a powder
> fresh chopped basil or $1\frac{1}{2}$ teaspoons dried basil or a good pinch of dried rosemary pounded to a powder
> a little oil
> clarified butter (optional)

Pass the meat through the fine blade of a mincer, and turn it into a bowl. Add the breadcrumbs, tomato liquid, seasonings, herbs and spices, and mix everything together very thoroughly with your hands. Shape the mixture into 8 burgers about $\frac{3}{4}$–1 inch high.

The burgers are now ready for cooking – they can be grilled or fried. To grill, brush all over lightly with oil, and grill under medium heat for about 8 minutes on each side until lightly browned and cooked right through. Reduce heat a little if the burgers are browning too fast. To fry, cook the burgers gently over low heat in a mixture of oil and clarified butter, allowing about 8 minutes on each side to ensure the meat is cooked right through. Drain well and serve piping hot.

SLOW BAKED PORK WITH PRUNES
(serves 2)

Prunes, onions and thyme always go well with pork. Here they are combined in a very easy dish which can be left to cook while you are out. Lentils with tomatoes (see page 210) makes a good accompaniment and can be cooked in the oven simultaneously.

$\frac{3}{4}$ lb lean streaky belly of pork rashers
6 prunes
1 fat garlic clove
3 tablespoons fresh chopped parsley
$\frac{1}{2}$ teaspoon dried thyme
1 medium-sized onion
salt and freshly-ground black pepper
3 tablespoons dry cider or unsweetened apple juice

Choose a gratin or baking dish just large enough to take the pork in a single layer. De-rind the rashers and lay them in the dish. Tuck the prunes (which do not need to be soaked in advance) into the gaps. Sprinkle the crushed garlic over the meat. Mix the parsley and thyme together and scatter them over the top. Add a good seasoning of salt and pepper and lay the very thinly sliced onion on top. Pour on the liquid and cover the dish with a lightly buttered foil lid.

Place the dish on an upper shelf of a cold oven. Switch on to 300F, 150C, gas mark 2 and bake for 3 hours, or set timing and temperature controls so that the oven will turn itself on to 300F, 150C, gas mark 2, 3 hours before you plan to eat.

CRISPY PORK WITH POTATO PURÉE
(serves 2)

These rashers are almost as good as roast pork – but without the expense of a whole joint. The rind of belly doesn't make perfect crackling but it becomes pleasantly chewy and the fat crisps to perfection.

> 6 thick streaky belly of pork rashers
> 1¼ lb potatoes
> a little oil
> butter
> salt and freshly-ground black pepper

Lay the pork rashers on a grid suspended across the top of a roasting pan – I use the grid from my grill pan but a cake cooling rack would be equally suitable. To prevent the pork from sticking during cooking, brush the grid with a thin film of oil before placing the pork on it.

Peel the potatoes and cut them into chunks weighing about 1½ oz each. Put them in a casserole, add some salt and 1 pt cold water, and cover with a lid.

Place the roasting pan on the top shelf of a cold oven, and place the casserole on the bottom shelf. Switch the oven on to 400F, 200C, gas mark 6 and cook for 70 minutes. Or set automatic timing and temperature controls so that the oven will turn itself on to 400F, 200C, gas mark 6, 70 minutes before you plan to eat.

Just before serving, drain the potatoes from their cooking liquid and mash them with plenty of butter and pepper. Serve the pork and purée with a fresh watercress salad.

CHINESE PIE
(serves 4–5)

Sausagemeat, butter, onions, cabbage and potatoes are combined in this homely and very comforting meal-in-a-pot, which is one of my very favourite inexpensive dishes for a chilly winter evening.

1¾–2 lb Chinese leaves
1¾ lb potatoes
2 onions
3–4 oz butter
salt and pepper

For the sausagement:
¾ lb lean fresh belly of pork (boned and de-rinded weight)
¼ lb streaky bacon
4 garlic cloves
1 heaped teaspoon dried thyme
salt and freshly-ground black pepper

Slice the Chinese leaves thinly. Put them into a large pan of fast boiling water, bring quickly back to the boil and boil for 1 minute. Drain well, pressing with a wooden spoon to squeeze out excess liquid, and set aside.

Mince the pork, bacon and garlic for a pungent sausagemeat, then mix in the thyme, some salt, plenty of pepper and the finely chopped onions. Fry this mixture in 1½ oz butter for 4–5 minutes until lightly coloured.

Generously butter a large casserole. Slice the potatoes thinly and arrange them in the bottom of the casserole, seasoning with salt and pepper between layers. Cover the potatoes with half the Chinese leaves.

Spread the sausagemeat and its buttery juices on top, then cover with the remaining Chinese leaves. Arrange flakes of butter over the leaves, lay a circle of buttered greaseproof paper on top, and press it down on the mixture with a potato masher. Cover with the casserole lid and bake at 350F, 180C, gas mark 4, for half an hour. Then reduce oven temperature to 325F, 160C, gas mark 3, and bake for a further 1½ hours.

SUPERIOR SCOTCH EGGS
(makes 6)

Home-made Scotch eggs are good cold (and useful for packed lunches), but they are perhaps best served still piping hot and crisp from frying.

6 eggs hard-boiled
a little French mustard
a little flour
2 eggs beaten with a little salt
about 5 oz dry breadcrumbs
oil for deep-fat frying

For the sausagemeat:
$\frac{3}{4}$ lb lean fresh belly of pork (boned and de-rinded weight)
2 oz finely chopped onion
$\frac{1}{2}$ teaspoon dried thyme
good pinch allspice
a large bay leaf crumbled to a fine powder
$1\frac{1}{2}$ oz finely grated mature Cheddar cheese
$\frac{1}{2}$ teaspoon ground coriander seeds
at least 1 teaspoon salt and lots of freshly-ground black pepper

Mix the sausagemeat ingredients together then put them through the fine blade of a mincer twice to make a smooth mixture. Divide the mixture into 6 pieces, lay them on a damp work surface and flatten each into a circle large enough to wrap round a hard-boiled egg. Spread each circle with a little mustard, place an egg on top, then mould the sausagemeat firmly and evenly round the egg so there are no cracks.

Roll each egg shape in seasoned flour, dip in beaten egg and coat generously with dried breadcrumbs. Chill for a minimum of 15 minutes to firm up the coating. Then deep fry in oil heated to 350F/177C, for 7–8 minutes, and drain well on thickly-crumpled kitchen paper.

HUNGARIAN SAUSAGES
(serves 4)

Serve this quickly cooked dish with lots of rice or – better still – with boiled and buttered tagliatelle.

1–1½ lb good pork sausages
2 onions
2 green peppers
2 oz butter
1 × 8 oz can of tomatoes
1 large garlic clove
2–3 teaspoons paprika
a few spoonfuls of soured cream
salt and pepper

You will need a really large frying or sauté pan for this dish. Melt the butter in it, add the sausages and fry them gently for 10 minutes. Meanwhile quarter and thinly slice the onions, de-seed and chop the peppers, mash the canned tomatoes into their liquid.

Push the sausages to the edge of the pan, add the onions to the centre and increase heat slightly. Cook for 5 minutes more. Then add the peppers and continue frying over medium heat for about 12 minutes more, turning the vegetables as necessary.

Remove the sausages and keep them hot. Sprinkle on the paprika and stir it into the vegetables. Add the tomatoes seasoned with plenty of salt, the crushed garlic and a little pepper. Let the mixture simmer for 5 minutes or so, stirring occasionally, until the vegetables are well cooked and very hot.

Then stir in the soured cream, let it warm through gently, check and adjust seasoning to taste. Pour the sauce over the sausages and serve immediately.

FOUR-STAR SAUSAGE ROLLS
(makes 16)

If you have only eaten shop-bought sausage rolls, or made sausage rolls using commercial sausagemeat, I feel sure you will find these a very special treat – and they take only 1 hour from start to eating.

> 1 × 8 oz packet puff pastry
> 1 small egg
>
> *For the sausagemeat:*
> ¾ lb lean belly of pork (fresh or salted, boned and de-rinded weight)
> 1 teaspoon dried thyme or sage
> a good pinch allspice
> a large crumbled bay leaf
> ½ teaspoon ground coriander
> 2 oz very finely chopped onion
> plenty of salt and freshly-ground black pepper

Divide the defrosted pastry into 4 pieces, and roll out each to an oblong 4 inches by 12 inches. Set aside for 10 minutes in a cool place. Meanwhile, heat the oven to 425F, 220C, gas mark 7, and make the sausagemeat by mincing the pork meat quite finely and mixing in the chopped onion and other sausagemeat ingredients.

Using floured hands and a floured work surface, divide the sausagemeat into 4 and roll each piece into a 12 inch length. Lay one piece along each pastry strip. Brush the pastry edges with beaten egg. Fold the pastry over the sausagemeat and seal it well, pressing the seal with the prongs of a fork, then cut into 3 inch lengths.

Transfer the sausage rolls to a damp baking sheet. Space them well apart, brush the tops with beaten egg then make a few knife slashes across the top of each sausage roll. Bake for 25–30 minutes.

TURBIGO
(serves 6)

You will need lots of plain boiled rice to soak up the piquant sauce in this dish. I serve it on a large bed of rice, and garnish it with fried bread croûtons and chopped fresh parsley.

> 1 lb good, small pork sausages
> 1 lb lamb's kidneys
> 3 oz butter
> a few spoonsfuls of oil
> 2 onions
> 2 generous teaspoons French mustard
> 2 generous teaspoons tomato purée
> 2 teaspoons red wine vinegar
> a pinch of sugar
> $\frac{3}{4}$ pt stock
> 1 heaped teaspoon plain flour and softened butter mashed
>   together
> salt and freshly-ground black pepper

Fry the sausages in a mixture of butter and oil, drain well and keep hot. Fry the cored and halved kidney in the fat remaining in the pan, until nicely browned on the outside but still slightly pink within. Drain well and add to the sausages.

Add more butter to the frying pan, reduce heat and cook the chopped onions until softened and golden. Then tip the contents of the frying pan into a saucepan that has a large surface area; scrape the bottom of the frying pan well so as not to waste the tasty meaty sediment sticking to it.

Pour on the stock, add the sugar, tomato purée and vinegar. Stir to mix well then let it boil briskly until reduced by half. Season with mustard and plenty of salt and pepper. Whisk in the mashed butter-and-flour. As soon as it has thickened the liquid to give a syrupy textured sauce, pour it over the meats, garnish and serve.

CIDER SAUSAGES
(serves 1–2)

A simple and good dish for a cool day. The better the quality of the sausages used the better the dish will be.

$\frac{1}{2}$–$\frac{3}{4}$ lb sausages
1 onion
scant 1 oz butter
$\frac{1}{4}$ pt dry cider
1 teaspoon French mustard
$\frac{1}{2}$ teaspoon plain flour
salt and freshly-ground black pepper
fresh chopped parsley

Slice the onion very thinly. Melt $\frac{1}{2}$ oz butter in a frying pan. Add the onion and turn it to coat it all over with fat. Add the sausages and fry gently for 10 minutes or until browned on all sides. Pour on the cider. Let it bubble up then reduce heat very low and let the sausages cook, uncovered, for 25–30 minutes, just turning the sausages occasionally during this time.

Lift the sausages out of the pan and put them on a bed of creamy mashed potatoes. Mash the remaining half ounce of butter into the flour. Add it to the pan and cook, stirring well until the sauce has thickened slightly. Stir in the mustard and chopped fresh parsley, a little salt and pepper. Let the sauce bubble and cook for a minute or two to give it a good consistency. Then pour it over the sausages and serve immediately.

BACON, EGG AND LEEK PIE
(serves 4)

To make this I bought a $1\frac{1}{2}$ lb knuckle of bacon, blanched it and boiled it for 45 minutes. It yielded 9 oz lean meat, most of which went into the pie – the left-over meat scraps went into an omelette, and the bacon stock made a good soup next day.

6 oz diced cooked bacon meat
5 hard-boiled eggs

1 lb thin leeks
1 oz butter
2 tablespoons plain flour
¼ pt bacon stock
¼ pt milk
2 teaspoons French mustard
3 oz grated Cheddar cheese
2 tablespoons fresh chopped parsley
salt and pepper
1 × 8 oz packet puff pastry
1 small egg yolk for glazing

Trim, thoroughly wash and slice the leeks thickly – green parts as well as white. Steam them over some of the bacon stock until just tender (steaming will help them keep in good shape, and prevent them becoming waterlogged) and allow to cool.

Make a cheese sauce with the butter, flour, bacon stock, milk and Cheddar cheese. Stir in the mustard, chopped parsley, a good seasoning of black pepper and only a very little salt. Stir in the quartered hard-boiled eggs, diced bacon and leeks. Turn the mixture into a 2 pt pie dish (I use an oval Pyrex dish) and let it cool – this is important or the steamy hot filling will spoil the pastry.

Heat the oven to 425F, 220C, gas mark 7. Roll out the pastry and use it to cover the pie. Decorate it, make a steam slit and glaze with beaten egg yolk seasoned with a good pinch of salt. Bake for 35–40 minutes until the pastry is puffed up and golden crisp.

GAMMON STEAKS WITH FRUIT SAUCE
(serves 2)

Bacon chops can also be cooked this way. They are usually sweet-cured and mildly flavoured, about half an inch thick and will need 7–8 minutes grilling on each side.

2 gammon steaks, each weighing about 6 oz
6 oz canned pineapple chunks in syrup
2 tablespoons dried mixed fruit
$\frac{1}{4}$ teaspoon mustard powder
1 teaspoon soft dark brown sugar
1 teaspoon cornflour
a small pinch of allspice
a little melted butter

Make deep snips into the fat all round the edge of the gammon to prevent the steaks from curling up during cooking. Brush the meat with a little melted butter and cook under a medium-hot grill for 5–6 minutes on each side.

When the steaks are nearly ready make the sauce – which is an exceptionally easy one. Simply chop the pineapple chunks into tiny pieces, put them and their syrup into a small saucepan, add all the remaining ingredients and bring very slowly to boiling point stirring vigorously all the while. Simmer for 1 minute, pour the sauce over the gammon and serve immediately.

MASHED POTATO PIE

(serves 4)

Certainly not haute cuisine but quick and cheap, this makes a warming and comforting supper dish. I serve it with steam-fry cabbage (see page 200).

2 lb potatoes
6 oz butter
2 onions
$\frac{1}{4}$ lb streaky bacon
$\frac{1}{2}$ lb chicken livers
a pinch of mace
salt and freshly-ground black pepper

Peel and boil the potatoes. Press them through a sieve or vegetable mill, beat in $\frac{1}{4}$ lb butter and season with plenty of salt and pepper so they are fluffy, creamy and well-flavoured.

While the potatoes are cooking, cut each bacon rasher into about 4 pieces. Cook over gentle heat until the fat runs. Remove with a slotted spoon. Add 1 oz butter and the chopped onions and cook gently until softened. Remove with a slotted spoon. Increase heat and sauté the chicken livers just long enough to seal and brown the surfaces really well but keeping them tender and pink in the centre. Season with salt, pepper and mace and mix with the onion and bacon.

Grease a 2 pt dish with some of the remaining butter. Spread half the potatoes over the base, cover with the liver and bacon mixture, top with the remaining potatoes and dot with the rest of the butter. Bake without a lid at 350F, 180C, gas mark 4, for 30–35 minutes until the top is golden.

MATCHSTICK MACARONI
(serves 4–5)

Liver, bacon, macaroni and cheese are combined here to make a homely and economic supper dish.

$\frac{1}{2}$ lb lamb's liver
$\frac{1}{2}$ lb streaky bacon rashers
1 green pepper
2 onions
1 × 8 oz can of tomatoes
8 oz macaroni
butter
salt and freshly-ground black pepper
plenty of grated cheese

Ask the butcher to slice the liver very thinly. When you get it home cut the slices into long narrow strips, then cut across to make matchstick lengths. Cut the bacon into similar small pieces. De-seed and chop the pepper and chop the onion.

Cook the bacon over low heat in a large flame-proof casserole until the fat begins to run. Push the bacon into a ring round the edge of the casserole. Increase heat to high, add a knob of butter and, when foaming ceases, add the liver. Cook stirring and turning until the liver is coloured – just a minute or so. Then tip the contents of the casserole on to a plate and keep warm.

Add another knob of butter to the casserole and fry the onion and pepper hard for about 5 minutes, stirring as necessary. Reduce heat, add the tomatoes and their juices and mash them. Leave to cook without a lid until the mixture is quite thick, but stir occasionally to prevent sticking. Meanwhile, boil the macaroni.

Add the drained macaroni to the casserole, also the reserved bacon and liver. Stir to mix everything well and season to taste before serving. Offer grated cheese in a small bowl so everyone can help themselves.

LIVER STROGANOFF

(serves 3)

Nutritionists are always saying we should eat more liver and kidneys, and they stress the particular importance of these foods for anyone on a diet. Grilled liver is probably best for you, but some people dislike it. So here is a liver recipe which even professed haters of liver seem to enjoy.

$\frac{3}{4}$ lb lamb's liver, cut into matchstick strips
$\frac{1}{2}$ lb small onions, thinly sliced and pushed into rings
$\frac{1}{2}$ lb mushrooms, thickly sliced
6 oz thickened yoghurt, beaten to a smooth cream and seasoned with 4 tablespoons chopped parsley and plenty of salt and pepper
a little butter and oil
1 teaspoon plain flour

Sweat the onions in a little butter and oil in a covered pan for 20 minutes. Then tip the contents of the pan into a sieve placed over a bowl to drain off as much of the fat as possible.

Add a fresh half ounce of butter to the sauté pan and fry the mushrooms. Push the mushrooms into a ring round the edge of the pan and add another tiny nugget of butter. When it is very hot add the liver. Cook, turning the meat to colour it on all sides, for about 1 minute. Return the onions to the pan and stir in the flour to blot up any fat remaining in the pan.

Pour on the yoghurt mixture and cook, stirring continuously, until the sauce is hot and coating all the ingredients nicely. Serve immediately.

WILTSHIRE KIDNEYS
(serves 4)

I love kidneys. If you don't like them you could always serve this delicious sauce with beefburgers; it would give them a good 'lift'.

12 lamb's kidneys
6 oz onions
2 oz butter
2 tablespoons red wine and $\frac{1}{4}$ pt light chicken stock (or 6 fl. oz chicken stock)
3–4 teaspoons French mustard
$\frac{1}{4}$ pt soured cream
salt and freshly-ground black pepper
fresh chopped parsley

Skin the kidneys, halve and core them carefully. If frozen kidneys are used, check that they are thoroughly defrosted and dry.

Heat a large frying pan until very hot. Add 1 oz butter and, when the butter foam begins to die down, add the kidneys. Sauté them for a few minutes until well browned and sealed on the outside – but they should remain juicy and pink within.

Lift the kidneys out of the pan with a slotted spoon, lay them on a bed of freshly boiled rice and keep warm. Add the remaining butter to the pan and the very finely chopped onion and cook over very low heat for 12–15 minutes until quite tender. Then pour on the liquids, let them bubble up and reduce by about half to give a syrupy consistency. Stir in the mustard and soured cream and cook gently until well blended and heated through. Season to taste with salt and pepper, stir in a good quantity of chopped parsley, pour the sauce over the kidneys and serve immediately.

OX TONGUE WITH SALSA VERDE
(serves 8 or more)

Sainsbury's often sell ox tongue which is particularly good, smoked as well as salted. Cooked, pressed and served cold with this delicious Italian sauce, it makes an admirable cut-and-come-again meal for all sorts of occasions.

> Salted and smoked ox tongue weighing approximately 4 lb
> 2 carrots
> 2 onions
> 2 celery sticks
> a pig's trotter (or gelatine powder)
> bay, thyme and black peppercorns
> a bottle of cider
>
> *For the sauce:*
> 1 oz parsley
> a bunch of chives
> 2 fat garlic cloves
> 3 tablespoons capers
> salt and freshly-ground black pepper
> the juice and zest of a lemon
> 7–8 fl. oz oil

Soak the tongue in plenty of cold water for 12–24 hours to get rid of excess salt, changing the water several times.

Next day drain the tongue, put it into a heavy-based saucepan or a flame-proof casserole. Add the chopped vegetables, the pig's trotter (if available), a bay leaf, some thyme and half a dozen black peppercorns. Pour on the cider and add water as necessary to cover the meat. Bring slowly to simmering point, cover with a well-fitting lid and simmer gently (on top of the stove or in an oven heated to 300F, 150C, gas mark 2) for about 4 hours or until the tongue is absolutely tender.

Strain the liquid and let it boil fast until reduced and well flavoured – the long soaking of the tongue before cooking and the use of cider should mean the liquid is not too salty. Meanwhile, skin the cooked tongue while it is still hot, cut away the fat and gristle from the root and remove all small bones. Curl the tongue and squeeze it into a round casserole or dish with straight sides. Pour a little slightly cooled cooking liquor into the dish to fill any gaps. (If you did not use a pig's trotter, dissolve some gelatine in the liquor first so it will set to a jelly when cold.) Put a plate on top, weight it and leave in a cold larder for 24 hours before unmoulding and serving.

To make the sauce, first chop the garlic, then crush it with the back of a knife. Put it into a liquidiser with the herbs, capers, lemon and oil and reduce to a thick green purée. Season with pepper and salt — just a hint of salt in view of serving the sauce with ox tongue.

TONGUE AND MUSHROOM VOL-AU-VENTS

Raw vol-au-vent cases are a boon for freezer owners, particularly in holiday time — they mean you can make snacks and picnic food very quickly and effortlessly. The pastry can be baked from frozen and this hot savoury filling is easily prepared while the pastry cooks to a golden brown.

24 medium-sized vol-au-vent cases (I use Jus-rol)
an egg beaten with a little salt for glazing the pastry
$\frac{1}{4}$ lb tongue
$\frac{1}{4}$ lb mushrooms
1 oz butter
$\frac{1}{2}$ oz plain flour
8 fl. oz milk
1 teaspoon French mustard
4 tablespoons chopped fresh parsley
salt and freshly-ground black pepper

Heat the oven to 425F, 220C, gas mark 7. While it heats up make a smooth white sauce with half an ounce of butter, the flour and the milk. Season it with salt and pepper, cover and set aside to keep hot.

Brush the outer rims of the still frozen vol-au-vents with beaten egg. Space them out on baking trays and bake in the hot oven for 18 minutes, changing over the positions of the baking trays halfway through this time.

Meanwhile, slice the mushrooms, or chop them if very large, and fry them in the remaining half ounce of butter. Gently reheat the sauce, stir in the chopped tongue, the mushrooms and their buttery juices. Stir in the mustard and parsley, then use the mixture to fill the piping-hot vol-au-vent cases.

CHICKEN LIVER GOUGÈRE
(serves 4–6)

Cheesy baked choux with a savoury chicken liver filling makes a lovely and rather unusual main course dish.

For the choux:
$3\frac{3}{4}$ oz plain flour
a good pinch each of mustard powder and cayenne pepper
$\frac{1}{2}$ teaspoon salt and a grinding of black pepper
3 oz butter
$7\frac{1}{2}$ fl. oz water
2 oz grated mature Cheddar cheese
2 oz mature Cheddar cheese cut into small dice
3 eggs

For the filling:
1 lb chicken livers
$\frac{1}{2}$ lb mushrooms
2 onions
1 garlic clove
1 × 14 oz can of tomatoes
2 oz butter
half a small lemon
Worcester sauce, salt and freshly-ground black pepper

First make the choux pastry. Sift the flour, mustard and cayenne on to a sheet of greaseproof paper. Dice the butter, put it into a small pan with the salt, pepper and water. Bring to a rapid boil. Immediately remove from the heat, shoot in the flour and beat until the dough is quite smooth and leaves the sides of the pan clean. Turn the ball of dough into a large mixing bowl. Beat the eggs lightly in a separate bowl, then beat them, a large spoonful at a time, into the dough to make it very smooth and glossy. Beat in the grated cheese and finally the diced Cheddar. Shape the mixture into fat blobs placing them round the edge of a large buttered gratin or flan dish, stand it on a preheated baking sheet and cook for 45–50 minutes at 425F, 220C, gas mark 7, until well risen and browned.

Meanwhile sauté the livers in half the very hot butter until well sealed and browned. Continue cooking more gently for another 2–3 minutes if you don't like pink-centred chicken livers. Remove the livers. Add the remaining butter to the pan. Fry the finely chopped onions, crushed garlic and thickly sliced mushrooms for about 7 minutes. Add the tomatoes (mashed) and their juices and stir over high heat until the sauce is thick and well reduced — about 8–10 minutes. Away from the heat season to taste with lemon juice, Worcester sauce, salt and pepper. Stir in the chicken livers and some of their juices — but don't thin the sauce too much. Pile the filling into the centre of the cooked gougère. Return the dish to the oven for 5 minutes, then sprinkle with finely grated lemon zest and serve.

Vegetables and Pulses

SPINACH GNOCCHI

These well-flavoured, feathery light savoury dumplings make a lovely first course for 4 people or an excellent supper dish for 2.

    1 lb fresh spinach
    ½ lb Ricotta cheese (from an Italian shop) or cottage cheese
    yolks of 2 eggs
    3 tablespoons flour
    4 tablespoons freshly-grated Parmesan cheese
    butter
    salt, freshly-ground black pepper and freshly-grated nutmeg

Thoroughly wash the spinach, discarding any tough stalks and yellowing leaves. Weigh out ¾ lb spinach and save the rest for a salad. Pack the ¾ lb spinach into a saucepan, cover and cook over medium-low heat – turning the leaves occasionally – for 6–7 minutes, until perfectly tender. Turn the spinach into a sieve and press with a wooden spoon to extract as much moisture as possible. Then turn the spinach on to a board and chop it finely. Set aside to cool. (This dish can also be made using ½ lb frozen chopped spinach – simply thaw and squeeze out all moisture.)

    Sieve the Ricotta or cottage cheese into a mixing bowl. Add the spinach and beat to mix well. Lightly whisk the egg yolks and beat them into the mixture. Then sift in 2 tablespoons plain flour, add 2 tablespoons grated Parmesan and beat again. Season to taste with salt, pepper and nutmeg. Spread the mixture on a plate and chill for at least 2 hours, or overnight if more convenient.

Sprinkle a tablespoon of flour on a working surface. Drop small blobs of the mixture on to it, one at a time. Turn them over, then roll between the palms of your hands to shape into small balls — this quantity will make about 32 in all.

Bring some salted water to the boil in a large sauté pan. Reduce heat to a bare simmer. Drop about half the gnocchi into the pan and cook, uncovered, at the gentlest simmer for about 5 minutes (if the fluid is boiling or the pan overcrowded the gnocchi will disintegrate).

Lift out with a draining spoon, blot on kitchen paper and keep warm in a low oven while you cook the remainder. Sprinkle the remaining 2 tablespoons Parmesan cheese over the gnocchi. Serve with extra grated Parmesan cheese and a bowl of melted butter.

ITALIAN PEAS WITH PROSCIUTTO
(serves 6–8)

A useful vegetable dish for entertaining since it comes to no harm if cooked early in the evening, covered and kept hot in a low oven. If you don't grow your own peas, use frozen petits pois — a much better bet than the ungraded bullets on offer in most greengrocers.

> $1\frac{1}{2}$ lb young peas (shelled weight)
> 2 oz butter
> 1 tablespoon olive oil
> $\frac{1}{4}$ lb onion
> $\frac{1}{4}$ lb prosciutto crudo or cooked lean ham
> 4 fl. oz light chicken stock
> salt and freshly-ground black pepper

If frozen peas are used, turn them into a colander and leave until completely defrosted — this takes several hours. Warm the butter and olive oil in a flame-proof casserole. Chop the onion finely, add it to the casserole and fry gently for 6–8 minutes until slightly softened. Add the peas and the stock and bring to simmering point stirring all the while. Cover the casserole and cook gently until the peas are tender – about 4 minutes if the peas were frozen, nearer 15 minutes if using fresh peas.

Cut the prosciutto or ham into small strips. Stir into the peas and continue cooking very gently – without a lid this time – for a further 5–10 minutes, just stirring and turning the ingredients occasionally, until most of the liquid has been absorbed or evaporated. Season to taste with salt and freshly-ground black pepper.

Good with pollo al Parmigiano (see page 93) and a crusty loaf warmed in the oven.

LATKES
(serves 4)

Served piping hot with fried eggs, bacon, or sausages, these make a good supper dish.

> 4 large potatoes
> 1 medium-large onion
> 2 eggs
> 4 tablespoons self-raising flour
> salt and freshly-ground black pepper
> oil for frying

Peel and finely grate the potatoes (peeled weight should be 17 oz). Peel and grate the onion. Put both pulps into a sieve and leave to drain for 15 minutes – this is important or the mixture will be too sloppy.

Beat the eggs in a mixing bowl with a generous seasoning of salt and pepper (add a few herbs if you wish). Add the drained potatoes and onion, sift on the flour, and beat everything together well to make a sort of pancake batter.

Heat about $\frac{1}{2}$ inch oil in a large frying pan. Add heaped tablespoons of the latkes mixture, spacing them well apart and flattening each with the back of the spoon. Fry over medium heat for 4 minutes on each side, until crisp and a rich golden brown.

Drain well and keep very hot while you cook the rest, then sprinkle with salt and serve immediately.

COURGETTES WITH TOMATOES AND HERBS
(serves 2)

In this dish vegetable juices mingle with butter and herbs to make a delicious natural sauce. Half a small, tender marrow could be used in place of courgettes: peel, seed and dice it, then salt as described in the recipe. Marrow may need slightly longer cooking time.

> $\frac{1}{2}$ lb courgettes
> generous $\frac{1}{2}$ lb firm tomatoes
> fresh chives and fresh basil
> 1–1$\frac{1}{2}$ oz butter
> salt, celery salt and freshly-ground black pepper

Wipe the courgettes clean and slice them – there is no need to peel them. Put them in a colander, sprinkle salt between the layers, cover with a soup plate and put a few weights on top. Leave for 30 minutes or so to drain off excess liquid. Then rinse and dry well with kitchen paper towels. Skin, seed and quarter the tomatoes, or cut into one-eighths if large.

When ready to cook, heat the oven to 350F, 180C, gas mark 4, and use about $\frac{1}{2}$ oz or so of butter to generously grease the base and sides of a casserole.

Put the vegetables into the casserole. Add about 1 tablespoon each fresh chopped chives and basil, a good grinding of black pepper, and a little each of celery salt and ordinary salt. Mix everything together, then dot with another half ounce or so of butter. Lay a circle of buttered greasproof paper on top but there is no need to cover with a lid. Bake for about 45 minutes until the courgettes are tender but still retaining a little crispness. Check seasoning and serve.

FLAGEOLETS WITH FRESH HERBS
(serves 6)

Minted new potatoes and peas are the traditional English accompaniments to roast lamb. These pretty pale green dried beans (available from good delicatessens, specialist French shops and some health food stores) make a more unusual alternative, and are particularly delicious when spiked with lemon juice and fresh herbs.

> 12 oz dried flageolet beans
> 2 lemons
> 5 or 6 sprigs of thyme (preferably lemon thyme)
> a good bunch of parsley and a good bunch of mint
> 2–3 oz butter
> salt and freshly-ground black pepper

Put the beans into a large bowl, fill it up to the brim with cold water and leave the beans to soak for 2–3 hours. Drain the beans, rinse them well and put them into a saucepan. Add enough fresh cold water to cover the beans very generously. Thinly pare the lemon rind and tie it into a muslin bag with the thyme and lightly crushed parsley stalks.

Add the herb bag to the saucepan (do not add any salt to the pan or the bean skins will harden) and bring to boiling point. Cover the pan and simmer gently for an hour or until the beans are quite tender.

When cooked, drain the beans thoroughly. Melt the butter in the bean pan over very low heat. Away from the heat add the beans, a good 2 tablespoons of lemon juice, a generous seasoning of salt and pepper, 8 tablespoons of chopped mint and 4 tablespoons of chopped parsley. Toss lightly to mix everything together, and serve.

CHICORY WITH SOURED CREAM SAUCE

This is based on a dish I remember from my childhood in which chicory was wrapped in sheets of ham and covered with a cheese sauce. I have retained both cheese and ham, but replaced the flour-thickened sauce with soured cream. The result is slightly more delicate, but nonetheless rich in flavour. Serve with hot French bread for a satisfying lunch or supper dish for 2 people.

> 4 chicory, each weighing about $\frac{1}{4}$ lb
> $\frac{1}{4}$ lb thinly sliced ham
> 1 oz butter
> $\frac{1}{4}$ pt soured cream
> 2 oz mature Cheddar cheese
> salt and freshly-ground black pepper

Wipe the chicory clean and trim the bases. Steam over a pan of simmering water for about 18 minutes or until just tender. As soon as cool enough to handle, squeeze each chicory with paper kitchen towels to extract excess liquid.

Butter a gratin dish, then cover the base with the ham cut into matchstick strips. Lay the chicory on top in a single layer, dot with flakes of butter and add a good grinding of black pepper. Add just a little salt, since both ham and cheese will provide a certain amount of saltiness. Cook under the grill for 4–5 minutes, turning the chicory to brown it lightly on all sides.

Beat the soured cream with a fork until smooth and well blended. Pour it over the chicory and sprinkle the finely grated Cheddar on top. Return the dish to the grill for another $1\frac{1}{2}$ minutes or so until the cheese is just melted. Serve immediately.

BRAISED CHESTNUTS
(serves 4—6)

To peel chestnuts first score them round the 'waist', drop in boiling water and simmer for 10 minutes. Drain and wrap in a towel to keep them hot (the warmer the chestnut, the easier it is to remove its shell). Insert the point of a knife into the scored shell and lift away shell and bitter tasting skin simultaneously. Throw away any nuts that do not look completely wholesome.

1½ lb chestnuts
1 onion
1 celery stalk
3 oz butter
1 heaped tablespoon arrowroot
3 tablespoons dry sherry or dry cider
about 1 pt good brown stock
salt and freshly-ground black pepper
cubes of slightly stale bread fried in butter until golden and
    crisp

Heat the oven to 300F, 150C, gas mark 2. Melt half the butter in a flame-proof casserole. Chop the onion and celery finely and 'sweat' them in the fat for 10 minutes or so until softened. Blend the arrowroot in a cup with the sherry or dry cider. Add the peeled chestnuts to the casserole. Pour on the arrowroot mixture and enough stock to cover the vegetables and nuts completely. Stirring gently and continuously, bring the mixture to simmering point. Let it simmer for a couple of minutes then season with salt and a good grinding of black pepper. Cover with a lid and transfer to the oven. Cook until the nuts are quite tender but not disintegrating. This may take 30–45 minutes or even more if the chestnuts are very large – check by piercing with a knifepoint. If the sauce has not reduced to a scant syrupy consistency by the time the chestnuts are tender, strain it off and reduce by fast boiling. If the sauce is very syrupy and the chestnuts still not tender, add boiling water or more stock to the casserole. In either case, check seasoning and stir in the remaining 1½ oz butter just before serving, then sprinkle on the fried croûtons.

LEEK AND POTATO CROQUETTES
(serves 4)

A delicious and unusual vegetable dish which can be partially prepared ahead.

1 lb potatoes (peeled weight)
½ lb leeks (trimmed and sliced weight)
2 eggs
2 oz grated Cheddar cheese
salt, freshly-ground black pepper and freshly-grated nutmeg
about 3 oz dry white breadcrumbs
oil for frying

Boil the potatoes. Mash them or put through a vegetable mill to make a smooth dry purée. Spread on a shallow dish and leave uncovered overnight to become cold and firm. Steam the leeks until tender then squeeze lightly with kitchen paper towels to absorb moisture, chop finely and set aside uncovered overnight.

Mix the cold vegetables together flavouring them with the cheese, salt, pepper and nutmeg, and binding the mixture with one egg yolk. Shape into 16–18 rolls, each about 1 inch in diameter and 2 inches long. Roll lightly in flour. Dip in the lightly beaten whole egg plus the leftover egg white, and coat all over with dry breadcrumbs.

Shallow fry in a large pan of hot oil over medium-low heat. Cook the croquettes in batches, turning them over from time to time to brown on all sides – each croquette will need a total of about 4 minutes. Drain well and serve piping hot.

STEAM-FRY CABBAGE
(serves 4)

Waterlogged cabbage is revolting! Here is a good way to cook cabbage so that it becomes tender but still retains slight crunch.

a generous 1 lb white cabbage
2½–3 tablespoons sesame or sunflour oil
2 oz very finely chopped onion
1½ teaspoons coriander seeds
salt and freshly-ground black pepper

Crush the coriander seeds with mortar and pestle, or grind them coarsely in a peppermill, or crush them with the back of a spoon (a wooden spoon pressed against a chopping board will make the seeds fly around less than using a metal spoon and saucer). Shred the cabbage finely, after removing tough core and outer leaves.

Warm the oil with the finely chopped onion and coriander in a large sauté pan over low heat, and cook gently for 5 minutes or so until the onion is just softened. Increase heat to medium-low. Add the cabbage and cook, stirring continuously for about 2 minutes until the cabbage is coated all over with fat. Then reduce heat as low as possible, stir in a good seasoning of salt and pepper, and cover the pan with a well-fitting lid – or improvise a lid using kitchen foil. Cook very gently, just stirring the mixture occasionally to encourage even cooking for 8–10 minutes until the cabbage is tender but still slightly crunchy. Serve immediately.

STUFFED ONIONS

These little stuffed onions make a good winter vegetable dish, or they could be served with spiced brown rice to make a vegetarian main course dish.

12 onions, all of the same size and weighing about 2 oz each
1 green pepper
a little butter and oil
2 tablespoons chopped and toasted nuts
2 tablespoons chopped parsley
salt and freshly-ground black pepper

One of the useful things about this dish is that all the preparations can be done well in advance; when mealtime approaches you only have to put the dish into the oven to complete cooking.

Peel the onions keeping them whole, drop them into a pan of fast boiling water and simmer for 5 minutes. Drain well and leave until cool enough to handle. Then cut a small lid off the top of each onion and use the tip of a sharp knife and your fingers to ease out the centre of the onion leaving thin onion shells. This takes a little patience as the onions are slippery at this stage. Finely chop the onion centres and the pepper and fry gently in 2 tablespoons butter and 1 tablespoon oil for 8 minutes or so. Away from the heat, stir in the nuts and parsley and plenty of salt and pepper. Push the stuffing into the onion shells, and stand the shells in a buttered gratin dish. Replace onion lids and cover the dish with a dome of foil.

To cook, bake at 350F, 180C, gas mark 4, for 50–60 minutes until piping hot and very tender.

GRATIN OF LEEKS
(serves 4)

The heavy wallpaper paste of a sauce in which leeks are so often served is anathema to me, the kiss of death to fresh vegetables. Leeks delicately coated in a little creamy béchamel can be very good indeed, but just as delicious and even simpler to prepare is this gratin.

> 12 young leeks
> 1 or 2 slices ham
> 2–3 tablespoons chopped fresh parsley
> $\frac{1}{4}$ pt double cream
> 3–4 oz grated cheese
> salt and freshly-ground black pepper

Thoroughly clean the whole leeks, steam them and pat dry. Lay them in a buttered gratin dish. Cut the ham into snippets, mix with the parsley and sprinkle over the leeks. Beat the cream with some salt, plenty of freshly-ground black pepper and 2–3 oz grated cheese. Pour this over the leeks and scatter a little more grated cheese on top. Place the dish under a grill heated to medium-hot and cook for 5 minutes or so until the topping is bubbling hot and golden brown.

SPINACH COULIBIAC
(serves 6)

Winter varieties of spinach have tough stalks which are best removed before cooking. This means you may lose up to half the bought weight so use the larger quantity given in the recipe.

2–3 lb spinach
3 oz brown rice
4 hard-boiled eggs
$\frac{1}{4}$ lb mushrooms
1 onion
$2\frac{1}{2}$ oz butter
1 chicken stock cube
salt and freshly-ground black pepper
1 × 13 oz packet puff pastry
1 beaten egg
$\frac{1}{2}$ pt soured cream
5–6 tablespoons yoghurt

Wash and thoroughly drain the spinach, discarding any tough stalks. Cook the leaves until they wilt. Steaming is definitely the best method for this: don't overfill the steamer, but cook the leaves in batches turning them occasionally so the steam penetrates evenly. Turn the cooked spinach into a colander and leave until cool enough to handle, then squeeze out all moisture and chop roughly.

Meanwhile, cook the rice in the spinach water, boosting flavour with a stock cube; sweat the finely chopped onion in $1\frac{1}{2}$ oz butter. Sauté the sliced mushrooms in the remaining butter, drain well and sprinkle with plenty of salt and pepper. Away from the heat, stir the cooked and drained rice into the onion pan. Add the squeezed and chopped spinach plus a generous seasoning of salt and pepper and mix well. (All these preparations can be done well ahead.)

Roll out the pastry very thinly to about 18 inches square and cut into 2 oblongs, one slightly larger than the other. Put the larger oblong on a greased baking sheet and pile half the spinach, onion and rice mixture on top, leaving a clear 1 inch rim round the edges. Lay half the sliced hard-boiled eggs on top of the spinach mixture, then the mushrooms, the remaining hard-boiled eggs and the rest of the spinach mixture. Cover with the second oblong of pastry and trim to fit. Brush the raw edges with beaten egg, roll and seal firmly. Cut steam slits into the top, decorate with leaves made from pastry trimmings and brush all over with beaten egg. Bake at 425F, 220C, gas mark 7, for about 25 minutes, until golden and well risen.

Serve with a cold sauce: season the yoghurt with salt and pepper, then vigorously stir in the sour cream until smooth and well blended.

MUSHROOMS WITH HAM AND ALMONDS

Served on rounds of crisply fried bread, this makes a delectable first course or savoury snack for 4 people.

$\frac{1}{2}$ lb large flat mushrooms
2 oz ham
$1\frac{1}{2}$ oz flaked and toasted almonds
4 tablespoons fresh chopped parsley
$1\frac{1}{2}$ teaspoons lemon juice
$\frac{1}{4}$ teaspoon coriander seeds
about 2 oz unsalted butter
4 tablespoons freshly-toasted breadcrumbs
salt and freshly-ground black pepper

Wipe the mushrooms clean but do not peel them, and trim stalks level with the caps. Chop the mushroom stalks very finely indeed and also the ham. Put them into a bowl, add the parsley, lemon juice, a little salt and a good grinding of black pepper. Crush the coriander seeds with the back of a spoon and add them.

Put the toasted almond flakes into a polythene bag, squeeze out the air and tie it, then crush with your hands or a rolling pin to break the almonds into small pieces — but not a powder. Stir the almonds into the bowl and check the mixture for seasoning.

Heat the oven to 400F, 200C, gas mark 6. Melt the butter in a small saucepan over low heat. Away from the heat, dip the flat mushrooms into the melted butter, one at a time, to moisten them. Lay them gill side up on a baking tray. Cover each one with a heaped mound of the ham and almond mixture. Sprinkle a few of the toasted breadcrumbs on top, and drizzle a little melted butter on top of that.

Bake the stuffed mushrooms for about 15 minutes, and serve piping hot.

POTATO GNOCCHI

A good and cheap supper dish for 2–3 people. I serve a ragú Bolognese with the gnocchi, or — better still — a pesto sauce.

> 1 lb potatoes
> $\frac{1}{4}$ lb self-raising flour
> 1 oz grated Parmesan cheese
> 1 egg
> about $\frac{1}{2}$ oz butter
> salt, freshly-ground black pepper and freshly-grated nutmeg

Peel and boil the potatoes, then put them through a vegetable mill to make a smooth, dry purée. Season generously with salt, pepper and nutmeg, stir in half the Parmesan and all the sifted flour, then beat in the egg. Spread the mixture on a shallow dish and chill, uncovered, until cold and dry – overnight if you wish.

Divide the mixture into portions. Make each into a long roll about $\frac{1}{4}$ inch in diameter, then cut into $\frac{3}{4}$ inch lengths. Bring a shallow wide pan of salted water to a bare simmer (it must not boil or the gnocchi might disintegrate) and cook the gnocchi in batches, poaching them for about 3 minutes. Lift out with a slotted spoon, drain well and keep hot in a buttered gratin dish while you cook the rest (brush the gnocchi with a little melted butter and sprinkle the remaining half ounce of Parmesan between layers to prevent sticking).

RATATOUILLE
(serves 4)

The important things about ratatouille are not to chop the vegetables too small and not to cook them for too long — or you will end up with mush instead of a tender richly-flavoured vegetable stew.

$\frac{1}{2}$ lb courgettes
$\frac{1}{2}$ lb aubergines
$\frac{1}{2}$ lb small onions
$\frac{3}{4}$ lb tomatoes
2 red peppers
1 green pepper
2 garlic cloves
3 dozen coriander seeds
olive oil
lemon juice
caster sugar
salt and freshly-ground black pepper

Cut the courgettes, without peeling them, into $^1/_3$ inch slices. Cut the aubergines, again without peeling, into $\frac{3}{4}$ inch cubes. Put each vegetable into a separate colander, sprinkling coarse salt between layers. Cover with plates and weigh down. Leave for 30–60 minutes to drain off excess liquid.

Meanwhile, prepare the other ingredients. Slice the onions thinly. De-seed and cut the peppers into chunks. Skin, quarter and de-seed the tomatoes. Pound the coriander seeds with mortar and pestle and mix the spice with 1 teaspoon each lemon juice and sugar, and a good quantity of salt and pepper. Chop the garlic finely.

Warm 6 tablespoons olive oil in a heavy-based pan. Add the onions and garlic and soften over low heat for about 10 minutes. Rinse the aubergines and squeeze them dry gently but thoroughly with kitchen paper towels. Add the aubergines and the peppers to the pan. Turn to coat with oil, then cover the pan and leave to cook very gently for 20 minutes just stirring occasionally.

Rinse and dry the courgettes. Add them to the pan together with the coriander and other seasonings. Stir gently to mix the ingredients, cover the pan and cook for 5 minutes more before adding the tomatoes. Just lay the tomatoes on top of the mixed vegetables, cover the pan and cook for 5 minutes. Finally, stir the tomatoes into the other ingredients and simmer for 5 or so minutes more, this time without a lid, to evaporate some of the juices. Adjust seasoning to taste and serve hot or cold.

CAULIFLOWER WITH CUMIN SAUCE
(serves 4)

This dish can be served alone or as an accompaniment to a meat main course – its delicate and unusual flavour goes well, I think, with boiled ham. But it has the sort of special taste that may not appeal to everyone.

>1 small cauliflower
>a few large and crinkly outer leaves from a cabbage
>3 large egg yolks
>1 tablespoon tarragon vinegar
>$\frac{1}{4}$–$\frac{1}{2}$ teaspoon caster sugar
>$\frac{1}{2}$ teaspoon cumin seeds
>salt and pepper
>2 tablespoons single cream

Leave the cauliflower whole just trimming away tough stalk and leaves. Take out the removable central handle from the steamer so that the cauliflower can be placed whole on the base of the basket. (Thread loops of string through perforations in the 'petals' to make alternative handles for lowering and raising the steamer from the saucepan.)

Steam the cauliflower until tender – about 15–20 minutes. Then arrange it on a warmed shallow dish lined with cabbage leaves which have been blanched in boiling water for 5 minutes, drained and dried.

To make the sauce, reduce the cumin to a powder with pestle and mortar, and put it into the top part of a double-boiler. Add the egg yolks, sugar, salt and pepper. Place over barely simmering water and whisk steadily until thickened and fluffy – about 4 minutes. Away from the heat, whisk in the cream, a spoonful at a time. Pour the sauce over the cauliflower and serve immediately.

NEWLY MINTED CARROTS

Serve this with some hot crusty bread as a first course for 4 people. It will take the edge off their appetites very deliciously before you serve a meat course. Or, if you follow the carrots with, say, an omelette and cheese, the meal will be well-balanced, satisfying — and inexpensive, too.

    1½ lb carrots
    1½ oz butter
    1 tablespoon olive oil
    a good pinch of caster sugar
    3 tablespoons fresh chopped mint
    2 tablespoons fresh chopped chives
    a little salt and a generous grinding of black pepper

Scrub the carrots and top and tail them, then cut them lengthways in half (and in half again if they are thick) and then across to make sticks about 1½ inches long and about ¹/₃ inch thick.

Bring a large pan of salted water to the boil, add the carrots, bring back to the boil and simmer for 3–4 minutes.

Turn the contents of the pan into a colander and let the liquid drain away. Put the pan back on the heat, add the butter and oil and leave to melt. Then add the carrots, 2 tablespoons each of mint and chives, the sugar, a pinch of salt and some pepper. Stir gently to mix everything well, cover with a lid and cook over the lowest possible heat for 10 minutes or so until the carrots are tender but still retain a little bite. Stir occasionally during this time to ensure even cooking.

When the carrots are ready, adjust seasoning to taste, turn them into a hot serving dish, sprinkle another generous tablespoon or so of chopped mint over them, and serve immediately.

RED CABBAGE WITH BACON AND BAKED POTATOES
(serves 2)

I find this warming and cheap supper dish very useful on busy days when I have no time to spend by the stove. To ring the changes I sometimes omit the bacon and serve the vegetables instead with grilled or boiling sausages.

$\frac{1}{2}$ lb streaky bacon rashers
2 oz dried chestnuts (optional)
1 lb red cabbage
1 small onion
4 smallish potatoes weighing about 8 oz each
a little butter and oil
2 tablespoons red wine vinegar
2 tablespoons redcurrant jelly
1 teaspoon coriander seeds
a pinch of allspice
salt and freshly-ground black pepper

De-rind the bacon. Cut each rasher in half, stretch with the back of a knife and roll up. Lay the bacon rolls in a well-buttered casserole (buttering the sides as well as the base of the dish) and scatter the chestnuts among them. Shred the cabbage, mix it with the finely chopped onion, vinegar, redcurrant jelly, crushed coriander, allspice and plenty of salt and pepper. Pile this mixture on top of the bacon, lay a sheet of buttered greaseproof paper over it and cover with a lid.

Scrub the potatoes and prick them. Rub them with a mixture of oil and salt, a messy job but worth it: instead of ending up with elephant-grey, wrinkled skins, the potatoes will be pleasantly crisp and savoury. Place the potatoes on a baking sheet and put it on to a lower shelf in a cold oven. Put the casserole on an upper shelf, and set time and temperature controls to give $3\frac{1}{4}$ hours cooking at 300F, 150C, gas mark 2.

LENTILS WITH TOMATOES
(serves 2)

This is a cold-start recipe which takes a few minutes to prepare in the morning and can be cooked while you are out using the automatic timing and temperature controls on your oven. It makes a good vegetable accompaniment to many of the cold-start meat recipes given in this book (for a full list see under cold-start in the index).

$\frac{1}{4}$ lb whole greeny-brown lentils
a knob of butter
1 × 8 oz can of tomatoes
1 small garlic clove (optional)
cold water
salt and freshly-ground black pepper

Be sure to use whole lentils, not the split variety, for this dish. Rinse the lentils in cold water and remove any little bits of grit. Turn the lentils into a well-buttered ovenproof dish, stir in a good seasoning of pepper (but do not add salt until *after* cooking) and a little crushed garlic if you wish. Roughly chop the tomatoes into their juices and mix with enough cold water to make a generous $\frac{1}{2}$ pt of liquid in total. Pour the liquid over the lentils and cover the dish with a buttered foil lid. Place the dish on the bottom shelf of a cold oven, and set automatic timing and temperature controls so that the oven will turn itself on to 300F, 150C, gas mark 2, 3 hours before you plan to eat.

MUSHROOM, PEPPER AND BARLEY PILAF
(serves 4)

If you like chewy grains, this mixture of barley and autumn vegetables makes a pleasant meatless main course. Serve it with plenty of freshly-grated Parmesan cheese.

$\frac{1}{2}$ lb pearl barley
10–12 oz small cap mushrooms
1 small red pepper
1 small green pepper
6 oz onion
2 fat garlic cloves
$1\frac{1}{2}$ lb tomatoes
a little butter and olive oil
fresh chopped basil
coriander seeds
salt and freshly-ground black pepper

Halve the onions and slice them. Halve or thickly slice the

mushrooms. De-seed the peppers and cut them into strips. Pour boiling water over the tomatoes, drain and peel away skins. Chop the tomato flesh roughly, put it into a liquidiser and reduce to a purée. Crush the garlic.

Heat 2 tablespoons olive oil and about 1 oz butter in a large heavy-based saucepan or a flame-proof casserole. Add the onions and garlic and cook gently for 4–5 minutes until slightly softened. Increase the heat to fairly high, add the mushrooms and cook, stirring occasionally, for 4–5 minutes.

Pour on the tomato purée and bring it quickly to the boil. Season generously with salt and pepper, 3–4 tablespoons chopped fresh basil (use parsley and chives mixed together with a little fresh mint if fresh basil is not available) and some coriander.

Either crush the coriander seeds very thoroughly with a wooden spoon or – easier – grind them in an empty peppermill. Stir in the barley and red and green peppers. Reduce heat to a bare simmer, cover the pan with a well-fitting lid and cook very gently for 45–50 minutes until the liquid is absorbed, the barley swollen and the vegetables perfectly tender.

ALL-PURPOSE TOMATO SAUCE
(makes about 1½ pt)

This is a very useful basic sauce – for example, you can add basil and use it with pork chops, add tarragon to serve with chicken and lamb, add crushed coriander seeds and spoon the sauce over oven-baked fish, and, of course, spike it with garlic and serve it with pasta. The quantity given here is large; it is worth making a lot while you are at it and to freeze any not wanted for immediate use – flavour remains true for 8 months, providing you do not add herbs or garlic until just before serving.

    4 lb ripe tomatoes
    2 celery stalks
    3 tablespoons olive oil (or peanut oil if you prefer)
    1 tablespoon caster sugar
    1 tablespoon lemon juice
    salt and freshly-ground black pepper

Put the tomatoes into your largest mixing bowl. Pour on boiling water to cover and leave for 2 minutes to loosen the skins. Drain, peel away skins and roughly chop the tomato flesh. Heat the oil in a large pan over low heat – choose a good wide pan if possible as a large surface area will help to speed up the evaporation of surplus tomato liquid. Scrub the celery stalks, then chop them up as finely as possible. Put them into the pan and cook very gently for 5 minutes.

Add the tomatoes, sugar and lemon to the pan. Bring the mixture to simmering point quite quickly and give the mixture a good stir. Cook uncovered at a gentle simmer over medium-low heat for about 40 minutes – that is to say until the tomato flesh is reduced to a smooth pulp and most of the liquid has evaporated to give a good sauce consistency.

Stir the sauce from time to time as it cooks to prevent sticking: this is particularly important towards the end of cooking time.

When the sauce is ready, season it with a little salt and pepper plus extra lemon juice and sugar if you wish, and a spoonful or so of concentrated tomato purée if you want a richer mahogany-coloured sauce. But do remember that it is always best to be mean when seasoning foods to be frozen: you can always add more after defrosting.

PIZZA NAPOLITANA
(serves 4)

The filling, like the shape of the pizza, can of course be varied to taste. Those with robust digestions may like to replace some or all of the tomatoes with onions chopped and gently stewed in olive oil. Sliced and sautéed mushrooms, or strips of grilled red pepper, or slices of spicy sausage (such as chorizio or cabanos) make good alternatives to anchovies and olives.

For the dough:
½ lb strong plain flour
¼ oz dried yeast
a pinch of caster sugar

1 teaspoon salt
1 medium-sized egg
2 tablespoons olive oil

For the filling:
$\frac{3}{4}$ pt all-purpose tomato sauce (see page 211)
about 3 teaspoons fresh marjoram or $1\frac{1}{2}$ teaspoons dried
   oregano
1 or 2 garlic cloves
1 teaspoon caster sugar
salt and freshly-ground black pepper
$1 \times 1\frac{3}{4}$ oz can of anchovy fillets
about 18 small black olives
a Mozzarella cheese (optional)

Measure 3 tablespoons warm water into a cup. (One part boiling water mixed with two parts cold water is ideal for reactivating dried yeast).

Stir a pinch of sugar into the warm water and, as soon as dissolved, sprinkle on the dried yeast. Set aside for 10–15 minutes until the yeast has frothed up.

Meanwhile, warm a large mixing bowl by filling it with freshly boiled water, lightly oil a sheet of clingfilm large enough to cover the top of the bowl, weigh the flour, and assemble the other dough ingredients.

Empty the water out of the mixing bowl and thoroughly dry it. Sift the flour and salt into the bowl and make a well in the centre. Measure the oil into the well. Add the egg, mixing it lightly into the oil with a fork.

Immediately pour the frothy yeast mixture into the well, mix it with the egg and oil, then quickly draw the flour into the liquid and mix until the dough begins to bind together and leaves the sides of the bowl to form one mass. (Add an extra spoonful or so of warm water if necessary – some brands of flour absorb liquid more readily than others.)

Press the dough into a ball with your hands and turn it out on to a work surface.

Flour your hands lightly and knead the dough until it is plump, smooth and quite elastic. How you knead does not really matter (the most popular method involves pushing part of the dough away from you, folding the dough back on itself, giving it a quarter turn, then repeating these movements over and over again). The aim is simply to push and stretch the dough so that the gluten in the flour is strengthened, which will give a good rise.

Put the kneaded dough back into the mixing bowl. Cover the bowl with oiled clingfilm, and set aside until the dough has doubled in size, becomes spongy and light and slightly sticky when touched. How long it will take to rise depends on the ambient temperature – about $1\frac{1}{2}$–2 hours in a warm place such as an airing cupboard (*don't* put it over a radiator: this would heat and toughen the bottom of the dough instead of surrounding the dough with even warmth), or about twice as long at average room temperature (65–70F, 18–21C) or about 8 hours in a cold larder.

To make the filling, put into a saucepan $\frac{3}{4}$ pt all-purpose tomato sauce. Add to the saucepan about 2 teaspoons chopped fresh marjoram or 1 teaspoon dried oregano, 1 teaspoon caster sugar and garlic crushed with a little salt. Simmer the sauce, uncovered, until reduced to half a pint or less – it should be very well flavoured and very thick. Stir occasionally while it cooks, particularly towards the end to prevent sticking and burning. Season to taste with salt and freshly ground black pepper.

Turn the risen dough onto a work surface – it will be puffy and soft. Knock it back, that is, punch it a few times with a clenched fist to flatten it and get rid of air pockets.

Knead it again, just for a minute or two, then shape it – into 4 individual rounds about 4 inches in diameter (placing them on a baking sheet), or to fit two 8 inch flan tins with removable bases, or to fill one baking tray measuring about 9 × 12 inches. Whichever shape you choose, first brush the metal base with oil (olive oil gives the right Italian flavour). Put the ball of dough on to the oiled surface, flatten it and push it into shape using your knuckles.

Raise the edges slightly to make a rim to contain the filling nicely.

Spoon the warm tomato mixture directly onto the dough, spreading it evenly. Top with anchovy fillets, just snipped into little pieces or cut in half lengthways and arranged in a lattice pattern if you like.

Sprinkle on the olives and another seasoning of marjoram or oregano, then drizzle a little oil from the anchovy can on top. Switch the oven to 425F, 220C, gas mark 7 and set the pizza(s) to one side. During the 15–20 minutes the oven takes to heat up the dough will recover from handling and start to rise again – called proving, that is, proving that the yeast is still active.

Bake the pizzas for 15 minutes in the hot oven. Then reduce heat to 375F, 190C, gas mark 5, (if you are using Mozzarella, slice it and lay it over the top of the pizza at this stage) and bake the pizzas for a further 10–15 minutes.

Puddings

EASY APRICOT SOUFFLÉ
(serves 6)

A rather impressive store-cupboard pudding, and a good way to use up leftover egg whites.

> 1 lb apricot jam
> finely grated zest of 1 orange
> 1 scant teaspoon ground cinnamon
> 5 large egg whites
> 1 tablespoon ground almonds
> 1 tablespoon flaked almonds

Heat the oven to 400F, 200C, gas mark 6, placing a baking sheet on an upper shelf. Toast the flaked almonds in the oven while it heats up. Reserve them. Lightly butter a large soufflé dish and sprinkle the base and sides with the ground almonds. Turn the jam into a large mixing bowl. Add the grated orange zest and cinnamon, and beat with a wooden spoon until the mixture is smoothly blended and slightly runny.

When the oven has reached the correct temperature, whisk the egg whites until they stand in peaks. Fold them gently but thoroughly into the apricot mixture. Turn the mixture into the prepared soufflé dish.

Place the soufflé dish on the hot baking sheet, immediately reduce oven temperature to 375F, 190C, gas mark 5, and cook for about 25 minutes. Sprinkle flaked almonds over the top and serve immediately while hot, golden and well risen — alone or with pouring cream.

APPLE MARMALADE

This must be the most useful of all apple recipes. It freezes very well indeed and, because it is fairly reduced, won't take up the whole of your freezer. It is equally good served hot or cold and forms the basis for literally dozens of delicious puddings.

You can fold the purée into whisked egg whites to make apple snow, fold it into thick yoghurt or crème patissière to make apple fool, top it with chilled whipped cream and glaze it with sugar to make apple brulée, use it to sandwich meringues or a sponge cake, spread it over the base of a blind-baked pastry case to make apple tart, layer it in glasses with crumbled shortbread biscuits and grated chocolate for an instant pudding, top it with meringue mixture and bake, and use it as the filling for a traditional apple charlotte or apple cheesecake.

> 2 lb Bramley apples
> 1 quince (if available)
> 1 lemon
> 4–5 oz caster sugar
> 1 oz unsalted butter
> ground cinnamon, allspice or cloves to taste

Heat the oven to 325F, 160C, gas mark 3. Peel, core and thinly slice the apples and put them into a flame-proof casserole. If a quince is used (and I find that even a small one adds greatly to the fragrance of the dish), peel, core and grate it into the casserole. Add the juice and finely grated zest of lemon. Cover with a lid and cook in the oven for 40 minutes or so until the apples are very tender but not disintegrating.

Turn the fruit into a sieve and leave for 5 minutes or more to drain off all the juices. Then return the fruit to the casserole, and beat it with a balloon whisk to make a fluffy purée. Add the butter, sugar and spices. Place over medium heat and cook, stirring fairly frequently, for a good 15 minutes to drive off as much moisture as possible. Use hot or cold.

APPLE BRULÉE
(serves 6)

An excellent and inexpensive alternative to the popular dinner party pudding of peeled grapes with brulée topping.

1 quantity of apple marmalade (see page 218)
½ pt double cream
caster sugar (or a few spoonfuls of praliné)

Spoon the apple marmalade into 6 individual soufflé dishes, so that it half fills each of them, and chill very thoroughly. Whip the cream until stiff and spread it over the top of each pudding, so that the dishes are nearly filled. Chill again − preferably overnight. For a very simple and delicious praliné topping, sprinkle a little crushed praliné over the top of each pudding just before serving: don't add it far in advance or it may start to soften and seep into the cream.

To make a classic brulée topping, about 2 hours before you plan to serve the puddings, heat the grill until very hot indeed. Sprinkle a thin, even layer of caster sugar over the top of each pudding, taking care to cover the cream completely at the edges as well as the centre of the dish. Arrange the dishes on a baking sheet, stand it on the grid of the grill pan, and place the pan under the piping hot grill. If the sugar topping comes almost to the brim of the dishes and the dishes are placed really close to the heat, the sugar should melt and caramelise quickly without danger of melting the cream. Turn the dishes as necessary (I've never yet come across a grill that provides really even heat) to colour the sugar evenly, then chill the puddings again so that the toppings set to brittle golden brown sheets of sugar.

FIG PUDDING
(serves 4–6)

Steamed puddings can be a bit stodgy and heavy. This one has a lovely light open texture, and spicy warm flavour.

$\frac{1}{2}$ lb dried figs
juice and finely grated zest of 1 large lemon
$\frac{1}{4}$ lb butter
$\frac{1}{4}$ lb soft dark brown sugar
2 eggs
2 oz fresh white breadcrumbs
2 oz self-raising flour
$\frac{1}{2}$ teaspoon each baking powder, ground cinnamon and mixed spice

Remove fig stalks, chop the flesh and soak it in the lemon juice and zest while you prepare the rest of the pudding.

Bring a large pan half-filled with water to the boil. Generously butter a 2 pt pudding basin and a large circle of kitchen foil.

Cream the butter and sugar together until soft and fluffy. Beat in the eggs one at a time. Sift the flour, baking powder, cinnamon and mixed spice together. Fold them into the butter, sugar and egg mixture. Fold in the breadcrumbs, and finally the chopped figs and all their juices. The mixture should be of slightly stiff dropping consistency – if the lemon was rather small it may be necessary to add a few drops of milk.

Turn the mixture into the prepared basin. Cover it with the pleated and buttered foil, tie securely, lower carefully into the pan of boiling water, top with a well-fitting lid and cook at a fast simmer for 2 hours. Top up with extra boiling water as necessary. Invert the cooked pudding on to a warmed plate and serve with custard or a fruit sauce.

ANGEL CAKE
(serves 8–10)

This famous American recipe is superb and I know of no better way to use up a large number of leftover egg whites. For perfect results, be sure to handle the ingredients very lightly and quickly.

10 egg whites
1 oz cornflour
3 oz plain flour
½ lb caster sugar
a good pinch of salt
1 tablespoon lemon juice
1 tablespoon hot water
1 teaspoon cream of tartar
2 oranges
½–2 lb fresh strawberries or raspberries

You will need an angel cake tin or similar mould about 8½ inches in diameter and 4 inches deep, with a central funnel and a removable base. Be sure it is absolutely greaseless.

Heat the oven to 350F, 180C, gas mark 4. Sift both flours into a bowl. Sift the salt and about one-third of the sugar into the same bowl. Then sift the combined ingredients at least twice more, lifting the sieve high above the bowl to aerate the mixture as much as possible. Set aside. Grate the orange zest finely and set aside.

Divide the egg whites, lemon juice and water between your two largest mixing bowls. Whisk the contents of one bowl until foamy, add half the cream of tartar and whisk again until the egg whites stand in stiff peaks.

Using a rotary whisk is best: it is admittedly more tiring on the wrists than using an electric whisk, but it will give greater volume to the egg whites and therefore result in a lighter cake. If you have to use an electric whisk, add a little sugar with the cream of tartar – this will minimise the risk of overbeating the egg whites.

Whisk the contents of the second bowl in exactly the same way, incorporating the remaining cream of tartar (plus a little sugar if you have to use an electric whisk), then tip the contents of the first bowl into the second.

Sift and whisk in the remaining caster sugar, a tablespoon at a time, adding the orange zest with the last spoonful of sugar. Then gradually sift the flour mixture on to the egg whites and fold it in thoroughly but very delicately indeed. Don't add more than a spoonful or two of the flour mixture at a time.

Turn the mixture into the cake tin or mould. Draw a knife through the mixture to release any large air pockets, and level the surface. Bake just below the centre of the oven for 45 minutes or until the surface of the cake feels firm and springs back when lightly pressed.

Invert the cake tin on to a cooling rack, but do not lift the tin away from the cake until the cake is absolutely cold – about $1\frac{1}{2}$ hours.

Just before serving, fill the centre of the cake with hulled fresh strawberries or raspberries (you will need about $\frac{1}{2}$ lb) and very lightly dust the top of the cake with sifted icing sugar. If you wish to serve an accompanying sauce, sieve the rest of the berries. Heighten fruit flavour by stirring in a little fresh fruit juice (about 1 tablespoon lemon juice and 2 tablespoons orange juice) and, if you wish, sweeten with a spoonful or so of sifted icing sugar.

BANANA CUSTARD CREAM
(serves 4–6)

This delicious variation on the ever-popular sliced bananas with cream is a good way to encourage children to take their daily quota of milk, but adults seem to love it too. It is very quick to prepare: cook the custard one day, then top and serve it when cold the next day.

$\frac{3}{4}$ pt milk
3 medium-sized eggs
2 tablespoons caster sugar
2 medium-sized bananas
$\frac{1}{4}$ pt double cream

Put 2 whole eggs plus one egg yolk into a bowl. Scald the milk and, away from the heat, stir in the sugar. When melted, pour the sweetened liquid on to the eggs in a thin stream – whisking all the time. Strain through a nylon sieve into a soufflé dish.

Cover the dish with a foil 'lid' and stand it in a roasting pan containing enough freshly-boiled water to come halfway up the sides of the dish. Bake for about 45 minutes in an oven preheated to 325F, 160C, gas mark 3. Uncover the cooked custard and let it cool, then cover it again and refrigerate overnight. Shortly before serving, peel and slice the bananas. Arrange the slices, like tiles on a roof, over the top of the custard. Whip the cream softly. Whisk the remaining egg white until stiff, then gently fold it into the cream. Spread the soft creamy mixture over the bananas, and the pudding is ready to serve. For extra flavour and colour, a little grated chocolate or ground cinnamon can be sprinkled on top of the cream if you wish.

GOOSEBERRY CRUMBLE
(serves 6)

Not a traditional hot crumble, but an attractively layered cold pudding.

1 lb gooseberries
$\frac{1}{4}$ lb caster sugar
scant 1 teaspoon gelatine powder
$\frac{1}{2}$ pt double cream
1–2 tablespoons icing sugar

For the crumble:
3 oz wholemeal flour
$1\frac{1}{2}$ oz desiccated coconut
$1\frac{1}{2}$ oz demerara sugar
$1\frac{1}{2}$ oz butter

Rinse, top and tail the gooseberries. Put them into a casserole, strew with the caster sugar and add 1 tablespoon water. Cover and cook at 325F, 160C, gas mark 3, for about 45 minutes or until the fruit is tender. Set aside, still covered, until cold.

Increase oven temperature to 400F, 200C, gas mark 6. Rub the flour, coconut, sugar and butter together. Spread the mixture on a baking tray and cook for 10–15 minutes. Allow it to become quite cold before crumbling finely.

Turn the contents of the casserole into a sieve placed over a bowl to drain off the liquid. Dissolve the gelatine powder in 3 tablespoons of water and blend it into the gooseberry liquid. Pour the mixture into a glass bowl and chill until set to a jelly. Crush the gooseberries lightly with a fork and sprinkle them with 1–2 tablespoons icing sugar. Whip the cream, fold it into the crushed gooseberries and pile it on top of the set jelly. Sprinkle the crumble mixture over the top just before serving the pudding.

ZABAGLIONE
(serves 3–4)

This sophisticated and foamy Italian pudding takes little more than 5 minutes to cook, but it must be cooked just before serving. If you always keep eggs and a bottle of Marsala in the house, it is the perfect pudding for emergency occasions.

4 large egg yolks
2 oz caster sugar
6 tablespoons Marsala
1 teaspoon finely grated lemon zest

Fill 3 or 4 small wine glasses with hot water and let them stand for 5 minutes to warm them through, then empty and dry them. Meanwhile bring some water to a bare simmer in the bottom part of a double-boiler. Away from the heat, break the egg yolks into the top part of the double-boiler and add the sugar.

Place the egg and sugar mixture over the pan of barely simmering water. Whisk with a rotary or electric whisk for about 2 minutes until the mixture begins to thicken. Add the Marsala and lemon zest and continue whisking until the mixture is the consistency of very softly whipped cream and has almost doubled in bulk – about 4–5 minutes. Pour the zabaglione into the warmed glasses and serve immediately – with sponge finger biscuits or macaroons if available.

PUFFED PEARS
(serves 4)

This is a good way to cook little green pears that are so hard you think they must be carved from wood.

1 lb cooking pears
1 tablespoon lemon juice
2 tablespoons unsalted butter
4 tablespoons runny honey
3 oz plain flour
3 tablespoons icing sugar
generous ½ teaspoon ground cinnamon
2 eggs
¼ pt milk

Heat the oven to 425F, 220C, gas mark 7, and peel, core and quarter the pears. Measure 1 tablespoon butter, the lemon juice and honey into a casserole and put the casserole into the oven for a minute or so to warm and mingle the ingredients. Turn the pears in the mixture, lay them in a single layer, cover the casserole and cook for 30–40 minutes until the fruit begins to soften.

Make the batter by sifting the flour, icing sugar and cinnamon together. Beat the eggs and milk, then whisk them slowly into the dry ingredients to make a smooth cream.

Heat a really large flan dish – I use a Pyrex one which is 12 inches in diameter – and melt the remaining tablespoon of butter. Transfer the partially cooked pears to the flan dish (reserve the casserole juices to serve as a sauce with the pudding). Pour on the batter and bake for about 35 minutes until puffed up and golden.

PLUM PUDDING
(serves 4–6)

Not a Christmas pud but an autumnal version of summer pudding. Stoning the plums is a nuisance but important if the pudding is to slice well for serving.

2 lb plums
1 large orange
4 inch cinnamon stick broken into small pieces and tied up in
    butter-muslin with 4 cloves
about 3 oz each caster and soft brown sugar
about 8 slices slightly stale bread

Halve and stone the plums. Put them into a casserole. Add the bag of spices and the juice and finely grated zest of the orange. Cover and bake at 325F, 160C, gas mark 3, for 20 minutes. Stir in the sugars (sugar tends to harden plum skins which is why I don't add it at the beginning) and continue baking until the fruit is tender. Remove the spice bag and squeeze the juices back into the casserole.

Line the base and sides of a $1\frac{1}{2}$–2 pt pudding basin with the crustless bread. Lift the fruit out of the casserole with a slotted spoon and pack it into the basin with some of the juice. Cover with a bread lid, top with a plate, weight it down and chill for several hours.

Run a palette knife between the bread and the basin sides to loosen the pudding. Invert it on to a serving dish and baste with some of the casserole juices until well coloured and juicy. Serve any leftover juices in a sauceboat.

CRÊPES SUZETTE
(serves 4–6)

Crêpes can be made up to 5 days before serving if you wish. Cool them on a cake rack – this allows steam to escape which prevents them from becoming rubbery. Stack when cold, interleaving them with sheets of greaseproof paper, wrap the stack in foil and refrigerate. Reheat by placing the foil-wrapped parcel in an oven heated to 375F, 190C, gas mark 5 for about 20 minutes, then finish off the crêpes in the Suzette sauce.

For the batter:
$\frac{1}{4}$ lb plain flour
1 teaspoon caster sugar
a pinch of salt

2 eggs
½ teaspoon orange zest
1 tablespoon Cointreau
4½ fl. oz each milk and water
2 tablespoons melted butter

For the sauce and for flaming:
1 oz caster sugar
2 oranges
3 oz unsalted butter
1 tablespoon Cointreau
about 3 tablespoons brandy

Sift the flour, sugar and salt into a bowl, and make a well in the centre. Lightly beat the eggs, orange zest, Cointreau, milk and water, pour them into the well and gradually whisk in the dry ingredients to make a creamy, perfectly smooth batter. Stir in the cool, melted butter.

Rub a 6 inch pancake or omelette pan with lightly buttered paper and thoroughly warm it over medium-low heat. Draw the pan to one side. Hold it in one hand and a spoon in the other hand. Add about 1½ tablespoons of batter to the pan, shaking and tilting the pan until the entire base is thinly coated.

Place the pan over the heat and cook for 45–60 seconds until the bottom of the crêpe has dried out to a pale golden brown. Shake the pan to check that the crêpe is not sticking. If necessary loosen the edge of the crêpe with a palette knife, then turn over. (Toss it if feeling flamboyant!)

I lift one edge of the crêpe with my fingers and flip it over gently. Cook on the second side for less than 30 seconds, then slide the crêpe out on to a warm plate.

Cook the rest of the batter in the same way, making a total of 16–18 very thin and very tender crêpes. Stir the batter occasionally to check that the orange zest is evenly distributed.

Rub the base and the sides of the pan with buttered paper occasionally, barely filming it with fat — the aim is to prevent sticking, the crêpes must not be fried in fat or they will be crisp and tough. Keep the cooked crêpes warm in a low oven, arranging them slightly overlapping in a circle on a warm plate.

To make the sauce and to finish the crêpes, first mix the caster sugar with the finely grated orange zest on a saucer. Squeeze the orange juice and measure it – you will need $4\frac{1}{2}$–5 fl. oz. Put the diced butter into a 10–12 inch frying pan. Add the orange-flavoured sugar, the orange juice and the Cointreau. Set over very low heat.

When the butter and sugar are completely melted, and the ingredients are well blended, add the first crêpe to the pan. Turn it to moisten both sides with the sauce, then fold it in half and in half again to make a triangle. Waiters do this with a flourish of spoons but using fingers is quicker and easier for mere mortals.

Slide the folded crêpe to the edge of the pan farthest from you. Soak and fold the rest of the crêpes, one at a time, and arrange them slightly overlapping, at the back of the pan. Tilt the pan occasionally so that the sauce runs to the front to moisten each crêpe as you fold it.

When all the crêpes are folded, increase heat very slightly. Let the crêpes slip and slide round the pan very gently until very hot and the sauce is bubbling.

Strew the crêpes with a little extra caster sugar and switch off the heat. Quickly warm the brandy in a small pan. Pour it over the crêpes, set it alight, and triumphantly carry the dish to the table.

GINGERED BUTTERSCOTCH PUDDING
(serves 6)

Loved by children and appreciated by many sweet-toothed adults – but for my taste a squeeze of lemon juice is needed.

    1 oz butter
    3 oz soft brown sugar
    3 oz golden syrup
    1 pt milk
    3 tablespoons cornflour
    4 ginger biscuits
    1–2 bananas

Heat the butter, sugar and syrup together very slowly, stirring until the sugar has lost its grittiness. Continue cooking over very low heat for a further 3–4 minutes until the mixture becomes a rich butterscotch. Draw the pan to one side and pour in all but 3 tablespoons of the milk – take care, the mixture may bubble up angrily. Return the pan to the heat and stir gently until the milk is hot and smoothly blended into the butterscotch.

Mix the remaining cold milk and cornflour together in a cup. Carefully blend the contents of the cup into the pan and stir continuously until the mixture boils and thickens. Pour into a shallow dish and set aside in a cool place for 3 hours or so. Top with crushed ginger biscuits and sliced banana just before serving.

BLACKBERRY CRUMBLE
(serves 2)

Blackberries gently warmed until their juices flow make one of the most heady scents in the world. The contrast between warm fruit, thick chilled cream and crumbly shortbread is delectable.

$\frac{3}{4}$ lb fresh blackberries
$2\frac{1}{2}$ oz caster sugar (preferably from a jar in which vanilla pods are stored)
1–$1\frac{1}{2}$ teaspoons fresh lemon juice
3 shortbread finger biscuits
3–4 fl. oz double cream

Hull and pick over the blackberries, then rinse and drain them. The best way to wash blackberries (and all other soft, easily bruised berry fruit) is to put them into a colander, then dip the colander gently in and out of a sinkful of cold water. Do this several times, then leave the colander on the draining board for 10 minutes or so.

Turn the berries out on to kitchen paper to dry them.

Chill the cream for several hours beforehand, but cook the blackberries only shortly before serving. Reduce the biscuits to very coarse crumbs, either breaking them up with your fingers or putting the biscuits into a polythene bag and beating it a few times with a rolling pin.

Whip the cream softly. Put the blackberries into a saucepan

with a large surface area so they lie in a shallow layer. Sprinkle them with the lemon juice and strew them with the sugar. Cover the pan with a lid and shake it to distribute the sugar among the fruit. Place the pan over very low heat for as long as it takes to melt the sugar and to start the blackberry juices flowing, about 4–5 minutes.

Shake the pan again and switch off the heat but leave the covered pan where it is for a further 5 minutes or so. The residue heat will continue to warm and soften the fruit, but there will be no danger of the berries disintegrating.

Pile the blackberries and their juices into 2 glasses or individual bowls. Sprinkle on most of the biscuits. Spoon on the cream: some of it will trickle down the sides of the glasses to melt and mingle with the fruit juices. Top with the remaining shortbread crumbs and serve immediately.

RICH CUSTARD TART
(serves 6–8)

Quiche Lorraine is the classic savoury custard baked in shortcrust. This spicy sweet custard tart is made in the same way.

For the pastry:
6 oz plain flour
3 oz butter
1 heaped teaspoon caster sugar
2 tablespoons cold water

For the filling:
3 eggs
$\frac{1}{4}$ pt single cream and 8 fl. oz gold top milk (or 8 fl. oz single cream and $\frac{1}{4}$ pt milk)
2 tablespoons soft brown sugar
the zest of 1 orange
$\frac{3}{4}$ teaspoon ground cinnamon
a pinch of ground cloves and a good scrape of freshly-grated nutmeg

Put a baking sheet in the oven and heat the oven to 350F, 180C, gas mark 4. Make the pastry in the usual way and use it to line a

9 or 10 inch flan tin with removable base. Prick the pastry with a fork, place the flan tin on the baking sheet and blind bake for 15 minutes. Separate one of the eggs and use the white to brush the inside of the pastry case. Blind bake for a further 5 minutes, then reduce oven temperature to 325F, 160C, gas mark 3. Meanwhile prepare the custard. Lightly beat the 3 egg yolks and 2 whites in a bowl. Add the spices and beat again. Scald the liquids and stir in the sugar, then carefully blend the liquids into the eggs.

Sprinkle the finely grated orange zest over the base of the pastry case. Carefully pour on the custard, straining it through a nylon sieve. Place the flan tin on the hot baking sheet and bake for 30–40 minutes until the custard has set. Let the custard cool slightly before serving (it is at its very best eaten warm, I think) or allow it to become completely cold.

SCENTED LEMON SORBET
(serves 12 or more)

The inclusion of herbs adds subtle fragrance to this refreshing sorbet. It is worth making a large quantity as the sorbet will, of course, keep well in a freezer or icemaking compartment of a fridge for many weeks.

> 6 juicy lemons
> a good bunch of fresh garden mint (or pineapple mint or lemon balm)
> $\frac{3}{4}$ lb caster sugar
> 2 egg whites
> $1\frac{1}{2}$ pt water

Put a loaf or cake tin of at least 3 pt capacity into the icebox to chill, and turn the fridge to its coldest setting. Measure the sugar and water into a pan. Add the grated zest of the lemons, and set over low heat. When the sugar is melted, bring the syrup to the boil and simmer gently for a few minutes. Remove the pan from the heat and stir in about 10 tablespoons of freshly chopped herbs. Add the juice of the lemons (there should be 8 fl. oz or just over) plus the fleshy pulp and pips, and stir again. Turn the mixture into a bowl and set aside until completely cold.

Strain the liquid into the chilled loaf or cake tin, using a nylon sieve and pressing the pulp with a wooden spoon to extract all the juices. Cover the tin with a double layer of foil and freeze for $1-1\frac{1}{2}$ hours.

Just before taking the mixture out of the icebox, whisk the egg whites, but not stiffly. Scrape the semi-frozen lemon mixture out of the tin into a large bowl and beat it with a rotary whisk until slushy. Then beat it gradually into the egg whites — I add about one-sixth of the mixture at a time. Spoon the mixture back into the tin, cover and freeze for a further hour or so.

Turn it out and beat with the whisk again (this second beating makes for a smoother textured sorbet). Then return the mixture to the tin, cover and freeze to a solid white snow before returning the fridge to its normal setting.

ASCOT PUDDING
(serves 6)

Chocolate and meringue combine deliciously in this pudding which is a winner with children.

For the sponge:
$\frac{1}{4}$ lb butter
$\frac{1}{4}$ lb caster sugar
2 egg yolks
$\frac{1}{4}$ lb plain flour
$\frac{1}{4}$ teaspoon bicarbonate of soda
$\frac{1}{2}$ teaspoon cream of tartar
3 tablespoons cocoa powder
up to $\frac{1}{4}$ pt milk

For the sauce:
2 oz each granulated sugar and cocoa powder
8 fl. oz boiling water

For the topping:
2 egg whites
3 oz caster sugar

Heat the oven to 350F, 180C, gas mark 4, and lightly butter a 3 pt soufflé or baking dish. Cream the butter and sugar together until light and fluffy. Beat in the egg yolks, then the flour sifted together with the bicarbonate of soda, cream of tartar and cocoa powder. Stir in as much of the milk as is needed to give a very soft dropping consistency. Turn the mixture into the dish and hollow the centre. Dissolve the sauce ingredients in the boiling water and pour them carefully over the pudding, put the dish in the oven and bake for 45 minutes – by the end of which time the sauce will have seeped through the sponge to make a chocolatey pool at the bottom of the dish.

Make a meringue mixture with the egg whites and 3 oz caster sugar. Use it to cover the sponge, taking it right up to the edges of the dish. Reduce oven temperature to 300F, 150C, gas mark 2, and bake for a further 45 minutes. A little longer will do no harm; in fact I think a crisp meringue is nicer.

CLAFOUTIS LIMOUSIN
(serves 6)

This sweet batter has a relatively small proportion of flour to liquid; and the texture of the finished dish is more custard-like than a Yorkshire pudding batter. Traditionally made with fresh cherries, it works well with tinned cherries too, and I've made it successfully using peeled and thickly sliced apples.

$\frac{3}{4}$–1 lb black cherries
3 eggs
3 oz caster sugar
$2\frac{1}{2}$ oz plain flour
$\frac{1}{2}$ teaspoon of ground cinnamon
$\frac{1}{2}$ pt creamy milk (or, for a special occasion, scant $\frac{1}{2}$ pt milk plus 2 tablespoons kirsch or rum)
2 tablespoons melted butter
a little icing sugar

Heat the oven to 375F, 190C, gas mark 5. Butter a really large shallow dish – I use an 11 or 12 inch flan dish – scatter the cherries over the base and sprinkle them with a tablespoon of the sugar.

Tip the rest of the sugar into a mixing bowl. Add the eggs and beat them into the sugar with an electric or rotary whisk. Sift in the cinnamon and flour mixed together, and continue whisking until the mixture is perfectly smooth.

Gradually beat in the milk (and kirsch or rum if using) and, finally, the cool melted butter. Pour the batter over the fruit and bake for 45 minutes until puffed up and lightly browned. Clafoutis is best served warm rather than hot from the oven – it will sink slightly as it cools. Dust with sifted icing sugar and serve, cut into wedges, with cream.

NOT-SO-FATTENING CHEESECAKE
(serves 10–12)

No cheesecake can hope to help you lose weight of course but this one is relatively low on calories. Of the various commercial varieties of fromage blanc available in delicatessens (and some of the more enlightened supermarkets, such as Waitrose) I think Gervais green label is the best.

For the biscuit base:
7 oz digestive biscuits
1½ teaspoons ground cinnamon
3 oz butter

For the filling:
1 lb thickened slimline yoghurt or fromage blanc
½ lb curd cheese
1 orange
1 lemon
3 eggs (separated)
2½ oz caster sugar
2 tablespoons gelatine powder

Lightly oil the sides of a 9 inch cake tin with springclip sides. Reduce the biscuits to crumbs (the easiest way is to put the biscuits into a heavy-duty polythene bag, to secure it tightly excluding all air and to crush with a rolling pin). Add the cinnamon and shake the bag of crumbs well to distribute the flavouring. Gently melt the butter, stir in the cinnamon crumbs, press the mixture firmly and evenly over the base of the tin and refrigerate. Grate the orange and lemon zest very finely into a large mixing bowl.

Squeeze the citrus juice into a small saucepan, sprinkle on the gelatine, soak for 5 minutes, then dissolve over low heat and set aside to cool slightly.

Meanwhile add the sugar and egg yolks to the mixing bowl, and cream them with the citrus zest until fluffy and light. Sieve the curd cheese into the bowl and beat vigorously until the mixture is very smooth and thick. Gradually beat in the fromage blanc or thickened slimline yoghurt and then the cooling gelatine.

Finally, whisk the egg whites until they stand in peaks, and fold them gently but thoroughly into the cheesecake mixture. Pour it into the prepared tin and level the creamy surface with a palette knife. Cover the tin with a dome of foil and refrigerate the cheesecake for 4 hours or more before serving.

CHOCOLATE JUNKET
(*serves 2*)

Cool, creamy and marvellously quick to prepare. Bottles of liquid rennet can be bought from old-fashioned grocers. Supermarkets usually sell junket tablets: crush them and follow manufacturer's instructions.

$1\frac{1}{2}$ oz plain dessert chocolate
$\frac{1}{2}$ pt creamy milk
$\frac{1}{2}$ teaspoon caster sugar
$\frac{1}{2}$ teaspoon liquid junket rennet
3–4 fl. oz double or whipping cream
a spoonful or two of soured cream (optional)

Grate 1 oz chocolate into a small pan. Add the sugar and milk and stir gently over low heat until the sugar and chocolate are melted and the liquid is warmed to blood temperature – 98F/37C. Don't let it get any hotter than this or the milk won't make junket successfully. If, like me, you are bad at gauging temperatures it is wise to use a thermometer.

Away from the heat, stir in the rennet. When the mixture is well blended divide it between 2 small bowls and leave undisturbed at room temperature for about 3 hours or until set. Just before serving, whip the cream. Fold in the stiffly whisked egg white if using (it makes the cream lighter and fresher tasting as well as increasing its bulk). Cover each junket with generous dollops of the creams (the inclusion of soured cream is optional but it makes for lighter and fresher-tasting results). Cover each junket with generous dollops of the cream and grate the remaining chocolate over the top.

PROFITEROLES
(serves 4–6)

Profiteroles, freshly-salted almonds and ripe red cherries all have one thing in common for me — they are compulsive eating.

For the choux pastry:
2½ oz plain flour
2 oz butter
a pinch of salt
1 teaspoon caster sugar
2 eggs

For the cream filling:
generous ¼ pt double cream
3 tablespoons soured cream or single cream

Heat the oven to 425F, 220C, gas mark 7. Rub a baking sheet with buttered paper.

Sift the flour on to a sheet of greaseproof paper. Put ¼ pt cold water into a small saucepan, add the butter, cut up into small dice, the salt and the sugar. Set over low heat until the butter and sugar are melted, then bring to a rapid boil. Immediately remove the pan from the heat, quickly shoot the flour into the pan, and beat with a wooden spoon until the dough is smooth and leaves the sides of the pan clean. Turn the ball of dough into a mixing bowl.

Break the white of one egg into a small bowl by itself. Put the yolk and the other whole egg into a second bowl and whisk lightly with a fork. Beat the egg white with a balloon whisk only long enough to make a very soft, snowy foam.

Add the yolk mixture to the dough, a large spoonful at a time, beating it in with the wooden spoon. Then beat in as much of the egg white as is needed to make a very smooth, glossy dough (with some brands of flour you may not need every drop). Beat swiftly but thoroughly – because it is the beaten eggs which will make the pastry swell into large featherlight golden bubbles during baking.

I'm too ham-fisted to pipe the dough. Instead I use two teaspoons to shape it into 30 flat blobs, spacing them at intervals on the baking sheet – homely looking rather than professionally perfect but the end results taste just as scrumptious!

Quickly put the baking sheet into the oven, on a shelf just above the centre, and bake for 15 minutes. Then reduce the oven temperature to 375F, 190C, gas mark 5, and bake for a further 15 minutes.

I must admit that I find it very tempting indeed to peek and/or to remove the tiny choux buns from the oven before the full half hour is up – they smell mouthwateringly inviting and puff up very quickly. But I have learned from bitter experience that it really is worth being patient. Those golden bubbles need time to set: if removed from the oven too soon they quickly collapse and become flabby.

When the half hour is up remove the baking sheet from the oven and turn off the heat. Quickly make a slit half-way round the 'waist' of each bun, then return them to the cooling oven for 4–5 minutes. This is to allow the steam trapped inside each bun to be released and the centre of the pastry to dry out.

Let the profiteroles cool on a wire tray. Once cold, the sooner they are served the better they will taste. Whip the creams together (I think a mixture of double and soured cream is particularly good). Fill the hollow centres of the profiteroles with the cream, pile them into a pyramid, pour chocolate sauce over them, (see recipe overleaf) and serve.

BITTER CHOCOLATE SAUCE

This is my mother's recipe – excellent, very quick and easy to make. The hint of coffee, like the inclusion of soured cream in the profiterole filling, makes for a more sophisticated dish than the sometimes sickly, over-rich versions I have eaten in restaurants.

1–2 tablespoons unsalted butter
2 tablespoons golden syrup
1 tablespoon caster sugar
3 tablespoons cocoa powder
1 teaspoon instant coffee powder

Put the ingredients into a small pan in the order given. Set over very low heat and stir until everything is melted and well blended, the sauce is perfectly smooth and very hot – but do not let it boil. Set the pan aside, sprinkling 2 teaspoons of cold water over the surface of the sauce. Let it cool slightly before stirring the water into the sauce. The sauce is then ready to use.

FRESH LEMON MOUSSE
(serves 6–8)

The clean fresh taste of a lemon pudding is wonderfully refreshing after a rich main course, and I particularly like the feather-light texture of this creamless mousse.

3 large, thin-skinned, juicy lemons
5 medium-sized eggs
6 oz caster sugar
1 very slightly heaped tablespoon gelatine powder
$1\frac{1}{2}$ oz flaked and toasted almonds

Measure $\frac{1}{4}$ pt water into a small pan. Sprinkle on the gelatine powder, soak for 5 minutes, then dissolve gently over low heat and set aside to cool. Meanwhile, grate the lemon zest finely into the top part of a double-boiler. Add the strained lemon juice, the sugar and the egg yolks. Whisk the mixture for 1 minute then set it over a pan of barely simmering water. Continue whisking steadily for about 6 minutes so that the sugar dissolves completely and the mixture becomes warm and slightly thickened. Now remove the top part of the double-boiler from the heat and set it over a bowl of cold water instead. Continue whisking for a further 6 minutes or so until the mixture is very pale, billowy and thick. Then gradually whisk in the cool gelatine mixture. Chill the mixture until it approaches setting point – it will reach this stage in a matter of minutes. Then whisk the egg whites until they stand in peaks. Fold them delicately but thoroughly into the lemon mixture. Turn the mousse into a pretty 3 pt dish, cover and refrigerate overnight. Scatter with toasted almonds just before serving, and accompany the mousse with a small jug of thin pouring cream.

KIWI CREAM
(serves 4–6)

I'm not usually keen on condensed milk, but its pronounced flavour is undetectable in this creamy rich pudding. Very quick to make and a pretty-looking pudding.

$\frac{1}{4}$ lb cream cheese
$\frac{1}{4}$ pt double cream
1 × 14 oz can condensed milk
$\frac{1}{4}$ pt freshly-squeezed lemon or lime juice
3 kiwi fruit
4–5 shortbread finger biscuits

Beat the cheese and cream together until soft and smooth. Gradually beat in the condensed milk. Then slowly pour on and beat in the fresh fruit juice – which will cause the mixture to thicken considerably. Turn it into a shallow, pretty dish and refrigerate for 4 hours or more.

Just before serving, crumble the biscuits and sprinkle them over the centre of the pudding. Peel and thinly slice the kiwi fruit and arrange them, overlapping, round the edge of the dish.

FRESH FRUIT TRIFLE
(serves 6)

Non-alcoholic trifles are usually reserved for the nursery, boozy versions supposedly being superior and better suited to adult tastes. I can only say that, although I've tried making trifles with brandy and other heady concoctions, I honestly think this one, made with raspberries and freshly-squeezed orange juice, is the best of all.

A slightly stale Victoria sponge cake
2 large oranges
$\frac{1}{2}$ lb raspberries
$\frac{1}{2}$ pt single cream
$\frac{1}{2}$ pt double cream
a little caster sugar
2 eggs
2 oz flaked and toasted almonds

Break the sponge cake into pieces and arrange it over the base of a glass bowl. Squeeze the orange juice and pour it over the sponge. Sprinkle the raspberries with a tablespoon of caster sugar and the very finely grated zest of half an orange, crush lightly with a fork and spread on top of the sponge.

Beat the 2 egg yolks and one white with 1 oz sugar in the top part of a double-boiler. Gradually blend in the scalded single cream, then stir the mixture over barely simmering water until it thickens slightly. Cool the custard slightly before pouring it over the raspberries. When the custard is cold, whip the double cream (if you want a very light tasting cream, whisk the leftover egg white until stiff and fold it into the whipped cream). Spread the cream over the custard and chill the trifle for several hours. Sprinkle with the flaked and toasted almonds just before serving.

CINNAMON RICE
(serves 2)

As is the case in all cold-start recipes given throughout this book, quantities here are for two servings — although I have known one very hungry person scoff the lot! But I've found that these dishes (with the exception of potato purée) work just as well if you halve, double or treble all ingredients to suit the numbers in your family. You will need larger dishes for larger numbers of servings of course – bigger surface area is preferable to extra depth – but there is no need to alter oven temperatures or timings.

2 tablespoons short grain pudding rice
generous $\frac{3}{4}$ pt creamy milk (or, preferably, $\frac{1}{2}$ pt milk plus $\frac{1}{4}$ pt single cream)
2 teaspoons caster sugar
$\frac{1}{4}$ teaspoon ground cinnamon
the finely grated zest of half a lemon
a little butter

Butter a small baking dish. Mix the sugar, cinnamon, rice and lemon zest together, sprinkle them over the base of the dish and pour on the liquid(s). Stir gently. When the surface has settled float wafer thin flakes of butter all over the top of the pudding, and carefully place the dish on the bottom shelf of a cold oven. Set time and temperature controls so that the oven will switch itself on to 300F, 150C, gas mark 2, 3–3$\frac{1}{2}$ hours before you plan to eat the pudding. Serve with jam: whole cherry jam or bramble jelly are particularly good.

GENEROUS BAKED APPLES

(serves 2)

Apples swimming in sweetened water are pretty boring; interesting and well-flavoured stuffings make all the difference. Bake the apples in an oven pre-heated to 350–375F, 180–190C, gas mark 4–5, for about 1 hour, or slowly and gently using the cold-start method described here.

2 large Bramley apples
ground cinnamon
the finely grated zest of half a lemon
2 tablespoons hazelnut kernels
2 tablespoons sultanas or raisins
3 tablespoons golden syrup
2 tablespoons dry cider or unsweetened apple juice

Core the apples and cut a slit through the skin round the 'waist' of each apple to prevent bursting during cooking. Stand the apples side by side in a small ovenproof dish. Stuff the centre of each fruit with a good pinch of ground cinnamon, a little lemon zest, a few of the nuts and some syrup. Surround the apples with the remaining ingredients. Cover the dish with a dome of foil, place on the bottom shelf of a cold oven, and set time and temperature controls so that the oven will switch itself on to 300F, 150C, gas mark 2, 2½–3 hours before you plan to serve the apples.

RICH CHRISTMAS PUDDING

This recipe is ideal for those who like their Christmas pudding to be richly packed with goodies. It is moist, beautifully dark, spicy and boozy.

> 2 oz self-raising flour
> ¼ lb ground almonds
> ¼ lb fresh white breadcrumbs
> ¼ lb shredded suet
> 1 teaspoon ground cinnamon
> 1 teaspoon mixed spice
> a little freshly-grated nutmeg
> the finely grated zest of 1 orange and 1 lemon
> ¼ lb soft dark brown sugar
> ¼ lb currants
> ¼ lb seedless raisins
> ¼ lb sultanas
> 2 oz chopped candied orange and lemon peel
> 2 tablespoons black treacle
> 2 eggs
> 2 tablespoons brandy
> 7–8 tablespoons Guinness

Sieve the flour, cinnamon and mixed spice into a really large mixing bowl. Add the ground almonds, breadcrumbs, suet, nutmeg, orange and lemon zest, sugar, currants, raisins, sultanas and chopped candied peel. Stir everything thoroughly until the ingredients are well mixed.

Stand the tin of treacle (without its lid) in a pan of freshly boiled water for a few minutes to make the treacle liquid enough to measure easily. Measure 2 tablespoons into a small bowl in which you have lightly beaten the eggs. Stir in the brandy and the Guinness. Then scrape the mixture (using a rubber-bladed spatula so that nothing gets wasted) into the large mixing bowl full of the dry ingredients.

Using a big wooden spoon that really gets down to the bottom of the bowl, stir everything very thoroughly together – and don't forget to wish! Cover the bowl with a clean tea towel and leave it in a cool place overnight so that the mixture thickens slightly as it absorbs the liquids.

Stir the mixture briskly for a few minutes, then turn it into well-buttered pudding basins – either two basins each of which has a capacity of 1 pt or just over, or one basin with a capacity of just over 2 pt.

Cover each basin with generously buttered and pleated foil and tie securely with string just under the rim of the basin. It is important to allow a generous pleat in the foil so that the 'lid' can expand as necessary as the pudding rises during cooking.

Lower the pudding basin(s) into large pans containing enough briskly boiling water to come halfway up the sides of the pudding basin(s). Cover the pan with a lid and cook for 5–6 hours (the shorter time for small puddings), topping up the pan with fresh boiling water when the level falls too low.

When the cooked pudding(s) have cooled, re-cover them with fresh dry greaseproof paper, and store in a cool airy larder. On Christmas Day recover them with generously buttered and pleated foil and cook for $1\frac{1}{2}$–2 hours (the shorter time for the small puddings).

LIGHT CHRISTMAS PUDDING

This is paler in colour and more delicate in flavour since it contains fewer spices and no booze. In fact, it is like a steamed suet sponge pudding filled with the fruit and nuts traditional at Christmas. I find it is popular with children and with those who find most Christmas puddings too heavy to be easily digested.

$\frac{1}{4}$ lb fresh brown breadcrumbs
$\frac{1}{4}$ lb pale soft brown sugar
2 oz shredded suet
2 oz grated carrot
2 oz chopped almonds
2 oz currants
$\frac{1}{4}$ lb seedless raisins
$\frac{1}{4}$ lb sultanas
the grated zest of 2 lemons
1 teaspoon ground cinnamon
4 eggs

Mix all the dry ingredients together in a very large mixing bowl. Beat the eggs lightly and add them to the bowl. Stir very thoroughly, using a large wooden spoon that reaches right down to the bottom of the bowl, and make your wishes. Cover the bowl with a clean tea-towel and let the mixture stand in a cool place for several hours.

Then turn it into well-buttered pudding basins – either one basin of just over 2 pt capacity, or two basins each of which holds just over 1 pt.

Cover with buttered and pleated foil and tie securely with string. Lower the basin(s) into a pan containing enough briskly boiling water to come halfway up the sides of the basin(s). Bring quickly back to boiling point.

Cover the pan with a well-fitting lid, reduce heat slightly and cook steadily for 5–6 hours (the shorter time for small puddings), just topping up the pan with fresh boiling water as and when necessary.

When the cooked pudding(s) have cooled, re-cover them with fresh dry greasproof paper, and store in a cool airy larder. On Christmas day re-cover them with generously buttered and pleated foil, and cook for a further 1$\frac{1}{2}$–2 hours (the shorter time for the small puddings).

HOME-MADE YOGHURT 1 (RICH)

Commercial yoghurt is often thin and acid-tasting. Home-made is delectable (particularly this rich version), and I frequently use it in place of fresh or soured cream in cooking. Thickened yoghurt (see below) is best for hot dishes as it is less likely to separate when heated.

> 1 × 14 oz can evaporated milk
> an equal quantity of freshly-boiled water
> 1 teaspoon yoghurt (from the last batch you made or 1 teaspoon commercial yoghurt – a plain one not a fruit flavoured yoghurt)

Thoroughly mix together the evaporated milk and freshly boiled water. Take a wide-mouthed insulated jar (those made by Insulex, sold in Boots, Woolworths and many other stores, are ideal) and rinse it out with warm water. Put the teaspoon of yoghurt into it. Check the temperature of the evaporated milk mixture. It should be 120F/49C – warm it in a pan or leave it to cool until this temperature is reached. Then stir 2 tablespoons into the yoghurt. When smooth and thoroughly blended, slowly pour on the rest of the milk mixture, stirring vigorously all the while. (A metal spoon is fine if you use a plastic jar of the type I have mentioned; use a wooden spoon and be gentle if using a glass-lined jar.) Cover the jar with its lid and leave undisturbed at room temperature for 5 hours. Then carefully transfer the covered jar to the refrigerator. Chill for 3 hours before eating.

HOME-MADE YOGHURT 2 (SLIMLINE)

If you are serious about counting calories, then this less fattening milk mixture makes a more sensible choice for yoghurt-making.

> 2½ oz skimmed milk powder
> 1 pt boiling water
> 1 teaspoon yoghurt (from the last batch you made or commercial yoghurt – a plain one, not flavoured)

Measure the powdered milk into a bowl. Pour on the boiling water and stir until the powder is dissolved. Clip a thermometer to the side of the bowl and wait until the temperature of the liquid drops to 120F/49C. Then proceed exactly as described in home-made yoghurt 1.

THICKENED YOGHURT

Yoghurt that is as thick as softly whipped cream is lovely for puddings and the best choice for cooking purposes as it is less likely to separate when heated. A suitably firm curd is automatically produced if the incubation period is increased to about 8 hours, but this has the unfortunate side effect of making the yoghurt rather acid tasting.

It is preferable to make and chill yoghurt in the normal way, then to drain off some of its liquid. To do this, place a sieve over a bowl and line it with a double thickness of butter-mulsin.

Tip the freshly-made and well-chilled yoghurt out of the jar into the sieve (do this very gently so you break up the curd as little as possible) and leave it in a cool place for a few hours so that some of the liquid (whey) drips away.

I find 2–3 hours is usually enough for most purposes, but if you want the yoghurt to be thick enough to use in place of whipped cream for, say, filling brandy snaps, you may prefer to leave it for 4–5 hours.

YOGHURT CHEESE

Yoghurt cheese (or dry yoghurt as it is sometimes called) is nothing other than fresh home-made yoghurt that has been left to drip like thickened yoghurt, but for longer – about 8 hours – until a considerable quantity of whey has been drained off and the yoghurt is reduced to a chick creamy consistency akin to a fresh-tasting curd cheese.

This is ideal for making such things as slimline cheesecakes and coeurs à la crème, but it is equally good for savoury dishes and, perhaps best of all, I like it simply seasoned with salt, pepper and fresh chopped basil for stuffing tomatoes.

Baking, Sweets and Preserves

PLAIN SCONES
(makes about 10)

I think the combination of flour and raising agents given here produces the best scones. But you could use $\frac{1}{2}$ lb plain flour plus 4 teaspoons baking powder instead. Or $\frac{1}{2}$ lb self-raising flour plus 2 teaspoons baking powder. Or $\frac{1}{4}$ lb plain flour and $\frac{1}{4}$ lb wholemeal flour plus either 1 teaspoon bicarbonate of soda and 2 teaspoons cream of tartar or 4 teaspoons baking powder.

> $\frac{1}{2}$ lb plain flour
> 1 teaspoon bicarbonate of soda
> 2 teaspoons cream of tartar
> a pinch of salt
> 2 oz butter
> $\frac{1}{4}$ pt milk

All scones must be baked as soon as made so turn on the oven — to 425F, 220C, gas mark 7 — before you start assembling the ingredients. Sift the flour, raising agents and salt into a mixing bowl. Add the butter. Cut, then rub the fat into the dry ingredients.

Make a well in the middle and pour in the milk. Using a palette knife cut and fold the liquid into the mixture to make a soft ball of dough. Knead for half a minute on a floured surface. Turn the dough over then pat or roll it out to a $\frac{1}{2}$ inch thickness.

Cut into rounds 2 inches in diameter, cutting as many scones as possible from the first rolling — because they will rise best. Press the trimmings together to make the last one or two scones. Transfer to a floured baking sheet and dust the top of each scone with a sprinkling of flour. Bake near the top of the hot oven for about 12 minutes, until well risen and lightly brown.

WHOLEMEAL SCONE LOAF

A soured milk is used in place of sweet milk in this recipe. Because it is acid it contributes to the rise of the dough, so less cream of tartar is needed. A higher oven temperature is best for a loaf.

$\frac{1}{4}$ lb wholemeal flour
$\frac{1}{4}$ lb plain flour
1 teaspoon bicarbonate of soda
1 teaspoon cream of tartar
$\frac{1}{2}$ teaspoon celery salt or ordinary salt
2 oz butter
$\frac{1}{4}$ pt plain yoghurt, whey or buttermilk

Heat the oven to 450F, 230C, gas mark 8. Put the wholemeal flour into a large mixing bowl. Sift in the plain flour, raising agents and salt. Cut, then rub in the fat, blend in the liquid, and knead the dough as for plain scones (see page 247).

Shape into a flat round about $\frac{3}{4}$ inch thick and transfer to a floured baking sheet. Using a floured knife score the dough into 6 or 8 wedges. Dust with flour or glaze, and bake at the top of the hot oven for about 25 minutes.

FRUIT SCONES
(makes about 10)

The inclusion of an egg means that these delicious scones can be kept fresh and soft for 24 hours if stored in an airtight tin as soon as cooled after baking.

½ lb plain flour
1 teaspoon bicarbonate of soda
2 teaspoons cream of tartar (or any combination of flour and
    raising agent given in the introduction to the plain scone
    recipe)
a pinch of salt
1 teaspoon ground cinnamon
1½ oz butter
1½ oz caster sugar
2 oz sultanas
1 egg plus enough milk to come up to the ¼ pt level in a
    measuring jug

Heat the oven to 425F, 220C, gas mark 7. Sift the flour, raising agents, salt and cinnamon into a large mixing bowl. Cut, then rub the fat into the dry ingredients. Stir in the sugar and sultanas, then make a well in the centre of the mixture. Break the egg into a measuring jug, beat it with a fork and add enough milk to come up to the ¼ pt level.

Mix the liquids into the dry ingredients to make a soft ball of dough. Knead, roll out, cut and bake as for plain scones (see page 247) − about 12 minutes at the top of the oven − but instead of dusting the top of each scone with flour before baking, brush each with a little milk.

CHEESY SCONE SQUARES
(makes about 6)

These are delicious with lashings of butter and bowls of steaming soup. Water is used instead of milk or the scones would be almost too rich and cake-like in texture.

½ lb plain flour
1 teaspoon bicarbonate of soda
2 teaspoons cream of tartar
a pinch each of salt, mustard powder and cayenne pepper
2 oz butter (or margarine)
3 oz grated slightly stale Cheddar cheese
¼ pt water

Heat the oven to 425F, 220C, gas mark 7. Sift the flour, raising agents, salt, mustard powder and cayenne into a large mixing bowl. Cut then rub in the fat. Stir in the grated cheese. Blend in the liquid and knead as for plain scones (see page 247).

Roll out to a generous $\frac{1}{2}$ inch thickness and cut into 3 inch squares. Transfer to a floured baking sheet, dust the tops with more cayenne or a pinch of Parmesan or sesame seeds, and bake at the top of the oven for about 15–18 minutes.

CINNAMON DROP SCONES

This is one of my favourites for tea after a brambling expedition: drop scones topped with a dollop of whipped cream and a few blackberries. They are also good served more conventionally with butter and jam.

$\frac{1}{4}$ lb plain flour
1 teaspoon bicarbonate of soda
1$\frac{1}{2}$ teaspoons cream of tartar
1 egg
1 oz caster sugar
$\frac{1}{2}$ teaspoon ground cinnamon
$\frac{1}{4}$ pt milk

Sift the first 3 ingredients into a bowl. Add the sugar and spice and stir to mix well. Make a well in the centre and break the egg into it. Beat the milk into the egg with a whisk, then gradually incorporate the dry ingredients to make a very smooth, thick batter.

Heat a griddle or cast iron frying pan until very hot. Grease it lightly with buttered paper, using just enough fat to prevent the scones from sticking. Drop a few small rounds of batter into the pan, using a dessertspoon held point downwards, and spacing them well apart. When bubbles rise to the surface and the undersides of the scones are browned – about 2–2$\frac{1}{2}$ minutes – loosen them with a palette knife, flip them over and cook for a further minute or so. Keep the cooked scones warm between the folds of a tea towel, lightly re-grease the pan and cook the rest of the scones in batches in the same way.

SAVOURY DROP SCONES

These savoury drop scones are delicious for tea, lavishly spread with butter or cream cheese. Good, too, for a children's supper, when I serve them with grilled tomatoes or bacon.

2 oz wholemeal flour
2 oz plain white flour
1 teaspoon bicarbonate of soda
1½ teaspoons cream of tartar
1 egg
1 teaspoon salt
a good grinding of black pepper
2 tablespoons each chopped fresh chives and parsley
¼ pt milk

Sift the first 4 ingredients into a mixing bowl. Make a well in the centre and break the egg into it. Add the salt, pepper, herbs and milk. Using a whisk (an electric one is quickest) beat the egg into the milk then incorporate the dry ingredients to make a very smooth, thick batter.

Heat a griddle or cast iron frying pan until very hot. Grease it lightly — just enough to prevent sticking. Drop a few small rounds of the batter into the pan, using a dessertspoon held point downwards, and spacing them well apart. When bubbles rise to the surface and the undersides of the scones are browned — about 2–2½ minutes — loosen them with a palette knife, flip them over and cook for a further minute or so. Remove the scones from the pan and keep them warm between the folds of a tea towel. Lightly re-grease the pan and cook the rest of the scones in batches.

MOIST CHOCOLATE CAKE

All-in-one sandwich sponge mixtures are very quick to make. The inclusion of ground almonds gives this one lovely texture, and the creamy, chocolatey filling is luscious.

3 tablespoons cocoa powder
$4\frac{1}{2}$ oz self-raising flour
$1\frac{1}{2}$ teaspoons baking powder
6 oz caster sugar
6 oz soft margarine
3 eggs
3 tablespoons ground almonds

For the filling:
$\frac{1}{4}$ pt double cream
2 tablespoons soured cream
4 teaspoons drinking chocolate powder
$\frac{1}{4}$ teaspoon instand coffee powder
a pinch of ground cinnamon
2 teaspoons boiling water

Heat the oven to 325F, 160C, gas mark 3. Grease 3 × 7 inch sandwich tins, line them and grease again. Sift the cocoa powder, flour and baking powder together. Add the remaining cake ingredients and beat with an electric whisk until everything is light, well blended and of good dropping consistency. Turn the cake mixture into the prepared tins and bake for about 35 minutes. Cool for half a minute before loosening the cakes and turning them out on to a wire cooling rack.

To make the filling, put the chocolate powder, coffee powder and cinnamon into a large mixing bowl. Pour on the boiling water, stir until dissolved and leave until cold. Add the fresh and soured creams to the bowl and whisk until fairly stiff. Spread the flavoured cream over the tops of two of the sponges. Place one sponge on top of the other, place the third sponge on top of that and dust lavishly with sifted icing sugar.

FAVOURITE GINGERBREAD

It is the inclusion of pieces of stem ginger which makes this cake so good.

½ lb plain flour
½ teaspoon bicarbonate of soda
2 teaspoons ground ginger
1 teaspoon mixed spice
1 teaspoon ground cinnamon
1 lemon
3 oz stem ginger plus 2 tablespoons syrup from the jar
2 tablespoons milk
2 eggs
6 oz butter
4 oz black treacle
4 oz golden syrup
2 oz soft brown sugar

Grease, line and grease again the base and sides of an 8 inch square cake tin. Heat the oven to 325F, 160C, gas mark 3.

Sift the first 5 ingredients into a bowl. Stir in the zest of the lemon and make a 'well' in the centre. Melt the treacle, syrup, butter and sugar in a small pan over low heat and set aside to cool slightly while you beat the eggs with the milk, ginger syrup, 2 tablespoons lemon juice and the roughly chopped stem ginger.

Scrape the treacle mixture out of the saucepan and turn it into the 'well'. Gradually draw in the dry ingredients and beat to a thick smooth batter. Add the egg mixture and continue beating until the cake mixture is glossy and well blended. Pour into the prepared tin and bake for 1¼ hours.

Let the cooked cake stand in the tin for 30 minutes before turning it out on to a cake cooling rack. When cold, store the gingerbread in an airtight tin. Store it whole to conserve the moist texture, and cut into squares just before serving.

PANFORTE DI SIENA

Chewy and sticky rich, this is more like nougat than a cake. I serve it in tiny slivers, with after-dinner coffee on special occasions.

> 3 oz almonds
> 3 oz hazelnuts
> 3 oz candied orange peel
> 3 oz candied lemon peel
> 2 oz plain flour
> 1 oz cocoa powder
> $1\frac{1}{2}$–2 teaspoons ground cinnamon
> $\frac{1}{4}$ teaspoon ground cloves
> 1 teaspoon orange flower water
> $\frac{1}{4}$ lb liquid honey
> $\frac{1}{4}$ lb caster sugar
> a little icing sugar

Heat the oven to 325F, 160C, gas mark 3. Thoroughly grease the base and sides of an 8 inch cake or flan tin with removable base, line with greaseproof paper and grease again.

Put the nuts into a frying pan and place over the heat until lightly toasted and some of the skins begin to loosen and rub off. Chop the peel quite finely. Put it into a bowl. Add the nuts, sift in the flour, cocoa powder and spices, and mix together well. Measure the orange flower water, honey and sugar into a large pan. Cook over low heat, stirring, until the sugar is melted then boil gently to 240F/116C (or when a little of the mixture forms a soft ball when dropped into a cup of cold water).

Quickly remove the pan from the heat, stir in the prepared ingredients and, when well mixed, turn it into the cake or flan tin. Spread the mixture flat and bake for 30 minutes. Let it cool in the tin, then turn out, peel away the paper and sift icing sugar over the top.

ISOBEL'S ALMOND SQUARES

This recipe was given to me by a friend — a special friend and special sweets.

$\frac{1}{4}$ lb ground almonds
$\frac{3}{4}$ oz flaked almonds
6 oz granulated sugar
$\frac{1}{4}$ lb unsalted butter
$4\frac{1}{2}$ tablespoons cold water
1 teaspoon orange blossom water

Measure sugar and liquids into a pan. Dissolve the sugar over low heat then cook to the softball stage, 235F/113C. (If you have no sugar thermometer, test by dropping a teaspoon of the syrup into a cup of cold water then gather the pieces together with your fingers; they should form a soft ball.) Remove the pan from the heat. Quickly beat in the ground almonds and butter, bit by bit. When smoothly blended, turn the mixture on to a baking tray lined with lightly oiled greaseproof paper. Level and shape the mixture with a palette knife, making an oblong 5 × 8 inches. Score lightly to make 40 × 1 inch squares and press a flaked almond into the centre of each square. Chill until set firm then cut into squares and peel away paper.

CHOCOLATE ORANGE TRUFFLES

Decidedly rich but irresistible, these make a marvellous present. Because they are so sticky the truffles are best stored in the fridge.

6 oz plain dessert chocolate
3 oz unsalted butter
the zest of 2 oranges
4 tablespoons Cointreau
5 oz icing sugar
2 tablespoons each cocoa and chocolate powder

Melt the chocolate with 1 oz of the butter. Remove from the heat and stir in remaining butter. Add the very finely-grated orange zest; blend in the Cointreau and sifted icing sugar, a little at a time, beating until the mixture is quite smooth. Cool, then refrigerate until nearly set. Using hands rinsed under a cold tap, roll the mixture (a small lump at a time) between your palms to make about 30 small balls. Coat the truffles by rolling them in cocoa and chocolate powder sifted and mixed on a plate. Refrigerate until set firm.

CHOCOLATE ALMOND DATES

Put these on your after-dinner coffee tray and I guarantee they will be gobbled up in a matter of minutes.

> $\frac{1}{2}$ lb fresh dates or 1 glovebox of dates
> about 15 whole blanched almonds
> about $\frac{1}{2}$ pt orange juice or sherry (optional)
> $\frac{1}{4}$ lb plain dessert chocolate
> 1 oz unsalted butter

Make a small neat slit in each date, remove stones and stuff the cavities with almonds cut in half lengthways. Put the dates in a small bowl, just cover with orange juice or sherry and leave for 3 hours. (This step is optional; it makes for stickier, fruitier results.) Drain, saving the liquid for a trifle. Melt the chocolate and butter. Remove from the heat. Spearing the dates on a skewer or trussing needle, swirl them in the chocolate to coat all over. Place on lightly oiled greaseproof paper and refrigerate until set firm.

TRADITIONAL BREAKFAST MARMALADE
(makes about 6 lb)

The first time I made marmalade I could hardly believe how easy it was, and I was pleasantly surprised to find that just one pound of fruit made enough glowing orange preserve to fill three jars.

Now I enjoy making several varieties each year — some with fine shreds, others with coarse cut peel, and I flavour each batch differently.

> 2 lb Seville oranges
> 2 lemons
> 4 pt cold water
> 4 lb preserving or granulated sugar (granulated is cheaper but preserving sugar makes less scum)

Wipe the fruit clean, cut each in half and squeeze out the juice.

Tear or cut the membrane out of each half shell together with some of the pith if very thick.

Chop the pith roughly and tie it up in a large piece of butter-muslin together with the membrane and pips. Cut the peel into shreds – fairly coarsely or very finely according to taste. Put the shredded peel, fruit juice and muslin bag into a preserving pan or other very large saucepan and pour on the water. If you wish the pan can now be set aside in a cool place for several hours or overnight.

Place the pan over a very low heat and let it simmer gently without a lid for at least 2 hours or until the liquid has reduced by about half and the pieces of peel are so tender they will disintegrate when squeezed between finger and thumb.

The peel must be really soft by the end of this first cooking because once the sugar is added to the pan the softening process ceases. Lift the muslin bag out of the pan. Place it in a sieve suspended over the pan and press it with a potato masher to squeeze all the pectin-rich juices out of the bag into the pan.

Clip a thermometer to the side of the pan and tip in the sugar. Cook, stirring, over the lowest possible heat until the sugar has completely dissolved – this is important or the finished marmalade may develop crystals during storage. The sugar will dissolve more readily if it is slightly warmed before adding to the pan: spread it out on a baking tray and warm through for a few minutes in a low oven.

As soon as the sugar is fully dissolved, bring the contents of the pan as quickly as possible to a rolling boil. Continue to boil the mixture, just stirring occasionally to prevent sticking, until setting point is reached – this usually takes 10–15 minutes – that is when the temperature reads 220F/104C.

If you don't have a thermometer, move the pan away from the heat and test setting quality by putting a spoonful of the marmalade on to a chilled saucer.

Let it cool for a few minutes before pushing a finger-tip lightly across the surface of the blob; if setting point has been reached the marmalade will form a skin as it cools and will wrinkle when touched.

Remove surface scum from the pan by skimming with a perforated spoon which has been dipped in boiling water and dried. Leave the marmalade to stand in the pan by the side of the stove for 10 minutes or so to cool slightly and start setting. Stir it gently so that the peel is evenly distributed and will remain suspended in the cooling jelly.

Pour it into warm, clean jars and cover immediately with discs of waxed or greaseproof paper. Let the marmalade become stone cold before sealing the jars with screw tops or clingfilm and rubber bands.

DARK SPICED MARMALADE

2 lb Seville oranges
2 lemons
4 pt cold water
4 lb preserving or granulated sugar
2 tablespoons coriander seeds
2 cinnamon sticks
2 tablespoons black treacle

This is made in exactly the same way as traditional breakfast marmalade. Simply crush the coriander seeds lightly with mortar and pestle and break the cinnamon sticks into short lengths and add the spices to the butter-muslin bag. Stir the treacle into the pan at the same time as the sugar.

GINGER MARMALADE

2 lb Seville oranges
2 lemons
4 pt cold water
4 lb preserving or granulated sugar
$1\frac{1}{2}$ oz fresh root ginger
4–6 oz ginger taken from a jar of stem ginger in syrup

In this delicious variation on the marmalade theme, the fresh ginger root is thinly peeled, grated coarsely and added to the butter-muslin bag. The stem ginger does not need cooking.

Chop it finely and stir it into the pan after setting point has been reached and the marmalade has been skimmed.

SCENTED ORANGE MARMALADE

2 lb Seville oranges
2 lemons
4 pt cold water
4 lb preserving or granulated sugar
4 tablespoons triple distilled orange flower water
3 tablespoons runny orange blossom or acacia scented honey

Follow the recipe for traditional breakfast marmalade simply stirring the orange flower water (which is available from chemists as well as from good grocers and delicatessens) and honey into the pan at the same time as the sugar.

BRAMBLE JELLY

Blackberries gathered for free from the hedgerows make an inexpensive preserve. I like to include a few sweet geranium leaves to give an extra dimension to the flavour.

6 lb blackberries
3 lemons
a handful of sweet geranium leaves (optional)
preserving or granulated sugar

Avoid over-ripe berries and try to include a few that are under-ripe. Rinse them but don't bother to hull them, and put them into a preserving pan. Squeeze the lemon juice over the berries, add the lemon pips, chopped up peel and geranium leaves. Pour on a scant pint of water and simmer gently until the berries are very tender.

Press the fruit with a potato masher, then turn the entire contents of the pan into a scalded jelly bag suspended over a large bowl and leave until the juices have dripped through.

Measure the strained liquid and return it to the cleaned out pan. Clip a thermometer to the pan and bring to the boil. Add sugar, allowing 1 lb for every pint of juice, and stir well until dissolved. Continue cooking fast until setting point is reached (for details see marmalade recipe), skim and pot immediately into small warm jars. Cover the surface of the jelly with greaseproof paper while still hot. Tie down, label and store when cold.

LEMON CURD

I like making marmalade and jams but few preserves are quicker and more fun than lemon curd – and home-made lemon curd is one of the greatest of all tea-time treats.

3–4 oz unsalted butter
½ lb granulated sugar
2 large juicy lemons
3 eggs (or 6 yolks if you prefer)

Grate the lemon zest and squeeze the juice into the top part of a double-boiler. Add the sugar and the butter cut up into small dice. Place over barely simmering water over low heat and stir occasionally until the butter is melted and the sugar is dissolved. Break up the eggs with a fork, add them to the pan and continue stirring over barely simmering water until the eggs begin to bind and thicken the mixture.

Remove the pan from the heat (and strain the curd through a fine sieve if you want to extract the strips of zest), then pour the curd into clean warm jars. Cover with greaseproof paper while hot and seal when cold.

Home-made lemon curd does not keep as well as most other preserves – about 4–5 weeks in a fridge or very cold larder – so it is best to make this sort of small quantity. It is also best to pot it in small jars, such as those in which redcurrant jelly is sold, as once opened and exposed to the air its keeping qualities are reduced.

SWEET GARLIC CUCUMBERS

My Mississippi friend Maggi Gordon gave me this recipe which was her mother's. I hope she won't mind but I have reduced the proportion of sugar to cucumbers, because the English are less sweet-toothed than the Americans.

> 2 × 1 lb 14 oz jars of pickled ridge cucumbers (jars of Polish pickled cucumbers, sold under the Krakus label, are widely available and excellent)
> 8 or 9 fat garlic cloves
> 1 lb granulated sugar
> 8 tablespoons malt vinegar
> 4 tablespoons pickling spice

This is a cheat recipe really since it is just a matter of adding to commercially pickled cucumbers, but it is well worth doing because the end result is so good. Sweet garlic cucumbers make a delicious snack to nibble with drinks. They are also excellent as a hamburger garnish and, perhaps best of all, chopped and stirred into soured cream to make a sauce to serve with roll-mops or marinated kippers. Place a large sieve over a preserving pan and tip the contents of the jars into the sieve to separate the cucumbers from the liquid.

Add to the pan the garlic cloves cut up into tiny slivers, the sugar, malt vinegar and pickling spice, and bring very slowly to the boil, then set aside to cool. Meanwhile cut the cucumbers lengthways into quarters and place them in a large ceramic bowl. Pour on the cool garlic sweetened vinegar, cover and leave in a cold larder or fridge for 2–7 days. Then pack the cucumbers into the cleaned out jars and pour on enough of the liquid to cover them completely. Seal and store.

FIG AND APPLE CHUTNEY

I love the aromatic bite of whole mustard and coriander seeds in chutney. If you don't, crush the seeds lightly with mortar and pestle and tie them in a piece of butter-muslin; remove and discard just before potting the chutney.

2 lb Cox's apples
1 lb dried figs
1 lb onions
½ lb sultanas
1 lb soft brown sugar
2 tablespoons each mustard seeds and coriander seeds
1 tablespoon salt
½ teaspoon each ground cinnamon and cloves
1¼ pt tarragon vinegar
plenty of freshly-ground black pepper

Peel, core and roughly chop the apples. Chop the stalks off the dried figs and cut up the flesh into little pieces. Chop the onions finely. Put these 3 ingredients into a preserving pan. Add the remaining ingredients (crushing the mustard and coriander seeds and tying them in a muslin bag if you wish) and stir to mix everything well. Bring very slowly to simmering point.

Then leave to simmer very gently without a lid and stirring the mixture quite often, particularly towards the end of cooking time – for 1 hour or until the ingredients are tender and well blended and the consistency is good and thick. Pot in warm clean jars, lay a double-thick disc of greaseproof directly on top of the chutney and seal with well-fitting lids.

RHUBARB AND RAISIN CHUTNEY

If rhubarb grows in your garden, there is probably so much of it that you have had your fill of rhubard pies and fools by mid-summer. This is a good way to use up any surplus.

2 lb rhubard
1 lb onions
1 oz coriander seeds
1 lb raisins
finely grated zest of 2 oranges
¾ pt tarragon or red wine vinegar
¾ lb soft dark brown sugar
1½–2 teaspoons salt
2–3 teaspoons curry powder

Trim the rhubarb and wipe it clean. Cut it into short lengths and put it into a preserving pan. Peel and chop the onions finely, and add them to the pan. Add all the remaining ingredients except the raisins and bring slowly to boiling point, stirring all the while. Cover the pan and simmer gently for about 20 minutes, until the rhubarb is tender and the onions are slightly softened.

Add the raisins to the pan and continue simmering gently, this time without a lid, for about $1\frac{1}{2}$ hours or until the rhubarb has pulped down completely, the flavour is mellow, the colour a rich brown and the texture is quite smooth and nicely thickened. Stir the ingredients occasionally during this time to prevent sticking.

Pot the chutney in warm clean jars and seal whilst it is still hot. Allow to mature for at least one month before eating.

SPICED PEACHES

At the time of year when peaches are really good value, I think it is a lovely idea to spice and bottle some which can be stored away for Christmas eating. These spicy pickled peaches are particularly good with gammon, ham and cold pork.

2 lb small unblemished peaches
1 lb soft pale brown sugar
$\frac{3}{4}$ pt white wine vinegar
3 cinnamon sticks
9 cloves

Bring a pan of water to the boil. Lower a few of the peaches into it, using a perforated spoon. Leave for about half a minute, then lift out the fruit and transfer them to a bowl of cold water. Scald the rest of the peaches in the same way. Then carefully peel away skins, halve the fruit and remove stones.

Break the cinnamon sticks in half. Place them in a preserving pan with the cloves, which should be lightly bashed with a wooden spoon. Add the sugar and vinegar and $\frac{1}{4}$ pt warm water. Stir over low heat until the sugar is dissolved then bring to the boil. Add the peaches to the pan and simmer gently for about 5 minutes or until tender. Lift them out of the pan with a perforated spoon and pack them into warm clean Kilner jars. Return the pan to the heat and continue boiling the spiced vinegar until slightly reduced and syrupy. Pour the liquid over the peaches, making sure it covers them completely. Cover, seal and store for at least 2 months before eating.

Index